World Tax Reform

Brookings Dialogues on Public Policy

The presentations and discussions at Brookings conferences and seminars often deserve wide circulation as contributions to public understanding of issues of national importance. The Brookings Dialogues on Public Policy series is intended to make such statements and commentary available to a broad and general audience, usually in summary form. The series supplements the Institution's research publications by reflecting the contrasting, often lively, and sometimes conflicting views of elected and appointed government officials, other leaders in public and private life, and scholars. In keeping with their origin and purpose, the Dialogues are not subjected to the formal review procedures established for the Institution's research publications. Brookings publishes them in the belief that they are worthy of public consideration but does not assume responsibility for their accuracy or objectivity. And, as in all Brookings publications, the judgments, conclusions, and recommendations presented in the Dialogues should not be ascribed to the trustees, officers, or other staff members of the Brookings Institution.

World Tax Reform
A Progress Report

Edited by JOSEPH A. PECHMAN

*Report of a conference held in Washington, D.C.,
on November 12–13, 1987, sponsored by the
Brookings Institution*

THE BROOKINGS INSTITUTION / Washington, D.C.

About Brookings

THE BROOKINGS INSTITUTION is a private nonprofit organization devoted to research, education, and publication in economics, government, foreign policy, and the social sciences generally. Its principal purpose is to bring knowledge to bear on the current and emerging public policy problems facing the American people. In its research, Brookings functions as an independent analyst and critic, committed to publishing its findings for the information of the public. In its conferences and other activities, it serves as a bridge between scholarship and public policy, bringing new knowledge to the attention of decisionmakers and affording scholars a better insight into policy issues. Its activities are carried out through three research programs (Economic Studies, Governmental Studies, Foreign Policy Studies), a Center for Public Policy Education, a Publications Program, and a Social Science Computation Center.

The Institution was incorporated in 1927 to merge the Institute for Government Research, founded in 1916 as the first private organization devoted to public policy issues at the national level; the Institute of Economics, established in 1922 to study economic problems; and the Robert Brookings Graduate School of Economics and Government, organized in 1924 as a pioneering experiment in training for public service. The consolidated institution was named in honor of Robert Somers Brookings (1850–1932), a St. Louis businessman whose leadership shaped the earlier organizations.

Brookings is financed largely by endowment and by the support of philanthropic foundations, corporations, and private individuals. Its funds are devoted to carrying out its own research and educational activities. It also undertakes some unclassified government contract studies, reserving the right to publish its findings.

A Board of Trustees is responsible for general supervision of the Institution, approval of fields of investigation, and safeguarding the independence of the Institution's work. The President is the chief administrative officer, responsible for formulating and coordinating policies, recommending projects, approving publications, and selecting staff.

Editor's Preface

The success of tax reform in the United States has stimulated many other countries to consider reforming their tax systems. Australia, Denmark, Canada, and the United Kingdom have already made significant changes in their corporate tax systems, and the Federal Republic of Germany, Sweden, Italy, France, Japan, and others have announced their intention to reduce tax rates and, in some cases, to broaden their income tax bases. Australia, Canada, and Japan are considering the enactment of a value-added tax.

The changes taking place will profoundly affect the distribution of tax burdens, as well as important domestic economic variables such as labor supply, saving, investment, growth of productivity, and exchange rates. The changes will also affect the competitive position of business firms in world markets and the flow of investment funds among nations.

Newspapers, technical journals, and the public have yet to catch up with the rapid developments in tax reform, even though knowledge of current issues is essential for intelligent business and government tax planning. This volume, in the series of Brookings Dialogues on Public Policy, reports on the proceedings of a conference to evaluate the tax developments throughout the developed world. The Brookings Center for Public Policy Education organized the conference, held at the Brookings Institution on November 12–13, 1987. The authors of the papers are government experts in charge of tax policy in their countries; to highlight different viewpoints, each paper is discussed by another expert not associated with the government of that country. Participants at the conference included tax experts from the public and private sectors, as well as business executives interested in the economic impact of tax policy.

Walter E. Beach organized the conference with the assistance of Lee Ann Sonnergren. Ruth Blau, Caroline Lalire, Jeanette Morrison, Brenda B. Szittya, and Theresa B. Walker edited the manuscript.

Richard S. Rice and Susan L. Woollen prepared the manuscript for typesetting.

Members of the staffs of the Washington embassies of the countries discussed in this volume were especially helpful in expediting the organization of the conference and the preparation of the volume.

This conference was part of a project on comparative tax systems, which is being conducted at the Brookings Institution, with the assistance of grants from the Alfred P. Sloan Foundation and the German Marshall Fund.

The Brookings Institution is grateful to the authors and discussants of the papers and to the experts who attended the conference. Their views, which are summarized in this volume, will help to improve public understanding of the worldwide tax reform movement.

JOSEPH A. PECHMAN

February 1987
Washington, D.C.

Contents

Introduction
JOSEPH A. PECHMAN

1

Australia
EDWARD A. EVANS

15

Comment by C. David Finch

40

Canada
DAVID A. DODGE & JOHN H. SARGENT

43

Comment by John Bossons

69

Denmark
JENS DREJER

79

Comment by Robert Koch-Nielsen

92

France
JEAN-CLAUDE MILLERON & DIDIER MAILLARD

95

Comment by Pierre-Andre Chiappori

113

Germany
ADALBERT UELNER & THOMAS MENCK

119

Comment by Gerold Krause-Junk

127

Italy
ALDO CARDARELLI & MICHELE DEL GIUDICE

141

Comment by Emilio Gerelli and Luigi Bernardi

147

Japan
ATSUSHI NAGANO

155

Comment by Keimei Kaizuka

162

Netherlands

HENDRIK ELLE KONING & DIRK WITTEVEEN   171
Comment by Flip de Kam   180

Sweden

CLAES LJUNGH   187
Comment by Leif Mutén   211

United Kingdom

IAN C. R. BYATT   219
Comment by John Hills   236

United States

LAWRENCE B. GIBBS   245
C. EUGENE STEUERLE   251

Overviews

SIJBREN CNOSSEN   261
RICHARD GOODE   269
KENNETH C. MESSERE   277

Conference Participants   291

JOSEPH A. PECHMAN

Introduction

The tax systems of the industrial countries of the world are changing rapidly and, in some cases, are undergoing major reform. In part, this movement is a reaction to the 1986 U.S. tax reform, which broadened the tax base and lowered the income tax rates to levels not seen since the 1920s. But it also reflects the almost universal recognition of the distortions and inequities created by high tax rates, years of inflation, and 'ineffective tax preferences. This volume presents a progress report, as of the end of 1987, on the tax revision programs of the United States and its principal trading partners.

CURRENT TAX SYSTEMS

Most of the countries discussed in this volume impose much higher taxes than the United States. In 1985 taxes ranged from 30.4 percent of gross domestic product (GDP) in Australia to 50.5 percent in Sweden, compared with 29.2 percent in the United States. Japan, with taxes amounting to 28.0 percent of GDP, had the lowest tax burden (table 1). All the countries rely on personal and corporate income taxes, consumption taxes, and payroll taxes to raise revenues, but they differ substantially in the degree of reliance. In general, payroll and consumption taxes (usually the value-added tax) are much heavier in Europe than in Canada, Australia, the United States, and Japan. The personal income tax is a major source of revenue in all the countries, whereas the corporate tax is a minor source.

Tax-policy makers in all the countries are impressed by the success of tax reform in the United States, particularly the large reduction in the top income tax rate. Each country has used its tax system to promote perceived social and economic objectives. As in the United States, the result has been to generate serious inequities and misallocations among industries and firms and to complicate the tax laws.

TABLE 1. *Tax Revenues as a Percent of Gross Domestic Product and Distribution of Tax Revenues, by Source, 1985*[a]

Country	Tax source						
	Individual income	*Corporate income*	*Payroll*	*Consumption*[b]	*Property*	*Wealth*[c]	*Total*
	Percent of gross domestic product						
Sweden	19.5	1.8	14.7	13.8	0.4	0.3	50.5
Denmark	25.5	2.4	2.3	17.7	0.9	0.5	48.5
France	5.8	2.0	20.8	15.4	1.2	0.4	45.6
Netherlands	8.8	3.1	19.7	12.1	0.8	0.4	44.9
United Kingdom	9.9	4.9	6.7	12.4	4.0	0.2	38.1
Germany	10.8	2.3	13.8	9.9	0.4	0.5	37.7
Italy	9.5	3.3	12.2	9.6	*	0.1	34.7
Canada	11.9	2.9	4.4	10.9	2.9	0.3	33.2
Australia	13.7	2.8	1.7	10.8	1.4	*	30.4
United States	10.4	2.1	8.6	5.2	2.7	0.2	29.2
Japan	6.9	5.9	8.5	4.8	1.6	0.3	28.0
	Distribution by source (percent)						
Sweden	38.5	3.5	29.1	27.3	0.9	0.7	100.0
Denmark	51.8	5.0	4.6	35.9	1.9	0.9	100.0
France	12.8	4.3	45.7	33.8	2.5	0.8	100.0
Netherlands	19.5	7.0	43.9	26.8	1.8	0.9	100.0
United Kingdom	26.0	12.9	17.5	32.4	10.5	0.6	100.0
Germany	28.7	6.1	36.5	26.3	1.1	1.3	100.0
Italy	27.4	9.5	35.3	27.7	*	0.2	100.0
Canada	36.0	8.4	13.3	32.8	8.6	0.9	100.0
Australia	45.1	9.2	5.5	35.5	4.6	*	100.0
United States	35.7	7.1	29.4	17.9	9.1	0.8	100.0
Japan	24.8	21.0	30.2	17.1	5.7	1.2	100.0

Source: Organization for Economic Cooperation and Development, *Revenue Statistics of OECD Member Countries, 1965–1986* (Paris: OECD, 1987). Figures are rounded.

* Less than 0.05 percent.

a. Includes national and local taxes.

b. Includes sales, value-added, and excise taxes, taxes on imports and exports, taxes on transfers of property and securities, other transaction taxes paid by enterprises, and miscellaneous other taxes.

c. Includes annual net wealth taxes and estate, inheritance, and gift taxes.

Despite considerable disenchantment with these policies, most countries are moving only slowly to broaden their tax bases for fear of adverse political repercussions. There is, however, strong pressure on governments to lower individual and corporate tax rates even though there is little or no room in their budgets to permit significant revenue reductions.

An important feature of European tax systems is the value-added tax (VAT). In most countries the various exemptions and tax rates complicate its administration. Harmonization of the rates and coverage of indirect taxes are mandated by the European Community by 1992, but progress toward this objective is slow. Australia, Canada, and Japan have been considering the adoption of value-added taxes, but in each country political opposition to a regressive consumption tax has forced the governments to postpone introducing the VAT.

The high payroll tax rates in Europe reflect the reliance on social security and welfare programs that are much more extensive than the U.S. system. Besides retirement and disability programs, the payroll tax is used to finance national health care or universal health insurance, unemployment compensation, employment and training programs, family allowances, income support for the poor, and child care. In several countries payroll taxes are used for general revenue purposes. Demographics are creating difficult problems for the retirement and health programs, but action to solve that problem is being deferred.

Thus the tax problems of other countries seem to be at least as intractable as they appeared to be in the United States before the 1986 tax reform was enacted. Budgetary restraint is required to bring down excessive deficits almost everywhere. Base broadening to raise revenues is appealing in principle but difficult in practice. Consumption and payroll taxes have already been raised to extremely high levels and so cannot be used to pay for income tax reduction. Yet the demand to reduce the high income tax rates is persistent. As may be expected, the reaction to these pressures varies widely and reflects the local social and political alignments on budget and tax issues.

MAJOR TRENDS

Although the tax reform plans of the countries discussed in this volume differ greatly, a number of trends are discernible.

TABLE 2. *Top Individual Income Tax Rates, 1984–90*[a]
Percent

Country	1984	1985	1986	1987	1988	1989[b]	1990[b]
Sweden[c]	82	80	80	77	75	75	75
Denmark	73	73	73	68	68	68	68
France	65	65	58	57	57	57	57
Netherlands[d]	72	72	72	72	70	70	70
United Kingdom	60	60	60	60	60	60	60
Germany	56	56	56	56	56	56	53
Italy[d,e]	65	62	62	62	60	60	60
Canada[e,f]	51	52	55	53	45	45	45
Australia	60	60	55	49	49	49	49
United States[e]	55	55	55	43	33	33	33
Japan	88	88	88	88	76	76	76

Sources: Papers presented at the conference, supplemented by various official government publications.

a. Combined national and local tax rates.

b. Assumes no unscheduled changes in current tax provisions unless otherwise indicated.

c. Assumes a local tax rate of 30 percent.

d. Assumes that proposed reforms will be enacted.

e. Takes into account the deductibility of local tax when calculating national tax.

f. Assumes the Ontario provincial tax rate and includes federal and provincial surtaxes.

Most countries will reduce individual income tax rates, particularly in the top brackets, and compress the number of brackets. In this respect, they are following the lead of the United States, although no country expects to emulate the reduction of twenty-two percentage points in the top U.S. federal tax rate (from 50 percent to 28 percent). Japan is cutting its top rate by twelve points, and Australia is cutting its rate by eleven points; most of the other countries are cutting theirs by two to eight points. Top bracket tax rates will therefore remain much higher in other countries than in the United States (table 2). Including local taxes, in 1989 the top bracket rates will range from a high of 75 percent in Sweden to 45 percent in Canada. In that year the combined federal and state rate to be paid by top bracket taxpayers in the United States will be about 33 percent.

Corporate tax rates are also coming down (table 3). Many believe

TABLE 3. *Corporation Income Tax Rates, 1984–90*[a]
Percent

Country	1984	1985	1986	1987	1988	1989[b]	1990[b]
Sweden	52	52	52	52	52	52	52
Denmark	40	50	50	50	50	50	50
France	50	50	45	45	42	42	42
Netherlands	43	43	43	42	42	42	42
United Kingdom	45	40	35	35	35	35	35
Germany[c]	56	56	56	56	56	56	50
Italy[d]	36	46	46	46	46	46	46
Canada[e,f]	51	52	53	52	48	44	44
Australia	46	46	46	49	49	49	49
United States[d]	51	51	51	45	39	39	39
Japan[c,d]	53	53	53	52	52	52	52

Sources: Papers presented at the conference, supplemented by various official government publications.

a. Combined national and local tax rates.

b. Assumes no unscheduled changes in current tax provisions unless otherwise indicated.

c. Tax on undistributed profits only; tax of 36.0 percent on distributed profits in Germany and 33.3 percent in Japan.

d. Takes into account the deductibility of local tax from national tax.

e. Rate for a nonmanufacturing corporation; tax for a manufacturing corporation will be lower.

f. Assumes a provincial tax rate of 15.5 percent.

that the investment tax incentives enacted in the 1960s and 1970s encouraged business executives to invest for tax advantages rather than to obtain the highest economic return. It is better, in this view, to have a level playing field for all business enterprise and let the market allocate resources. The United Kingdom led the way in 1984 by eliminating expensing for plant and equipment and using the revenues to reduce the corporate rate from 50 percent to 35 percent. The United States followed suit in 1986 when it reduced investment allowances and cut the federal corporate rate from 50 percent to 34 percent; with an average state rate of five percentage points, the combined U.S. rate on corporate profits will be 39 percent beginning in 1988. Canada has also eliminated its investment tax credit (except for some regional credits) and reduced its federal-provincial corporate

rate from 51 percent to 44 percent (39 percent for manufacturing corporations). Smaller corporate tax rate cuts are being made in France, Germany, the Netherlands, and Japan. Australia and Denmark have increased their corporate tax rates, but in both countries this rise will be partially offset by relief for dividends received by stockholders. Sweden and Italy have not made any changes in their corporate rates recently. In 1990 four countries will have corporate tax rates of 50 percent or more, and five others will have rates between 40 percent and 50 percent, according to present plans; only the United Kingdom and the United States will have rates below 40 percent. The countries with the higher rates recognize that they may be forced to lower their rates for international competitive reasons.

Aside from the elimination of tax preferences for investment, the base-broadening features of the tax revisions have not been as far-reaching as in the United States. The most unusual—and perhaps pathbreaking—reform is the Australian decision to tax noncash employee fringe benefits to the employer at the corporate tax rate. Canada converted personal exemptions and other deductions to tax credits, while Denmark limited the tax value of deductions to the first bracket rate of 50 percent. Deductibility of entertainment expenses has been curtailed in Australia, Canada, Denmark, and the United States. Japan has sharply cut exemptions for interest on small saving accounts; Italy has imposed a flat 12.5-percent withholding tax on government bond interest, which was previously tax exempt; and Germany has introduced withholding on all interest payments at a flat 10-percent rate. All countries are examining their tax structures to see whether they can pick up additional revenues by eliminating other unnecessary deductions or tax credits, but the general view is that the scope for such reforms is much more limited than it was in the United States.

Capital gains are taxed in Australia, Canada, Sweden, and the United Kingdom, although only Australia has followed the United States in taxing them as ordinary income. Most other countries tax capital gains realized from the sale of real estate, but not those from the sale of securities (except for gains of professional traders). None of these countries is considering the taxation of such gains, let alone treating them as ordinary income. This attitude reflects the long-standing European view that capital gains are not income. Moreover, Europeans believe it would be difficult to adopt the strict annual limit

($3,000) on the deduction for net capital losses imposed by the United States. Fear of the flight of capital to other countries is also a factor. The diffidence about taxing capital gains will make it difficult for these countries to make additional reductions in their top bracket rates without reducing progressivity.

Like the United States, Denmark and Sweden have limited their deductions for interest paid, but the methods used are somewhat different. The United States has eliminated the deduction for consumer interest (except for interest on home mortgages) and limited the deduction for investment interest to the amount of property income reported by the taxpayer. Sweden provides a full deduction for interest payments, but the tax value of the deduction is limited to the first bracket rate of 50 percent if it results in a capital income deficit. In Denmark interest is deductible only against capital income.

Most countries adjusted the personal exemptions and tax brackets for inflation during the 1970s. But as inflation receded, indexation was eliminated or deferred, usually for revenue reasons. The only countries that now automatically index their exemptions and tax brackets annually are France and the United States. Canada adjusts for the excess of the annual inflation rate over 3 percent. One perhaps significant development is the adjustment of the purchase price of assets for inflation in calculating taxable capital gains. Sweden and the United Kingdom already make this adjustment, and other countries will be under pressure to follow suit if inflation recurs.

Income tax simplification is a major objective of tax reform in all countries, but progress is slow everywhere, including in the United States. Australia, Canada, Denmark, and Sweden have reduced the number of tax brackets to five or fewer along with the compression of their tax rates; however, the simplification achieved is considered negligible. Denmark, Italy, Sweden, and the United States have increased their standard deductions to simplify tax return preparation for most taxpayers. In Japan, Germany, and the United Kingdom, most wage earners discharge their tax liabilities through withholding and are not required to file returns. The Netherlands is considering the integration of its income and social security taxes into one rate structure with four brackets; most Dutch taxpayers will be subject to the first bracket rate and will not be required to file tax returns. Sweden has undertaken to prepare tax returns for its taxpayers on the basis of information reported by employers and firms paying interest and dividends. By contrast, the United States is only now beginning to study the feasibility of a return-free tax system.

Most of the countries attempt to "integrate" their individual and corporate income taxes by providing some form of dividend relief. The exceptions are Sweden, the Netherlands, and the United States, which use the classical system of separate corporate and individual income taxes. (However, Sweden now provides a 10-percent deduction at the corporate level for dividends paid on new capital issues for a period of twenty years.) Australia recently enacted an imputation system along the lines adopted by France, Germany, Italy, and the United Kingdom; Denmark plans to introduce imputation in 1990. Under that system, the double tax on dividends is reduced or eliminated by a credit at the individual level for the corporate tax paid on the dividends. In enacting its 1986 reform, the U.S. Congress rejected a proposal by the administration to reduce the corporate tax on distributed earnings.

Although the value-added tax is usually regarded as a simple tax, in practice most countries have complicated it by adopting multiple tax rates for various goods and services and exempting others from taxation. The complications are particularly serious in France and Italy, but other countries have similar problems. The ideal would be to include all consumer goods and services in the tax base and to use only one tax rate. But the pressure to avoid burdening low-income families by providing zero or low rates for necessities is considerable everywhere. Some simplification may be achieved when the harmonization of indirect taxes in the European countries goes into effect in 1992, but most observers believe that there will be only limited revisions. As already noted, the governments of Australia, Canada, and Japan have officially proposed the adoption of a value-added tax but have delayed introducing the tax because of strong opposition to its regressive feature.

RECENT HIGHLIGHTS

The following are highlights of the tax reform movements in each country.

Australia has just completed a major overhaul of its tax system to improve both equity and efficiency. The marginal rates of the individual income tax have been reduced, particularly at the top, where the rate was cut from 60 percent to 49 percent; the number of tax brackets has been cut to four (excluding a zero-rate bracket); and real capital gains realized on assets acquired after September 19, 1985, are now taxed as ordinary income. Part but not all of the cost of the rate reductions was recouped by base-broadening measures, the most important being the taxation of employee fringe benefits and elimination of the deductibility of entertainment expenses. The corporate tax rate was raised from 46 percent to the 49-percent top individual rate, but this increase will be moderated by the introduction of an imputation system for corporate dividends. The government recommended the adoption of a retail sales tax but withdrew the proposal when it met with strong opposition. Consideration is now being given to broadening the corporate tax base with a view to reducing the corporate rate.

Canada has also made important changes in its tax system through base broadening and rate reduction. The fraction of capital gains subject to tax will be raised from 50 percent to 75 percent by 1990. A deduction of up to $1,000 of investment income under the individual income tax was eliminated, and deductions for home offices, meals, entertainment, and automobile expenses were curtailed. In addition, the personal exemptions and remaining deductions were converted to tax credits. The revenues from these changes were used to reduce the marginal income tax rates; including provincial taxes, the top rate was cut from 55 percent to 45 percent. The number of rate brackets was reduced to three. The investment tax credit was eliminated and depreciation allowances were reduced; the corporate tax rate went from 53 percent to 44 percent (again including provincial taxes). The government plans to replace the federal manufacturers sales tax with a value-added tax, but has delayed action in order to consult with the provinces on a possible method to combine direct federal and provincial sales taxes into one system.

Denmark has introduced a novel change in its tax structure to stop the revenue loss resulting from interest deductions. Under the new structure the individual income tax will consist of a tax on personal income and a tax on capital income. Personal income is essentially labor income; capital income consists of interest, dividends, taxable capital gains, rents, and profits from business enterprises. Personal income is subject to tax at three rates, ranging from 50 percent to 68 percent (down from the previous maximum of 73 percent), whereas capital income is taxed at a flat 50-percent rate. Interest is deductible in full against capital income, but any excess of interest payments over capital income cannot be deducted from personal income, so that the maximum tax value of negative capital income is 50 percent. Another novel feature of the new system is a special arrangement for self-employed persons. If the taxpayer elects to use this arrangement, the net income from the business is divided into capital income (computed by imputing a market rate of return to invested capital), which is taxable at the 50-percent rate, and personal income, which is taxable at the progressive rates. Most allowances under the personal income tax will be deductible only at the 50-percent tax rate; only 25 percent of entertainment expenses will be deductible at this rate. Denmark has also increased its corporate tax from 40 percent to 50 percent, but a new tax credit for dividends will be introduced in 1990.

France is restructuring its tax system to reverse the progressive tilt of tax policy in the early 1980s. The corporate tax rate has been cut from 50 percent to 42 percent, beginning in 1988. Since the tax credit for dividends has not been changed, this reduction in the corporate rate automatically reduces the double taxation of dividends. The unpopular "professional tax," which is a tax on the rental value of businesses plus their wage payments, has also been reduced. The top-bracket individual income tax rate has been cut from 65.0 percent to 56.8 percent, and all other rates, except the starting rate, have been reduced commensurately. Personal exemptions have been increased, but other deductions and allowances have remained unchanged. The annual net wealth tax, introduced in 1981, was repealed in 1986. The present government plans additional cuts in individual and corporate tax rates if it is successful in reducing public expenditures and the deficit. It has no plans to broaden the individual income tax base or to restrict investment allowances as other countries have done.

Germany is also emphasizing reductions of the individual and corporate income tax rates. Individual income tax rates have been reduced from a range of 22–56 percent to 19–53 percent, and personal exemptions have been increased. The tax rate on retained profits of corporations has been reduced from 56 percent to 50 percent. The tax reductions have been partially financed by a new 10-percent withholding tax on interest, reductions of certain targeted depreciation allowances, and some base-broadening measures, particularly related to fringe benefits. The main tax reform objective of the German government is to modify individual income tax graduation in order to reduce the tax rates in the middle brackets.

Italy has made only minor changes in its tax system. Personal exemptions and a special deduction for wage earners have been increased, and marginal individual income tax rates have been reduced somewhat. The top tax rate has been reduced from 62 percent to 60 percent. The only base-broadening provision of any consequence adopted recently is a new withholding tax of 12.5 percent on government bond interest, but since such interest remains outside the tax base, it is not subject to the progressive rates. Assets have been revalued for purposes of calculating depreciation and capital gains, and there has been a speedup in the collection of corporate taxes. However, corporate income tax rates have remained unchanged.

Japan was in considerable political turmoil because of a proposal by the government to enact a value-added tax as part of its plan to restructure the tax system. The value-added tax was temporarily shelved, and several significant tax changes that had been delayed were finally enacted. Both the national and local income tax rates were reduced, with the result that the combined top-bracket rate was cut from 88 percent to 76 percent. The tax exemption accorded to small savers was limited to persons over 65 years of age, the physically handicapped, and those in need of financial assistance, and the exemption for employee savings was restricted to savings for purchasing a home or being set aside for retirement. A flat withholding tax of 20 percent applies to interest on ordinary bank deposits, while interest on time deposits may be taxed separately at a flat rate of 35 percent or aggregated with other income at the taxpayer's option. The corporate income tax has been reduced from 53 percent to 52 percent.

The Netherlands is concentrating on the proposal of the Tax Simplification Committee to integrate the individual income tax and social security contributions into one combined levy. The new structure would consist of four tax rates, ranging from 40 percent to 70 percent. Eighty-eight percent of all taxpayers would be subject only to the first bracket rate. To implement this proposal without reducing take-home pay, it will be necessary to increase the gross wages of all employees by an amount equal to the share of the social security contributions now paid by employers. (This could be done without cost to employers.) Although the proposal contains some broadening of the tax base, the income tax base is already considered quite broad, and little rate reduction could be achieved, even if all tax deductions (other than the personal exemptions) were eliminated.

Sweden has the highest tax rates in this sample of countries, even after a recent restructuring of the individual income tax rates into four brackets, with rates ranging from 35 percent to 75 percent. The corporate tax rate has remained at 52 percent. The major changes emerging from recent reforms are the introduction of a limitation on the tax value of interest deductions to 50 percent, the discontinuance of joint taxation of married couples, and the abolition of indexation. Both the government and the private sector have shown considerable interest in further tax reforms. But action on such reforms has been delayed until the reports of parliamentary commissions established to study the individual and corporate income taxes.

The United Kingdom led the world in eliminating investment tax preferences and reducing the corporate tax rate. This policy was motivated by the conviction that freely operating markets allocate resources much more efficiently than those driven by tax incentives. In 1984 the government eliminated the 100-percent first-year write-off for plant and equipment and the 75-percent write-off for industrial buildings, using the revenue gain to reduce the corporate tax rate from 50 percent to 35 percent in four stages. Individual income tax rates have been cut, and personal allowances have been raised. The basic rate of income tax has been reduced from 33 percent to 27 percent, the top rate of tax on earned income has been cut from 83 percent to 60 percent, and a surcharge on investment income has been abolished. To offset part of the revenue loss from these changes, the government raised the standard rate of value-added tax from 8 percent to 15 percent. The former capital transfer tax, which applied to gifts as well as bequests, has been replaced by an inheritance tax (actually an estate tax) without a gift tax. Despite its support for a level playing field, the government has introduced tax incentives for individuals to invest in small enterprises and in equity funds. It has also introduced a unique tax scheme to promote flexibility in wage arrangements and to encourage workers to identify with their firms.

Under the scheme, one-half of profit-related pay is tax free up to £3,000 or 20 percent of pay, whichever is lower.

The United States is digesting the massive tax reform enacted in 1986. The corporate and individual income tax rate reductions became fully effective at the beginning of 1988. The principal base-broadening provisions—repeal of the investment tax credit, taxation of capital gains as ordinary income, restrictions of deductions for interest expenses, and limitations on tax shelter losses (called passive losses)— remain intact. The economy has done well since the act was passed, and there is little pressure to make changes in the reformed system before it has been fully tested. The administration and Congress have refrained from changing the income tax rates despite the urgent need for revenue to reduce the large federal deficit.

CONCLUSION

Judged by this sample of countries, the tax reform movement is almost universal. Many reforms have already been put in place, and others are being phased in over a period of years. By the end of the 1980s the developed world will have lower individual and corporate income tax rates and fewer tax preferences, particularly incentives for investment, than at the beginning of the decade. Since there is virtually no room in national budgets for net reductions in receipts, revenue for further tax rate reductions must come from public expenditure cuts or additional base broadening, but the prospect for such measures is slim. Although income tax simplification is a major objective of tax reform, little progress has been made in simplifying the tax laws or the tax returns. Payroll tax rates are higher in most other countries than in the United States, but they cannot be brought down because the revenues are needed to finance social welfare programs. Countries without a value-added tax have expressed interest in it, but efforts to introduce the tax have met with fierce political opposition.

For the benefit of the reader, table 4 presents the U.S. dollar exchange rates for the countries covered in this volume on January 1, 1988. These rates may be used to convert the values of revenues, exemptions, deductions, and rate brackets expressed in the various currencies to dollar values.

TABLE 4. *U.S. Dollar Exchange Rates of Ten Currencies, January 1, 1988*

Country	Currency	U.S. dollars per unit of foreign currency	Units of foreign currency per U.S. dollar
Australia	Dollar	0.7220	1.385
Canada	Dollar	0.7692	1.300
Denmark	Krone	0.1626	6.149
France	Franc	0.1878	5.325
Germany	Mark	0.6377	1.568
Italy	Lira	0.00088	1,164.500
Japan	Yen	0.00826	121.000
Netherlands	Guilder	0.5562	1.798
Sweden	Krona	0.1713	5.835
United Kingdom	Pound	1.8860	0.530

Source: *Washington Post*, January 1, 1988.

EDWARD A. EVANS

Australia

Taxation issues are seldom far from the forefront of a government's agenda, partly because revenue raising forms one side of the annual budget and partly because the extraordinarily complex tax systems that Western governments have devised seem to be in constant need of repair. Major structural reforms of taxation arrangements are more rare.

In Australia there was little structural change to the taxation system for most of the four decades following World War II—even though the growth of government during that period had necessitated a great increase in the overall tax burden. The inevitable increase in tax rates promoted, during the 1970s, tax avoidance and evasion—practices that exacerbated legislated and judicial narrowing of the tax base, leading, equally inevitably, to disrespect for the system.

Faced with these pressures, the present government foreshadowed, in the preelection context of December 1984, a major reform of the tax system during its next (up to three-year) term of office. Within nine months, the details of that reform were conceived, extensively debated, and announced in September 1985. In the following two years, the reforms were legislated. In the process, 700 pages were added to the tax law, reflecting the far-reaching nature of the reforms.

In the meantime, tax reform has proceeded in many other countries. While much can be said for allowing a period of consolidation in the Australian tax system, developments abroad are now requiring Australia to consider further tax reform—this time, confined to the taxation of business income.

This paper first describes the 1985 reforms, discussing their background, the reform proposals, and the unique Australian elements of the reforms. It then considers some of the most important economic implications of the reforms, and finally, indicates the general approach to the review of business income taxation now under consideration.

THE 1985 REFORMS

In recent years, tax reform has held a high profile on Australia's political and economic agendas. This has not always been the case, and the reform of the taxation system in the mid-1980s was the most far reaching of any in Australia to date.

Throughout most of the 1950s and 1960s there was a relative lack of interest in tax matters by both academic economists and the governments of the day. Only minor changes were made, and by the early 1970s the personal income tax rate scale was basically unchanged (at least in nominal terms) from that of two decades earlier. In the 1970s, however, an increased and more authoritative debate emerged. The growing impetus for change came largely from changes in Australia's economic circumstances (inflation, recession, and structural change), the election in 1972 of the first Labor government in twenty-three years, and numerous overseas reports on taxation. Two official inquiries into the taxation system and several others that touched on taxation matters reflected those influences.

Despite this growing momentum, changes to the tax system in the 1970s were largely one-time reactions to particular problems rather than part of an overall reform strategy. They included a reduction in the number of personal income tax marginal rates from twenty-eight to three, the introduction and subsequent abandonment of indexation of the personal rate scale, the introduction of measures to address tax avoidance, the adoption of a single rate of company tax in 1973, and big changes to the tax treatment of mining companies.

By 1984 it had become clear that this piecemeal approach would no longer suffice; the main effect of plugging one leak was to increase the pressure on other weak points. The basic problem was clear enough: high tax rates imposed on a narrow base. As in so many other countries, that combination was proving to be self-reinforcing. The high rates led to understandable demands for specific base-narrowing relief. When that was not forthcoming, evasion and avoidance produced much the same result.

The reports of the 1970s highlighted the following Australian symptoms of this international disease:

—Excessive reliance on the income base. In particular, Australia had no general tax on consumption, but rather had a narrowly based (and anomaly-ridden) tax on manufactured goods and hotchpotch of excises and taxes on specific activities (gambling, property transactions) and a few services.

—A far from comprehensive income base. In particular, Australia's tax system virtually excluded fringe benefits, capital gains, income from a foreign source, and a sizable, tax-free, first tranche of all income. The capacity to convert income into expenses for tax purposes, for example, deductions for work-related expenses and entertainment, was inadequately controlled.

—High marginal rates of tax. Average wage and salary earners faced a marginal rate of 46 percent, compared with only 19 percent some thirty years earlier; the top marginal rate cut in at incomes only one and one-half times average earnings, compared with about eighteen times thirty years earlier. Despite that lowering of the top marginal rate threshold (because of inflation), those above the top threshold contributed only 20 percent of total personal income tax, compared with a 50-percent contribution from the comparable group thirty years earlier.

—Corporate incomes subject to classical double taxation. Corporations in Australia faced a maximum rate of around 78 percent on distribution.

Given this situation, the driving force behind the 1985 reforms was a desire to lower the high marginal rates of personal income tax, to be financed by a broadening of the income and, more important, consumption tax bases.

THE REFORM PROCESS

Australia's approach to its first major taxation reform in many decades was molded largely by the government's requirements in two important respects: that any reform package have widespread community support and that the major elements be phased in within an electorally acceptable time frame.

The first requirement was to be met by the canvasing of options at a representative national conference, dubbed the National Taxation Summit and held in early July 1985, just seven months after the initiation of the reform process. Representatives of federal, state, and local governments, unions, business, welfare groups, women's groups, and others participated in the conference.[1]

As preparation for the summit, the government published a comprehensive *Draft White Paper,* which analyzed the problems of the Australian tax system, presented three basic approaches to reform, and analyzed those approaches for equity, efficiency, and macroeconomic effects.[2] Each of the three approaches involved reductions in the marginal rates of personal income tax, the extent depending on the base broadening involved in the graduated approaches. Approach A was confined to broadening the income tax base; approach B added a consumption tax at a moderate (5 percent) rate and on a restricted base; approach C added a full-blown consumption tax in terms of both rate (12.5 percent) and base. In the *Draft White Paper* the government expressed a preference for approach C, subject to the requirement of widespread community support.

In any event, that requirement was not met. Each of the major groups at the summit rejected approach C. Business groups rejected it, not because of the consumption tax, but because approach C incorporated all of approach A, which had some elements not to their liking. Most of the other groups were rejecting the consumption tax itself. By and large, rejection was based on fears about the perceived macroeconomic and, more important, distributional effects of such a tax.

The *Draft White Paper* had anticipated that such concerns would emerge and had examined the issue at some length. On the basis of that analysis, the government's preferred approach C included extensive compensation arrangements to ensure that low-income earners who might otherwise be adversely affected by the tax package would not be. For example, some 138 welfare programs and subprograms were targeted to receive compensation supplements. Nonetheless, the fears prevailed. In some measure, that response reflected the support they received from independent distributional analyses that drew strong conclusions from data that, on any objective assessment, were inadequate for the task.

1. The full proceedings of the summit are published in *National Taxation Summit: Record of Proceedings* (Canberra: Australian Government Publishing Service, 1985).

2. *Reform of the Australian Tax System: Draft White Paper* (Canberra: AGPS, June 1985).

Perhaps more fundamentally, however, the fears prevailed and approach C was rejected because there was inadequate time for the case to be made. Put another way, there was an inherent conflict between achieving widespread community support and implementing the program "within an electorally acceptable time frame," which would have required a decision to proceed with the introduction of a broad-based consumption tax by mid-1985. That deadline severely limited the time available to achieve widespread community support.

With the consumption tax rejected, the government set about molding a tax reform package around approach A, concentrating on income base broadening. In that process it examined, and rejected as impracticable, the possibility of grafting a tax on services onto the existing wholesale sales tax (though some rationalization of that tax was undertaken). It also examined, and rejected, several approaches to taxing the tax-free income tranche.[3] The tax reform package was announced in September 1985.[4]

THE REFORM PACKAGE

Table 1 lists the tax reform measures, separated into three broad categories: rate reductions, base broadening, and administrative measures directed at greater compliance. Revenue effects are included to indicate the relative importance, in revenue, of individual measures.

Table 1 does not show one or two minor measures announced as part of the 1985 package but not subsequently enacted. It does, however, include one measure (the so-called quarantining of negative gearing of rental properties) that was enacted but subsequently reversed in the 1987–88 budget.

The package largely reflected the income base-broadening elements of approach A in the *Draft White Paper*. As indicated earlier, the incorporation of approach A within approach C led to the business community's rejection of approach C at the tax summit (reflecting distaste for the foreign tax credit system and the form of the fringe

3. One such approach is canvased in G. Bascand, J. Cox, and M. Porter, *The Draft White Paper: Should There Be an Option 'D'?* (Monash University, Centre of Policy Studies, June 1985).

4. Paul Keating, *Reform of the Australian Taxation System: Statement by the Treasurer* (Canberra: AGPS, September 1985).

TABLE 1. Revenue Effects of the 1985 Tax Reform Package
Millions of dollars at 1987–88 prices, full year

Measure	Estimated revenue change	Measure	Estimated revenue change
Rate reductions		*Base broadening (cont'd)*	
Restructuring of personal rates	−4,560	Limitations on deductions	
		Deductions for entertainment expenses	330[b]
Base broadening		Negative gearing of rental property investments	[e]
Expanded inclusions		Concessions for Australian film industry	35[b]
Fringe benefits tax	750	Deductions for expenditure on conserving or conveying water	13[b]
Capital gains tax	75[a]	Capital subscribed to petroleum and afforestation companies	10[b]
Foreign tax credit system	60[b]	Concessional expenditure rebate	60[d]
Taxation of public-unit trading trusts	5[b]		
Tax-free threshold restrictions	85[b]	*Administrative measures*	
		Prescribed payments system extension	50[b]
Reduced inclusions		Substantiation requirements for employment-related expense claims	190
Imputation system of company tax	−300[c]	Quarterly installment system for provisional tax	[f]
Group loss transfer for petroleum and general mining expenditure	−65[b]	*Other*	
Depreciation on residential income-producing investments	−7[d]	Rationalization of wholesale sales tax	110[b]
		Total	−3,134

a. Revenue from capital gains tax currently estimated between $50 million and $100 million.

b. Estimated revenue changes in 1986–87 prices.

c. Includes abolition of branch profits tax, increase in company tax rate, and changes to imputation and dividend withholding tax arrangements announced on December 10, 1986.

d. Estimated revenue changes in 1985–86 prices.

e. This measure was abandoned in the 1987–88 budget; however, $11 million was raised in 1986–87.

f. The measure is revenue neutral in ongoing terms; however, $70 million associated with late payments will be brought forward to 1987–88, the first year of implementation. The smoother pattern of receipts will result in reduced sales of short-term government securities; associated interest savings are estimated to be about $120 million in 1987–88.

benefits tax). In recognition of that fact, the final package included one major proposal, the imputation system of company taxation, that was not included in approach A and that is highly beneficial to the business sector.

The other significant feature that can be seen in table 1 is that, unlike each of the approaches discussed in the *Draft White Paper*, the package is not revenue neutral. The reasons for that, and the implications, are considered later in this paper. Suffice to note that the total cost (in 1987–88 prices) of about $3.1 billion is substantial by Australian benchmarks; it is equivalent to about 4.0 percent of revenue and 1.1 percent of gross domestic product (GDP). Some of the revenue estimates, however, are necessarily highly speculative because of the absence of data bases where new taxes are involved. This is particularly the case with the capital gains tax, where the ultimate revenue yield of that tax could be orders of magnitude greater than indicated in the table.

THE MAJOR ACHIEVEMENTS

Many of the base-broadening measures, while not unimportant in the Australian context, will be of little interest to an international audience. This paper, therefore, concentrates on what the Australian reform may have to offer in the international context.

Marginal Rate Reductions

Reducing the higher marginal rates of personal income tax was the main objective of the reform. The extent of reduction is shown in table 2. The reform reduced the number of steps in the scale (including the tax-free tranche) from six to five. The reductions were heavily concentrated, as intended, in the top rates. The changes clearly reduced the progression of the rate scale, but the overall reform package was not regressive: the base-broadening measures heavily affected higher-income earners.[5]

5. See the quantitative analysis in Keating, *Reform of the Australian Taxation System*.

TABLE 2. *Pre- and Postreform Tax Rates*

Annual income (dollars)	Prereform marginal rates (percent)	Annual income (dollars)	Postreform marginal rates (percent)	
0– 4,595	0	0– 5,100	0[a]	0[b]
4,596–12,500	25	5,101–12,600	24	24
12,501–19,500	30	12,601–19,500	29	29
19,501–28,000	46	19,501–28,000	43	40
28,001–35,000	48	28,001–35,000	46	40
35,001 and over	60	35,001 and over	55	49

a. Effective December 1, 1986.
b. Effective July 1, 1987.

In comparing the postreform tax rates with those applying in other countries, the following points should be kept in mind:

—While Australia is a federation, the lower levels of government do not levy income tax as they do in most other federations.

—Australia's welfare system is largely noncontributory, being funded from general revenue.[6] Hence the marginal tax rates indicated in table 2 do not need to be adjusted on that score as is required in most other countries.

The Capital Gains Tax

The capital gains tax (CGT) has many of the features of those applying in other countries, but the following aspects might be noted:

—It is not a separate tax but part of the income tax, applying on a residual basis where other provisions of the income tax do not apply.

—It is levied, at the appropriate income tax rates, only on realized real capital gains (calculated by indexing the asset cost base by the Consumer Price Index), with nominal loss offsets allowed. While the taxation of real gains may be considered the most appropriate approach, in the context of a tax system otherwise based on nominal income (in particular, where full deductibility of interest expense

6. The one exception is the Medicare levy, imposed at the rate of 1.25 percent of taxable income, which partly finances the public health system.

applies) the nontaxation of the inflationary wedge represents a concession.

—Compared with CGTs in most other countries, Australia's version is more comprehensive in coverage (the main exemption is the taxpayer's principal residence), including nonresidents.

—Rollover provisions apply at the taxpayer's death and for certain business reorganizations but, in general, are less generous than in most other countries.

—It applies only to gains realized on the disposal of assets acquired after the announcement date, September 19, 1985.

The last-mentioned feature was adopted to ensure that the tax was entirely prospective, reflecting the extreme political sensitivity of retrospective measures in Australia. Its adoption created a privileged class of grandfather assets, exacerbating the lock-in problem associated with taxes levied on a realizations basis. Perhaps of equal importance, its existence has greatly complicated the legislation.

As indicated, Australia has been, to date, rather niggardly in its approach to rollovers. To some extent that reflects a learning process, and some possible extensions to the rollover provisions are currently under review. It also, however, reflects a recognition that the rollover provisions applying in several other countries, when coupled with selective financing arrangements, could readily lead to an indefinite deferral of tax liability.

The Fringe Benefits Tax

The fringe benefits tax (FBT) is imposed on employers for noncash fringe benefits provided to their employees (or their employees' associates). The tax is levied at the company tax rate (now 49 percent, also the top marginal rate of personal income tax) and is not allowed as a deductible expense to employers.

The FBT replaces provisions of the income tax law that sought to tax fringe benefits in the hands of the employee. That approach, as in many other countries, had proved extremely difficult to enforce, and the provision of fringe benefits in Australia had accelerated. The decision to levy the tax formally on the employer was not taken lightly and reflected administrative and industrial relations considerations. The judgment was made that, when the provision of fringe benefits had effectively escaped tax for so long and to such an extent as in Australia, the only effective way of taxing these benefits was in the hands of the employer.

The same approach had been adopted a little earlier in New Zealand but has not yet been pursued in other countries.[7] The New Zealand approach is somewhat more restrictive than Australia's, applying only to those benefits explicitly specified in the legislation. The Australian legislation operates on an exclusions basis, with only a small range of exclusions being specified; de minimus provisions and concessional valuation rules, however, deliberately soften the application of the tax.

The FBT remains the target of criticism by some employers, though less so than initially. In all but the short run, of course, the actual incidence of the tax is unlikely to differ greatly whether it were formally levied on the employer or employee. Furthermore, considerable evidence exists of benefits being cashed out or simply eliminated. Despite that, the revenue yield has greatly exceeded expectations, the extent of benefits provided in this form being even greater than anticipated.[8]

Imputation

A full imputation system of company taxation was introduced from July 1, 1987. It is, to my knowledge, the only such system currently operating in countries in the Organization for Economic Cooperation and Development (OECD), others stopping short of full relief.[9] The imputation system removes the double taxation of dividends by crediting tax paid at the company level to shareholders, making their dividend income effectively tax free if it has already borne company tax at the company rate. Dividends paid out of company income that has borne company tax are known as franked dividends. Dividends

7. It may be worth noting that, while New Zealand tax reform is not under consideration at this conference, that country has recently enacted reforms more extensive than in most of the countries represented here.

8. See *Budget Paper No. 1, 1987–88* (Canberra: AGPS, 1987), pp. 362–65.

9. The split-rate system operating in the Federal Republic of Germany provides full imputation in respect of the federal corporate tax; it does not, however, provide credits for the not insignificant income tax levied on corporations (and other business forms) by lower levels of government.

paid from profits that have not borne Australian company tax are known as unfranked dividends, do not carry imputation credits, and are assessable in shareholders' hands. Imputation ensures that only one level of tax, at shareholders' rates, is applied to all company income paid to taxable shareholders, while company income paid to tax-exempt shareholders is taxed in the hands of the company or not at all.

The method of calculating the extent of imputation credit attaching to dividend payments is disarmingly simple, relying on the maintenance of a "dividend franking account" by companies. The account is credited with the amount of any franked dividends received by the company and with the after-tax amount of any income on which tax has been paid after July 1, 1987 (that is, an amount equal to 51/49 of any tax paid, given the company tax rate of 49 percent). Dividends generally must be paid from the dividend franking account as long as that account has a credit balance, with the account being debited by an amount equal to the franked dividends paid. Where the dividend franking account has insufficient credit to fully frank a dividend, dividends may be franked in part to the extent of credit available.[10] Credits are nonrefundable and hence are not paid to exempt or nonresident shareholders. Coincident with the introduction of imputation, however, the branch profits tax was abolished, and the dividend withholding tax no longer applies to franked dividends paid to nonresidents.

The imputation system involves a considerable cost to revenue despite the limitation imposed by credits not being refundable. To finance the system partly, the company tax rate was increased from 46 percent to 49 percent, leaving an estimated overall cost of about $300 million a year.

Three features distinguish this imputation system from the ideal fully integrated system:

—It does not provide refunds of imputation credits, most notably to nonresidents or tax-exempt bodies such as retirement funds, principally because of the high cost of revenue.

—It imposes a layer of tax on tax-preferred income when distributed

10. For further detail, see Paul Keating, *Statement by the Treasurer: Business Tax Reform—Ending the Double Tax on Company Dividends* (Canberra: AGPS, December 10, 1986).

to shareholders. This means that tax concessions provided to corporate shareholders are clawed back when tax-preferred income is distributed. Besides specific concessions, this condition would also apply to the inflationary component of capital gains, which, under the Australian CGT, is not subject to tax. Thus income that would be freed from tax if earned directly by a taxpayer would eventually bear tax if earned by a corporation. Of course, a considerable deferral advantage accrues to the corporation compared with no concession at all, but a nonneutrality remains between corporate and noncorporate taxpayers.[11]

—It does not look behind the corporate veil to treat undistributed profits in the same way as distributed income, that is, by allocating imputation credits on undistributed income. This is, however, relatively minor. Companies can achieve the result for undistributed income simply by issuing bonus shares or by using a dividend reinvestment scheme. Because bonus shares are treated as dividend and reinvestment, the result is equivalent to imputing retained earnings to shareholders.

Expense Deductibility

The 1985 reform package completely denied deductibility for entertainment expenses, introduced much more stringent substantiation requirements for work-related expenses, and removed rebates for most expenses of a personal nature (the previous concessional expenditure rebate). In each case, the Australian approach would seem to have gone further than similar efforts elsewhere. While not ranking with many of the other measures in reform terms, such changes can be seen as an integral part of attempts to improve the fairness of the tax system.

11. Those who draw attention to this nonneutrality in the imputation system tend to ignore that it also applied under the classical system. Moreover, while the existence of clawback of tax preferences reflects the conventional wisdom, there is some doubt as to whether it actually occurs, or need occur, when one considers the implications of distributions for share prices and hence future capital gains tax liability. Although that is not pursued further here, early work on this topic concludes that the clawback is far from complete.

Quarantining Provisions

The package announced in September 1985 contained two explicit provisions to quarantine losses, generally associated with interest deductibility, one concerning farm incomes and the other concerning income from rental properties (the latter being dubbed, in the Australian context, "negative gearing"). The first of these proposals was not adopted; the second was applied for two years before being abandoned in the 1987–88 budget, delivered on September 15, 1987.

Apart from the treatment of income flows to and from nonresidents, therefore, there are now no explicit quarantining provisions in the Australian tax law. This is in contrast to legislation in many other countries. In particular, it contrasts markedly with the U.S. 1986 Tax Reform Act, which introduced a plethora of quarantining provisions.

The thinking on this issue was conditioned by a debate that has developed in Australia (and elsewhere) in recent years, primarily in the context of highly geared takeover and merger activity. The conclusions are, broadly, that quarantining is very much a second-best approach to dealing with defects in a tax system and, moreover, that it is most unlikely to be effective given the fungibility of money and debt.[12]

Those conclusions relate to taxation within one jurisdiction. Increasingly, not least because of the internationalization of capital markets, taxpayers have become adept at quarantining income or expenses in differing jurisdictions, providing sound grounds for fighting fire with fire. Accordingly, Australia's foreign tax credit system, like others, contains quarantining provisions and applies thin capitalization rules to non-arm's-length borrowing by foreign-controlled subsidiaries operating in Australia. Quarantining efforts in this sphere will no doubt require continuing attention by Australia and others.

SOME ECONOMIC IMPLICATIONS

The 1985 reforms focused on the objectives of equity and efficiency. There was no explicit macroeconomic intent and, as apparently has

12. See, for example, The Treasury, *Some Economic Implications of Takeovers*, Treasury Economic Paper 12 (Canberra: AGPS, 1986).

been the case with reforms in most other countries, macroeconomic considerations did not receive a lot of attention.[13] As the reforms were originally intended to be revenue (more correctly, deficit) neutral, that is not surprising. In any event, the 1985 package was far from revenue neutral, involving a full year (1987–88) cost of about $3.1 billion.

The package departed from revenue neutrality not because of tax reform issues but because, through a coincidence of timing, it came to incorporate personal income tax cuts designed for another purpose. In mid-1985 the government was grappling with the problem of preventing the effects of a sizable exchange rate depreciation from feeding through into the domestic wage and price structure. A real wage decline was required to maintain the improved competitiveness offered by the exchange rate depreciation.

As part of the approach to that problem, an agreement was reached between the government and the union movement that, in the forthcoming national wage round, wage demands would be reduced by 2 percent if equivalent personal tax cuts were provided. Those cuts were delivered by means of an increase in the tax-free threshold and reductions in the first two marginal rates (from 25 percent to 24 percent and from 30 percent to 29 percent). This wage-tax trade-off accounted for the shape of the lower end of the new rate scale and also, as indicated, for the overall net cost of the tax package.

Such a cost clearly raised macroeconomic issues, not least because of the imperative of reducing the overall budget deficit as part of the process of restoring the domestic saving and investment imbalance, which was reflected, at the time, in a current account deficit of the order of about 6 percent of GDP. The government was, then, following a medium-term fiscal strategy addressing that problem, which required significant expenditure restraint. The advent of the tax package intensified that requirement and, in my opinion, played no small role in the significant fiscal improvements since achieved. In particular, the budget deficit was cut from 3.1 percent of GDP in 1984–85 (and a peak of 4.1 percent in the previous year) to zero in 1987–88.

13. They were, however, addressed in the *Draft White Paper*. A fuller treatment, including of what follows in this paper, may be found in E. A. Evans and I. M. McKenzie, "Some Macroeconomic Implications of Tax Reform" (Canberra, 1986).

Revenue was held virtually constant as a proportion of GDP over that period, requiring a reduction in expenditures from 29.7 percent of GDP in 1984–85 to an estimated 26.8 percent this year.

This approach—using tax cuts to force the pace on expenditure reductions— is inherently risky. It did not work in the United States. It has worked in Australia. Clearly, governments control the process and political will, and priorities determine the outcome.

Aside from this overall aspect, the macroeconomic consequences of the 1985 reforms lie primarily in what efficiency gains might attach to base broadening and rate reductions and in the consequences of the reforms for capital formation.

The Taxation of Capital

The 1985 reforms concentrated on the personal income tax. While the *Draft White Paper* devoted some chapters to business tax matters, these did not figure prominently in the final reforms, though the capital gains tax, the foreign tax credit system, and, most notably, the imputation system all have implications for the taxation of business income and are worthy of some attention.

Some of those implications arise from the continued existence of sizable concessions in the tax base and the exemption of certain income. Information on the cost to revenue of these items is provided in the annual Tax Expenditures Statement published by the Treasury. In particular, the following might be noted:

—Accelerated depreciation for plant and equipment

—One hundred and fifty percent research-and-development deduction

—Two and one-half percent depreciation on buildings

—Generous concessions to the film industry

—Nontaxation of income from gold mining

In addition, retirement funds in Australia are not taxed on fund income, and beneficiaries are taxed on lump sum payments at a concessionary rate.

The net effect of the business tax component of the 1985 reforms has been to remove some of the tax discrimination against corporations and to reduce the importance of tax considerations in financing decisions. The combination of a slightly higher corporate tax rate and a more comprehensive capital gains tax will add somewhat to the corporate tax bill but, with the advantages flowing to shareholders from imputation, will not add to the overall rate of tax on investment earnings. If anything, the package of tax measures should add to aggregate saving and investment through lower personal marginal tax rates and a less distortionary tax system.

International Implications

The imputation system offers significant benefits for resident shareholders of resident companies. For nonresident shareholders and for foreign-sourced income, the situation is more complex. A number of features of the reforms have affected the international aspects of Australia's tax system, including the following:

—No refund of excess imputation credits, including those on dividends paid to nonresidents

—Abolition of dividend withholding tax on fully franked dividends

—Introduction of a foreign tax credit system

—No imputation credits for foreign tax paid

At the same time, the corporate tax rate has increased slightly, while the rate in a number of other countries has been falling, in some cases dramatically. Where does that leave Australian companies and shareholders and the attractiveness of Australia to foreign investors?

It is useful to distinguish three cases: foreign investment in Australia, investment abroad by Australian companies, and the conduit situation in which foreign income flows through an Australian company to foreign shareholders. In the first case, the reforms have reduced the total rate of tax on dividends paid by Australian subsidiaries of foreign companies. Dividends paid to foreign investors will now bear total tax (company plus dividend withholding tax) at 49 percent or 15 percent (under treaty) depending on whether the dividend is paid from fully taxed or from tax-preferred income. Under the previous system the rates would have been 54 percent and 15 percent respectively.

While the corporate tax rate has been strongly criticized as being too high by international standards, not all of this criticism has been well founded. Australia, unlike many other OECD countries, does not impose corporate tax at a state or regional level. When account is taken of taxes at all levels of government, Australia's rate does not stand out so markedly. Table 3 compares tax rates for seven countries

TABLE 3. *Corporation Tax Rates, Selected Countries, 1988*
Percent

Country	State or provincial rate	Federal or national rate	Total corporation tax rate
Australia	. . .	49.0	49.0
Hong Kong	. . .	18.0	18.0
United Kingdom	. . .	35.0	35.0
United States	9.6[a]	34.0	40.3
West Germany	25.0[a]	36.0[b]	52.0
Canada	15.5[a]	28.0[c]	44.3
Japan	20.1[d]	33.3[e]	58.5

Source: Author's calculations based on official sources.

a. The tax rates for California and Ontario are illustrative of the state rates for the United States and the provincial rates for Canada. The German trade income tax varies from 12.5 percent to 25.0 percent; the maximum rate of 25 percent is assumed. The California and German taxes are deductible, but the Ontario taxes are not deductible for federal corporate tax purposes.

b. The German corporate tax rate is 56 percent for undistributed income, with a refund of 20 percent of the taxable income on distributions. In other words, the tax rate for distributed income is 36 percent.

c. The Canadian statutory rate is 28 percent. An additional 3-percent surtax currently applies pending sales tax reform.

d. This consists of the 13.2-percent enterprise tax, which is deductible for Japanese corporate tax purposes, and the local inhabitants tax, which is not deductible. The local inhabitants tax is levied at 20.7 percent of the Japanese national corporate tax of 33.3 percent, or 6.9 percent ($.207 \times 33.3$).

e. A withholding tax of 20 percent is also levied on all dividends paid.

and shows that, while Australia has the highest federal statutory tax rate, it has only the third highest rate when all levels of government are considered. For distributions to nonresident shareholders, the total Australian tax rate of 49 percent is higher only than that in Hong Kong and the United Kingdom.

Comparisons such as these, however, can be very misleading and even become a little mindless. Several caveats are warranted. First, comparisons of statutory rates take no account of base differences, which, as the recent U.S. reforms have shown, make a big difference in the actual tax burdens faced by companies. Second, a tax system should not be seen as onerous, and certainly not as revenue efficient, purely because the tax rate is high. Firms find ways of evening out differences between countries and between different business forms. The widespread use of trusts and profit-shifting schemes and the recent advent of stock-stapling schemes provide some examples of the techniques used to minimize taxes by breaking down the barriers imposed by nonneutral tax systems.

Finally, there is a question of where the incidence of the tax falls. It is unlikely to fall completely on the holders of capital, who clearly will attempt not only to minimize taxes but also to shift the burden as much as possible. Some forward shifting will occur, but the precise incidence is uncertain. For a uniform tax, forward shifting will depend on the elasticity of the supply of capital. With perfectly elastic supply (the small country case), the tax can be fully shifted forward, thereby reducing demand for the produce, given fixed exchange rates. With flexible exchange rates, the capital outflow will depend on the extent to which the exchange rate adjusts in response to the forward shifting of the tax.

When the tax is not uniform (that is, different taxpayers or different activities are facing different effective tax rates), the elasticity of supply is still relevant, but other factors are also important. In particular, if the demand for capital in two activities is not independent, an increase in the tax on one activity will not be able to be fully shifted as demand would shift to the substitute. As a result, the tax will cause capital to move from the activity that is being taxed. How does the tax regime facing different types of investors compare?

As table 4 shows, Australian-sourced income distributed to resident or nonresident shareholders is taxed at the same rate of 49 percent (assuming fully franked dividends). For domestic shareholders, this is the maximum tax liability they can face. Nonresident shareholders, however, may face further taxation in their country of residence depending on whether that country has a foreign tax credit system and whether the investment is done directly or by a company in the country of residence. Thus some investors could well be disadvantaged by the high rate in Australia.

While domestic-sourced income is taxed at a uniform maximum rate, the playing field is not entirely even for income arising from investments abroad by Australian companies. When income is received directly by individuals, tax liability can only arise under the

TABLE 4. *Effective Personal and Corporate Tax Rates on Various Shareholders, Selected Countries, 1988*
Percent

Country	Taxable resident, individual shareholder	Tax-exempt resident, shareholder[a]	Nonresident shareholder
Australia	49.0	49.0	49.0
Hong Kong	18.0	18.0	18.0
United Kingdom	64.4	35.0	24.4[b]
United States	64.4	40.3	49.3[c]
West Germany	67.0	52.0	59.2[c]
Canada	59.3	44.3	52.7[c]
Japan	75.1	48.1[d]	55.9[c]

Source: Author's calculations based on official sources.

a. Assumes shareholder is taxable at the maximum personal income tax rate.

b. Assumes a tax treaty of the U.S. type (that is, full tax credit for advance corporation tax paid or 27/73 of dividends paid, and 15-percent dividend withholding tax on dividend plus tax credit).

c. Assumes a tax treaty, with the most common dividend withholding tax of 15 percent. In the United States the most common rate on direct investment is 5 percent.

d. Effective corporate rate reduced by a refund of the 20-percent dividend withholding tax; that is, refund equals 25 percent of cash dividend.

FTCS. However, if the income is received by a resident company, additional tax may be payable when the income is distributed to individual shareholders. Because no imputation credit is available on foreign tax paid, dividends paid by resident companies from foreign-sourced income will not be fully franked and will bear additional tax in the hands of the shareholder. This is shown in table 5.

If the foreign-sourced income has already borne tax at the rate of 40.0 percent, domestic corporate and personal income tax would amount to an additional 29.4 percent, for a total tax burden of 69.4 percent, much higher than for domestic investment. Table 6 repeats the exercise for a wide range of foreign tax rates, indicating that the total tax (foreign and domestic) paid on foreign income increases as the rate of foreign tax increases. Since the total tax paid on domestic

TABLE 5. *Effective Corporate and Personal Tax Rates on Distributed Foreign Income from a 40-Percent Rate Jurisdiction, Selected Countries, 1988*
Percent

Country	Corporate tax	Personal plus corporate tax		
		Distributed to resident individual shareholders[a]	Distributed to tax-exempt resident shareholders	Distributed to nonresident shareholders
Australia	9.0	29.4	9.0	15.2
Hong Kong	0.0	0.0	0.0	0.0
United Kingdom	22.2	36.0	22.0	9.0[b]
United States	5.8	27.7	5.8	5.8[c]
West Germany	0.0	33.6	0.0	9.0[c]
Canada	0.0	16.1	0.0	9.0[c]
Japan	18.3	35.0	7.9[d]	15.7[c]

Source: Author's calculations based on official sources.

a. Assumes shareholder is taxable at the maximum personal income tax rate.

b. Assumes a tax treaty of the U.S. type (that is, full tax credit for advance corporation tax paid or 27/73 of dividends paid, and 15-percent dividend withholding tax on dividend plus tax credit).

c. Assumes a tax treaty, with the most common dividend withholding tax of 15 percent. In the United States the most common rate on direct investment is 5 percent.

d. Effective corporate rate reduced by a refund of the 20-percent dividend withholding tax; that is, refund equals 25 percent of cash dividend.

income is constant at 49 percent (for a taxpayer on the top rate), an increasing disincentive to foreign investment by Australian companies is imposed as the foreign tax rate rises. This relative disincentive has been created by the removal of the second layer of taxation under the imputation system for domestic-sourced income but retention of the essentially classical treatment of foreign-sourced income.

This comparison ignores the deferral advantage available through the FTCS for income sourced in lower-tax countries, which will no doubt represent an important factor driving Australian offshore investment. This deferral arises simply because the FTCS applies only when income is remitted to Australia, not when the income

TABLE 6. *Tax on Foreign Income for Resident Individual Shareholder in Forty-Nine-Percent Personal Tax Bracket*

| Foreign | Tax rate (percent) Australian[a] | | | Total |
	Company	Personal	Total	
0	49	0	49	49.0
10	39	5.1	44.1	54.1
20	29	10.2	39.2	59.2
30	19	15.3	34.3	64.3
40	9	20.4	29.4	69.4
50	0	24.5	24.5	74.5
60	0	19.6	19.6	79.6
70	0	14.7	14.7	84.7

a. Rates are expressed as a percentage of the underlying income, not as a percentage of dividend received as in tables 4 and 5.

accrues. Putting aside all questions of timing (that is, delays both in remitting income to Australia and in distributing that income to individual shareholders), the FTCS has not increased the total tax burden on foreign income received by companies and distributed as dividends to resident individuals. This burden would be the same for an exemption system. The difference is that the FTCS ensures that foreign-sourced income is taxed when received by a corporate Australian shareholder, whereas under the former exemption system, such income was not taxed until received by individual shareholders. Under both systems, total Australian tax is levied at a maximum rate of 49 percent (and, as indicated by table 5, generally much less than that).

This is certainly not a unique Australian problem. As table 3 shows, the rate of tax on foreign-sourced income is high only compared with Hong Kong and Canada. In almost all countries, the total tax on foreign-sourced income exceeds that on domestic income. Interestingly enough, the United States is one exception (except for a minor difference arising from taxation at the state level): the combination of an FTCS and a classical system keeps the two rates equal for foreign tax rates that are less than the U.S. corporate rate.

Obviously the implications of this uneven taxation of foreign-sourced income depend on how much forward shifting of the tax burden is possible in the country of investment. They also depend on how significant the deferral advantage may be for investment by Australian firms in lower-tax countries. To eliminate this deferral advantage completely is not feasible (some countries do so partly by use of controlled foreign corporations legislation); hence it is impossible to achieve full capital export neutrality. But to argue in this case that the deferral advantage should be offset by taxing foreign-sourced income in an essentially classical way would be an imperfect way to compensate for a nonneutrality.

Given the other significant advantages of an imputation system of company tax, there may be merit in trying to move closer to taxation neutrality between domestic and foreign-sourced income even if, at this stage, there is no mechanism for countering the deferral non-neutrality. While some European countries have had at least a partial imputation system for many years, none apparently has seen a pressing need to address the problem. Two possible approaches, short of reverting to a classical system, would be to provide imputation credits for foreign tax paid, or to exempt from tax dividends paid from profits that have not previously borne tax.

It is doubtful that any country would be prepared to surrender the taxing rights implied by the first option, even though this would readily remove the problem. The second option raises a broader issue. The Australian imputation system, in common with the former classical system, effectively claws back some of the advantages provided by specific tax concessions when tax-preferred income is distributed and taxed in the hands of individual shareholders. To some extent this represents nonneutral treatment between companies and individuals investing directly, although the tax liability for the shareholder can elude a substantial deferral.

In adopting the imputation system, the decision was taken that tax-preferred income should continue to be subject to tax when distributed to individual shareholders. This design feature removed the need for the compensatory tax element of the original proposal and is one reason for the distinction between franked and nonfranked dividends. This distinction also prevents companies from distributing, free of tax, very large amounts of retained earnings predating the introduction of imputation.

Thus the franked dividend approach is unlikely to be bettered. It may, however, be possible to enable dividends paid from foreign-sourced income to be paid out by a company with no additional tax liability. This would represent a relaxation of the franked and unfranked dividend distinction. The advantages of this must be weighed against the continuing deferral advantage for investments in low-tax countries, and this matter has not yet been resolved.

The tax liability for nonresident shareholders in Australian trans-nationals can also be very high when income is sourced from outside Australia, that is, when an Australian company is acting as a conduit. The example in table 5 has an Australian tax liability of 15.2 percent on top of the foreign tax liability of 40.0 percent. Australian companies are considering ways to overcome this tax liability. One mooted approach—still subject to consideration by the Australian govern-ment—is by the use of stapled stock schemes, whereby dividends would be paid directly from foreign subsidiaries to foreign share-holders without going through the Australian tax system.

Two conclusions might be drawn from this analysis:

—Foreign-sourced income, when remitted to an Australian com-pany, can be taxed more heavily than domestic-sourced income, thereby providing an apparent bias in favor of domestic investment. This can be at least partly offset by a deferral advantage if the source country has a relatively low rate of tax.

—While the Australian corporate tax rate is relatively high by world standards, this is largely offset by the advantages to shareholders from the full imputation system.

Nevertheless, the high corporate tax rate, the imputation system, and the foreign tax credit system combined provide a less than even playing field for Australian corporations in organizing their interna-tional affairs. At present there is a major incentive for resident corporations to maximize their taxable deductions in Australia while minimizing reported income. Income may instead be recognized in a low-tax country so that the total tax liability can be minimized on a worldwide basis, with the major loser being the Australian revenue. My understanding is that the recent reductions of the U.S. and U.K. corporate tax rates have raised concerns in other countries that this type of practice will become widespread. Restrictions on profit transfer or quarantining provisions are unlikely to eliminate the problem because of complex corporate structures and the fungibility of debt.

The only effective reaction seems to be for other countries to follow the lead of the United States by lowering their corporate tax rates through a process of base broadening.

FURTHER REFORM

The dust from the 1985 reforms in Australia has not yet settled. Some of the legislation has still to be finalized, and there is a lot of tidying up to be done. More important, it will take some time for both individuals and businesses to adjust their economic behavior to the new system. Yet pressure for further reform has not abated and, indeed, was to the fore in the 1987 federal election campaigns.

In part the pressure for further reform comes from those with a preference for smaller government, and the reform proposals they prefer are usually to be financed in large part by expenditure reductions. In part it reflects a desire of some for flatter (less progressive) tax scales. And in part it reflects a more general questioning of why a country with a relatively low overall tax burden should require such high tax rates; thus the base-broadening, rate-reduction possibility remains a subject of debate.[14]

The present government has acknowledged the possibilities in the business tax area and has commissioned the Treasury to review the potential for reducing the corporate tax rate by sensible approaches to broadening the business tax base. It will be recalled that Australia increased the company tax rate from 46 percent to 49 percent to partly finance the imputation system. While such a rate was not out of line then with the developed world generally (the United Kingdom being an exception), the rest of the world has not stood still, and Australia's rate is now toward the upper end of the spectrum. Moreover, a more healthy skepticism is now afoot in many countries about the efficacy of those concessions that do so much to narrow business tax bases, as indicated in *Comparative Tax Systems*:

> There is growing disenchantment almost everywhere with investment incentives. Opinion is widespread that they distort the

14. Australia's public sector is relatively small by the standards of developed countries. In 1985 Australia ranked nineteenth out of the twenty-four OECD countries in overall tax and GDP ratios.

allocation of resources and generate numerous inequities among industries and firms. Britain has already replaced immediate expensing of plant and equipment with more realistic depreciation rates and lowered the corporate rate. Canada is phasing out its investment tax credit and reducing the corporate tax rate. Now that the United States has also eliminated its investment tax credit and lowered its corporate tax rate to 34 percent, other countries are reconsidering the structure and rates of their corporate taxes.[15]

The OECD also reported

The majority of the panel endorsed the idea of a broader corporate tax base with lower tax rates. Such a tax system would be more evenhanded than the systems of tax reliefs with high tax rates and is likely to be more efficient over the long run. The panel also felt that business would welcome a tax system that encouraged decisions on the basis of general commercial considerations rather than on the basis of tax considerations.[16]

Hence the emphasis is not on any simplistic comparison of tax rates internationally but on improving the structure of the tax system. Such an approach is nowhere more important than in Australia, given the restructuring of the economy required to overcome long-standing external account difficulties. The review of business taxation is part of a heightened attention to microeconomic policies with a generalized objective of removing impediments to structural adjustment.

The scope of the base broadening that might be undertaken must await the final review. Some obvious large-ticket items warrant consideration, such as Australia's system of accelerated depreciation for plant and equipment and other overly generous write-off provisions. Timing considerations apart, no restrictions have been placed on the scope of the review.[17] Australia shall also be looking at the

15. Joseph A. Pechman, ed., *Comparative Tax Systems: Europe, Canada, and Japan* (Arlington, Va.: Tax Analysts, 1987), p. 3.

16. For the conclusions of an International Symposium on Tax Reform, January 1987, see OECD, Committee on Fiscal Affairs, *Taxation in Developed Countries: An International Symposium* (Paris: OECD, 1987).

17. For a comprehensive listing of the base-broadening possibilities, see The Treasury, *Tax Expenditures Statement* (Canberra: AGPS, 1986).

potential for controlled foreign corporations provisions and the implications of that for the structure of the foreign tax credit system.

One area requiring particular attention is the arrangements for taxing retirement income. At present, concessions are applied to retirement incomes through the nontaxation of employer contributions to funds and the exemption of fund income. Benefits are taxed, though, notably for higher-income earners, at concessional rates. This review is not solely, nor even primarily, a matter of removing or reducing concessions, though the generosity of the concessions does require consideration. Rather it is a matter of reviewing what taxation arrangements would best mesh with other aspects of the government's retirement income policy and other aspects of the tax system. In particular, there is a need to address the distortions in the saving and investment intermediation process generated by the tax exemption of fund income. It is possible to envisage arrangements that might better meet both objectives without any noticeable effect on the overall concessionality of the provisions, but the full implications of such arrangements require further thought before any firm conclusions can be drawn.

It is intended that the results of this review will be announced either in or before next year's federal budget, due in August 1988. Beyond that review, there seems little doubt that continuing attention to measures to protect the tax base will be required, not least in respect to international transactions. The possibility of shifting the tax mix toward greater reliance on indirect taxation is not on the current agenda but may reemerge at some future date. Australia is also continuing to address the possibilities for comprehensive inflation adjustment of the income tax base.

Comment by C. DAVID FINCH

Being neither a tax expert nor a resident of Australia, my comments cannot follow the pattern set by other discussants. They will focus instead on some general issues, raised by the Australian experience described so lucidly in the paper.

Although Australia's tax reform in 1985 made several important innovations, it failed to achieve the main initial aim—the introduction of a consumption tax. This objective was lost at the special meeting held on tax reform—the National Taxation Summit—which allowed special interests, business, and unions to focus their objections against reform with enhanced publicity. Although the author attributes the loss in this forum to inadequate time for the case to be made, it seems clear, with hindsight, that the summit was a tactical mistake. A lesson for others would seem to be to avoid allowing too much attention to special interests that are virtually certain to oppose reform. Instead, particularly when the electoral cycle is short, act quickly when political decisions can be taken.

Given the outcome of the summit, the tax reform implemented without the proposed consumption tax involved a major loss of revenue. The paper relates this loss to a bargain made with the unions in which they accepted a wage settlement that was lower by the amount of the tax reduction so that their take-home pay was not affected. The Australian Compulsory Arbitration system gave this trade-off a special importance not matched in other countries. Nevertheless such considerations have a dubious role in tax reform. All too often wages quickly return to past patterns while the tax structure is much less adaptable.

This state of affairs highlights a general problem with tax reform. The effort to achieve political support for a reform featuring microeconomic gains almost inevitably weakens the capacity of the financial authorities to ensure that macroeconomic policy remains adequately strong. The major loss of revenue in the case of Australia fits the prototype.

The author, however, stresses that in Australia there were broadly equivalent cuts in expenditures, suggesting that the normal weakness was overcome. There were in fact important successes—although they were achieved primarily in state, not federal, expenditures. This undoubtedly was aided by the unusually favorable tactical position of the federal government on income tax cuts. Grants to the states were directly related to income tax receipts, as they were compensation for the states' conceding sole rights in this tax to the federal government. Nevertheless, even allowing this measure of success, questions can still be raised on the macroeconomic costs of the reform. Australia, at the time, had a serious current account deficit in the balance of payments. It seems likely that achieving tax reform delayed the urgently needed improvement in the fiscal position. Consequently, subsequent budgets had to be more restrictive.

In regard to international cooperation on taxation, Evans discusses the problems arising from Australia's innovations with corporate taxation. The introduction of a system of imputation to avoid double taxation by allowing personal taxpayers a tax credit for the income tax levied on the corporation raises interesting problems when transactions cross national boundaries. Further study of these problems by an international group is clearly urgent, and I am pleased to hear that the Organization for Economic Cooperation and Development has this task in hand.

However, the problems raised are not only ones of description of the issues. Any extension of the approach taken by Australia would multiply the value of international negotiations for the appropriate adaptations of tax laws. While these can be handled by bilateral negotiations, it would be much more efficient if multilateral negotiations were arranged, giving the broader setting needed. At this stage it is undoubtedly utopian to expect such an innovation, but upgrading the regularity and status of an international committee on such issues would be a useful step. This was done for banking by the creation by the Bank for International Settlements of the Cooke committee of bank regulators. A formal step on taxation taken now would give increased visibility and importance to the taxation issues arising in a rapidly integrating world. Later this could lead to multilateral negotiation on international taxation, perhaps eventually even to a secretariat that, like the General Agreement on Tariffs and Trade for trade issues, could provide the forum for multilateral resolution of the inevitable problems in this area.

DAVID A. DODGE & JOHN H. SARGENT

Canada

In June 1987, the government of Canada proposed major changes to the federal government's three leading revenue sources: the personal income tax, the corporate income tax, and the federal sales tax. The reforms would significantly reduce rates and broaden the tax base for the personal and corporate income taxes. The existing sales tax, which is levied on a relatively narrow base at the manufacturing level, would be replaced by a type of value-added tax (VAT) on a broad base of consumer goods and services. The general approach to tax reform is part of a broader economic strategy, which favors a less intrusive role for government in the private economy, adopted by the government that was elected in September 1984. This view has been reflected in reductions in subsidies to business, significant deregulation of the energy and transportation sectors, and privatization of a number of government-owned enterprises, as well as in the move toward a more neutral tax system with lower tax rates.

Following the tabling of the proposals in June, House of Commons and Senate committees held hearings and issued reports suggesting a number of modifications. The government responded to these reports and to representations received, in December. It announced its intention to modify the proposals in certain respects. Legislation is expected to be introduced early in 1988 to implement the personal and corporate income tax reforms, which will start to take effect in 1988. The sales tax reform—certain aspects of which are still being developed—would be implemented at a later stage.

BEFORE THE REFORM SYSTEM

A brief review of the overall structure of government revenues in Canada and of key features of the existing personal and corporate income taxes and the federal sales tax is important as background to the reform proposals. Tax revenues of all levels of government are equal to 33 percent of gross domestic product (GDP) in Canada; this figure is modestly higher than in the United States but less than in the major European countries. The central or federal government share in tax revenues in Canada is about 50 percent. Personal income tax revenues, which accounted for 36 percent of total tax revenues of all levels of government in 1985, are a somewhat larger share of total taxes than in the large European countries, although virtually the same share as in the United States. Corporate income tax revenues, which account for 8 percent of total revenues, are in the middle of the range for major developed countries. Social security contributions, at 13 percent of total taxes, are much lower than in most other countries, including the United States. General sales taxes, at 13 percent of total taxes, are somewhat lower than in most European countries that make substantial use of the VAT, but much higher than in the United States. However, revenues from tariffs, and excise taxes on specific goods, motor vehicle licenses, and other things are relatively important; total taxes on goods and services are a higher share, at 32 percent, of total government revenues than in any of the major developed countries except the United Kingdom. Local real property taxes are also relatively important.

Personal Income Taxes

Personal income taxes currently provide about 45 percent of federal government revenues. The personal income tax is a progressive tax on a reasonably comprehensive definition of income, with federal rates starting at 6 percent and rising to 34 percent[1] on taxable income in excess of roughly $60,000.[2] The taxpaying unit is the individual income recipient, with fixed personal exemptions for spouse and dependents. All Canadian provinces also levy personal income taxes; the federal government collects tax for nine of the ten provinces, one condition of the arrangement being that provinces express their taxes

1. In this description of the existing tax system, and in the later description of the reform proposals, a temporary 3-percent surtax currently applied to federal personal and corporate tax liabilities is not taken into account.
2. Unless otherwise indicated, dollar figures in the text refer to Canadian dollars.

as a percentage of federal tax. (Taxpayers in the nine provinces participating in the Tax Collection Agreement file a single return that covers both federal and provincial taxes.) Although there is some variation, provincial taxes average about 55 percent of federal tax, resulting in combined federal-provincial top marginal rates in the range of 53 percent.

A feature of the postwar evolution of personal income taxation in Canada, as in many other countries, has been the significant reduction over time in top-bracket marginal rates and the reduction in the income level—in real terms—above which the top rate applies. In 1972 the top combined federal-provincial rate was reduced from 80 percent on taxable income over $400,000 (or over $1,300,000 in today's prices) to about 61 percent on taxable income over $60,000 ($190,000 in today's prices). In 1982 it was further reduced to just over 50 percent on taxable income over $53,000 ($65,000 in today's prices).

Capital gains have been subject to tax since 1972, with one-half of capital gains included in taxable income. Capital gains unrealized at the death of a taxpayer are included as income in the final year's tax return. Gains on owner-occupied housing are exempt. In 1985 the government introduced a lifetime exemption, to be phased in, of $500,000 of net capital gains. At the same time, special treatment for gains on farm assets and on gains on shares in small business corporations transferred to the taxpayer's children was eliminated.

There are no deductions for property taxes or for home mortgage or other consumer interest. Retirement saving—in the form of pension plans or saving by the self-employed within special plans—are deductible up to an annual limit. Earnings on the plans accumulate tax free, and payments are subject to full taxation. There is, however, no supplementary tax on early withdrawals.

Indexation of personal exemptions and of tax brackets for inflation was implemented in 1974. As a deficit reduction measure, effective in 1986, the first three percentage points of annual increase in the Consumer Price Index were excluded in calculating the adjustment in the indexation factor. As an ad hoc measure to provide some recognition of the effect of inflation on the real value of interest income, a deduction was introduced for the first $1,000 of interest income in 1974 and later extended to dividend income and taxable capital gains. During a brief experiment in the early 1980s, taxpayers were offered an option that provided for taxation of capital gains on an inflation-adjusted but semiaccrual basis for listed common shares held in special plans.

There is some integration of the personal and corporate income tax system, implemented through a credit against personal income tax on Canadian corporate dividends received. Currently, a credit of roughly one-third of the dividend is allowed against personal income tax liabilities; the dividend is grossed up by one-third for inclusion in income. The credit approximately offsets the tax that would be expected to be paid on the income underlying dividends by a fully taxable private corporation eligible for the small business tax rate reduction.

There are two refundable credits under the personal income tax. A "child tax credit" was introduced in 1978 and is currently equal to roughly $500 per child. It is reduced by 5 percent of family net income in excess of roughly $24,000. A "sales tax credit," currently equal to $50 per adult and $25 per child and reduced by 5 percent of family net income over $15,000, was implemented in 1986 as an offset to the impact of an increase in the sales tax on the position of lower-income taxpayers. While, as noted, the taxpaying unit is generally the individual, these two refundable credits are reduced on the basis of family income (or, more precisely, the total income of the individual and his or her spouse) as this is considered more closely related to the need that these credits address.

An alternative minimum tax took effect in 1986. The base adds back selected tax preferences, including the deduction for retirement saving. The federal rate is 17 percent, which, given the automatic impact on provincial tax, results in an overall rate of about 25 percent. However, the first $40,000 in adjusted taxable income is exempt.

There are no inheritance or gift taxes; they were dropped at the federal level in 1972, when taxation of capital gains was introduced, and were gradually dropped by all the provinces over the ensuing thirteen years. There are no personal wealth or capital taxes, although local government real property taxes are important.

Corporate Income Tax

The corporate income tax currently accounts for 11 percent of federal government revenues. While financial statement income is the starting point for the tax base, the existing law generally provides capital consumption allowances that are accelerated relative to accounting depreciation. In addition, credits that reduce taxes are allowed, including an investment tax credit for the manufacturing, resource, construction, and transportation sectors, and a credit on current and capital research and development expenditures. The rates of investment tax credit for the manufacturing and resource sectors and the research and development credit are higher in defined regions that have experienced persistently above-average unemployment rates and below-average per capita income levels. Interest is fully deductible, and there is no alternative minimum tax at the corporate level.

Special provisions apply to the resource sector; the treatment of exploration and development expenses is generous relative to standard accounting. Instead of allowing deduction of provincial mining taxes and oil royalties, there is a "resource allowance" (deduction from taxable income) equal to 25 percent of resource profits measured before deduction of interest, exploration and development costs, earned depletion allowances, and resource taxes. This approach was designed to recognize a role for provincial royalty-type taxes on depletable resources, but to avoid the possibility of provinces' preempting an excessive share of the federal corporate tax base through royalty charges.

The general federal corporate rate on taxable income is 36 percent, with a rate of 30 percent applied to manufacturing and processing profits earned in Canada, a rate of 15 percent applied to the first $200,000 of active business income of Canadian-controlled private corporations, and a rate of 10 percent applied to the first $200,000 of manufacturing and processing profits of Canadian-controlled private corporations. Provinces also levy corporate income taxes at rates that vary but, for the most part, are in the 10-percent range on small business income and in the 15-percent range on other income. Thus the combined federal-provincial rate for public, nonmanufacturing corporations is generally just above 50 percent. The federal government collects the provincial corporate income tax for seven of the ten provinces. In these provinces, taxable income for provincial purposes is identical to the base for the federal tax. In the other provinces the base is similar.

As might be expected, given these features of the tax system, wide variation occurs in the ratio of taxable income to book income and in the effective tax rate on new investment. The ratio of taxable to book income for profitable corporations ranges from just under 50 percent in mining and the financial sector to above 95 percent in construction, wholesale and retail trade, and services. The combined federal-provincial effective tax rate on new investment for large, taxpaying corporations is estimated to range from −15 percent in mining to more than 35 percent in construction and wholesale and retail trade.

Many of the tax preferences in the corporate income tax were introduced in the 1970s. In 1972, in response to concerns that the U.S. domestic international sales corporation (DISC) provision might further weaken already depressed investment in Canadian manufacturing, the special, lower tax rate on manufacturing and processing income was introduced, and a special 50-percent straight line rate of capital cost allowance (depreciation) was introduced for machinery and equipment used in manufacturing and processing. In 1975, as a measure of general investment stimulus, the investment tax credit was introduced on depreciable property in the manufacturing and processing sectors. It was subsequently extended to the transportation and construction sectors and to research and development expenditures. A further special provision was the 3-percent inventory allowance introduced in 1978 as an ad hoc means of adjusting for inflation.

As noted, there is some integration of the corporate and personal income taxes.

Federal Sales Tax

The federal sales tax currently accounts for 14 percent of federal revenue. Canada's federal sales tax is a single-stage tax, generally levied on the manufacturer's sale price of goods produced in Canada and on the customs value of imported goods, including any applicable duty. A relatively narrow range of goods is taxable at the wholesale trade level.

The standard rate of tax for most manufactured goods is currently 12 percent, with construction materials taxed at 8 percent and alcohol and tobacco products at 15 percent. As it is essentially a tax on manufactured goods sold in Canada, the tax is not levied on services nor does it apply to exported goods. In addition, many items such as food, clothing and footwear, heating fuels and electricity, books and magazines, and certain health goods are exempted from federal sales tax.

The current federal sales tax applies not only to goods destined for sale to consumers, but also to business inputs, such as office supplies and materials used to construct business facilities. Although production, farming, and mining machinery, equipment, and raw materials are generally exempt from tax, business inputs are for the most part taxable for all firms beyond the manufacturer's level. In fact, approximately one-half of the total federal sales tax collected is derived from business inputs.

The sales tax has become something of an administrative nightmare; a vast number of detailed rules, often somewhat arbitrary in nature, are required to differentiate between taxable and exempt commodities, to define the exact point in the production-distribution process that should be used to measure value for tax purposes, and to provide adjustment to actual transactions prices when those transactions do not occur at the point in the process at which it was desired to levy the tax. These notional adjustments have recently been subject to court challenges. As well as these administrative considerations, the tax is known to result in widely varying effective rates—in terms of the ratio of tax to final retail selling price—even among similar, taxed products. Further, the tax base is defined in such a way that the effective rates applied to domestic manufactures are generally higher than the rates applied to imported manufactures. Finally, although the intent is to exempt exports and production machinery, some inputs in the production of exports and machinery are taxed.

This description of Canada's current tax system is, among other things, intended to convey the message that Canada shared rather fully in what seems to have been a tendency for tax incentives and other tax preferences to proliferate, especially in business taxation and, in Canada's case, in the federal sales tax.

CONSIDERATIONS IN REFORM

The government elected in September 1984 had or soon developed a number of concerns with the tax system. As noted, the new government had a preference for a less intrusive role for government in business activity. Two months after the government took office, the minister of finance published a paper, which saw government's role as "establishing a positive and stable climate for investment" and expressed the concern that government programs and tax provisions "should not override the economic basis for business decisions."[3] As discussed in the overview of the existing corporate tax system, the effective tax rates on new investment by industry sectors are widely dispersed. The intent to move toward a more even playing field was established early as a priority.

A second concern was that public confidence in the fairness of the tax system was eroding, in part because some high-income taxpayers and profitable corporations paid little or no tax. Tax preferences contribute to this result. It could be argued that taxpayers taking advantage of tax preferences will tend to pay a price in lower before-tax returns. However, concern remains that certain preferences still convey significant benefits. In any event one cannot dismiss the general public perception.

Dependability of revenue yield was the third major concern. A particular factor was the build-up of potential tax deductions and credits in businesses not in a position to take advantage of them currently. As well as adding directly to the uncertainty of future revenue yield, this build-up created pressure to find ways, not intended when the original provisions were introduced, to transfer the tax benefits to those with taxable income. Trading in tax losses by one means or another, including innovative use of limited partnerships, was becoming increasingly prevalent and expensive in revenue terms.

These general concerns with the tax system applied with particular force to the federal sales tax. As explained, besides suffering from severe problems of administration, this tax distorts economic decisionmaking in several dimensions, is unfair in that its incidence depends on particular consumption patterns, and has proved subject to erosion as new avoidance techniques were developed.

The constraint that the overall level of revenue had to be firmly protected was added to these concerns about personal, corporate, and sales tax structure. The government inherited a deficit equal to 6.8 percent of GDP in 1984.[4] It has set the objective of reducing the

3. Michael H. Wilson, *A New Direction for Canada: An Agenda for Economic Renewal* (Ottawa: Canadian Department of Finance, 1984), p. 39.
4. This figure is on the national income accounts basis.

deficit, by the early 1990s, to a level at which public debt will grow no faster than GDP; this aim will require a reduction in the deficit-to-GDP ratio of about five percentage points relative to the 1984 level. Roughly half the required reduction is expected to be achieved by the end of 1987. While the larger part of the reduction in the ratio of the deficit to GDP achieved to date has reflected a decrease in the ratio of expenditures to GDP, it has also been necessary to introduce net tax increases over the past three years to make adequate progress toward achieving the deficit reduction goals. With some distance still to go in reducing the deficit, it is not possible to remedy problems in tax structure in ways that reduce net revenues, and it is desirable to protect revenues through preventing erosion that could result from expanded use of existing tax preferences.

The government's initial inclination was to avoid comprehensive tax reform. Rather it intended to proceed to remedy individual problems in the personal and corporate income taxes and to start a process, begun several times by previous governments but never carried through, of major reform of the sales tax. The government started almost immediately to address the concerns relating to economic distortion, fairness, and revenue stability and reliability. Measures were introduced in 1985 and 1986 to restrict avoidance in each of the three tax areas. An alternative minimum tax provision was added to the personal income tax. The general investment tax credit, although not the special credits for research and development and for investment in certain regions, was phased out, and corporate rates were lowered, starting in 1987.

This period thus saw significant tax change. However, with further changes on the horizon for each of the three major revenue sources, the case for a comprehensive, integrated approach, in which the balance among the three taxes would also be reviewed, strengthened.

By mid-1986 it was also becoming clear that broad-ranging reform would occur in the United States. The U.S. reform would greatly lower corporate and top personal income tax rates while greatly cutting back personal and business tax preferences. The U.S. example raised the profile of comprehensive tax reform as an issue in public discussion in Canada and gave encouragement to the approach of lowering rates and broadening bases, which was the government's general inclination. Further, the changes in the U.S. regime had certain direct implications for the Canadian tax system. A situation in which statutory corporate tax rates were much higher in Canada than in the United States, besides influencing longer-run competitiveness of business activity in Canada, could be expected to inspire arrangements by multinational firms to direct income to the lower tax jurisdiction and expenses to the country with a higher tax rate. Any significant statutory rate differential could thus seriously threaten corporate income tax revenues. The sharp reduction in statutory corporate tax rates in the United States virtually forced some reduction in Canadian statutory rates.

Similarly, a situation in which average personal income tax rates were much higher than rates in the United States would tend to put Canadian businesses—including Canadian professional sports organizations such as National Hockey League teams—at a disadvantage in attracting key people. The U.S. example of rebalancing between the personal and corporate tax also had an influence. The fact that effective corporate tax rates on new investment were raised gave some room for adjusting effective rates in Canada without encountering immediate concerns and criticism about the impact on the competitive position of Canadian industry and the attractiveness of investment in Canada.

The government decided to proceed with comprehensive reform in July of 1986, having already done substantial background work, particularly in corporate income tax and sales tax. The general strategy chosen had two central thrusts. The first was to reduce tax rates, while broadening the tax base for all three taxes through eliminating or reducing tax incentives and other tax preferences. This approach of rewarding success, not effort, had clearly been foreshadowed in the basic position that government should set a favorable framework for business but should lessen the extent to which it was an active player. It had also been foreshadowed in several of the specific measures, particularly in corporate tax.

Great importance was attached to achieving a significant reduction in marginal tax rates. This aim reflects the basic judgment that lower rates are the most effective general incentive for better economic performance across the various dimensions of efficient allocation of investment, promotion of personal effort and innovation, increased saving, and so on. Furthermore, lower rates lessen the risk of diversion of income to other jurisdictions and contribute to international competitiveness. They also lessen the incentive for avoidance and thus contribute to the objective of revenue stability.

Given the constraint that revenues could not be reduced, the strategy of seeking substantial rate reductions put particular pressure behind the effort to broaden the tax base through elimination of, or reduction in, selective tax preferences. This second half of the first thrust had its own direct justification. It responded to the concern that tax rather than economic considerations were increasingly dominating business decisions, to the fairness concern that some high-income individuals and profitable corporations were paying little or no tax, and to the concern that the build-up of the overhang of tax losses—resulting from tax preferences—contributed to instability of revenues. But the drive to reduce tax rates greatly strengthened the willingness to cut back tax preferences.

The second strategic choice was that there should be a rebalancing of the mix among personal income tax, corporate income tax, and sales tax revenues, to arrest—and to some extent reverse—the trend of the past three decades that has seen an increase in the share of federal government revenues from the personal income tax and reductions in the share of corporate income tax revenues and sales tax revenues. The increase in personal income tax share reflected, in part, a significant increase in effective personal income tax rates. At the same time, a narrowing of the sales tax base and an increase in the relative importance of tax preferences under the corporate income tax contributed to the declining shares of these two revenue sources. The strategy of rebalancing the revenue mix reflected, among other things, the view that heavy dependence on one revenue source, and the accompanying high rates, invites serious problems of avoidance.

The strategy of rate reduction and base broadening would be carried out while retaining the fundamental approach of levying personal and corporate taxes on nominal income. The possibilities of switching from income to an expenditure or cash flow base, or alternatively of introducing adjustment of business and investment incomes for inflation, did not commend themselves to the government.

Income rather than expenditures is still viewed by the government as the base for personal taxation that best achieves the objective of equity of taxation based on ability to pay. There is a willingness to continue to accept one significant qualification to the income base by allowing a deduction, up to a limit, for saving for retirement. This emphasis on income as the basis for personal taxation does not preclude an important role for the sales tax as a significant additional revenue source, with the refundable sales tax credit making it possible to achieve consistency between the goals of increased use of the sales tax and equity. The balanced use of the income and sales bases makes it possible to avoid very high rates on either one.

For corporate income tax, income again continues to be viewed as the most appropriate base subject to partial integration with the personal income tax. In an economy in which the important resource sector, in particular, can be subject to substantial cyclical swings, the income base results in a more countercyclical revenue pattern than would a cash flow base. Thus businesses tend to be assisted during depressed periods, which is an important consideration. There are also big advantages in using the same general basis for business taxation as used by countries closely linked with Canada in trade and international investment.

The government's disposition has been to reduce rather than enhance the use of automatic adjustment for inflation and ad hoc offsets to inflation such as the inventory allowance and the investment income deduction. The marked reduction achieved in the actual rate of inflation and the determination to maintain noninflationary monetary and fiscal policy have lessened the case for inflation adjustment. Further, full adjustment of business and investment income for inflation would introduce substantial complexity for taxpayers and would add to the cost of compliance. Full inflation adjustment would obviously require limitation of the interest expense deduction to "real interest." This step would tend initially to more than offset, in cash flow, the benefits for many businesses from inflation adjustment of capital consumption and inventory allowances. The difficult issue of dealing with tax deductions and income connected with interest on outstanding debt also arises. Finally, the accounting profession has not yet reached consensus on the best approach to inflation adjustment, and there are unresolved issues concerning the choice of price index (for example, whether indexation should be provided on price changes that reflect sales tax changes or international price shocks).

It is significant that the 1984 U.S. Treasury proposals to move most of the way toward full inflation adjustment of business and investment income were dropped at a fairly early stage of public discussion. The complexity and unpopularity of the interest adjustment provision was apparently a major factor. Both the U.S. experience on this issue, and the advantages in keeping the Canadian tax system for business income broadly in line with the U.S. system, given the integration of the two economies, reinforced the government's initial view that inflation adjustment of business income was not appealing under current circumstances.

THE PROPOSED REFORMS

The major changes proposed for the three revenue sources must be examined against this background of the considerations that motivated the decision to proceed with tax reform and the general strategy adopted.

Personal Income Tax Changes

The existing personal income tax system was accepted as basically sound and in need of repair rather than fundamental change. In general, the Canadian system has fewer personal income tax preferences than the U.S. system and thus offers somewhat less potential for base broadening. As noted, the intent is to achieve a marked reduction in rates while taking base-broadening action to offset in part the revenue loss from lower rates and to ensure that high-income taxpayers bear a fair share of the tax. The conversion of personal exemptions and some deductions to credits is the third major element of personal income tax reform. Although there is no intent to achieve a major redistribution of the share of tax borne, on average, by different income groups, there is a desire to reinforce existing effective progressivity by eliminating tax on some low-income taxpayers and by modestly increasing the share borne by upper-income groups.

The federal rate schedule, which currently consists of ten brackets with rates starting at 6 percent and rising to 34 percent on income in excess of $63,000, will be replaced by three brackets with rates of 17 percent on the first $27,500 of taxable income, 26 percent on the next $27,500, and 29 percent on income over $55,000. Some 66 percent of taxpayers will be in the 17-percent tax bracket, 29 percent will be in the 26-percent bracket, and 5 percent in the 29-percent bracket. The top combined federal-provincial marginal rate should decline from an average of about 53 percent to an average of 45 percent.

TABLE 1. *Threshold Income Levels at which Positive Federal Income Tax Is Payable, 1988*
Income in dollars

Tax law	Single, under 65	Single, over 65	Married, 1 earner 2 children	Couple, over 65
Before reform	4,940	10,785	16,770	16,945
After reform	6,220	11,430	18,890	19,010

Source: Canadian Department of Finance, *Tax Reform 1987: A Summary for Taxpayers* (Ottawa, December 1987), p. 9.

An important change in the personal income tax is the replacement of personal exemptions by nonrefundable credits of fixed amounts, and of several deductions by credits equal to a given percentage of the base for the previously allowed deduction. This change in structure reflects the view that it is fairer to provide the same tax saving to all taxpayers in identical situations rather than tax savings that increase in value with marginal rates, as is the case for an exemption or deduction. The new basic personal credits have generally been set at levels that provide greater tax saving to lower-income taxpayers but a lesser saving to upper-bracket taxpayers than do the current exemptions. The switch from exemptions to credits at the levels chosen has the effect of significantly raising the threshold income levels at which positive tax is payable, as shown in table 1. By offsetting some of the benefit received by high-income taxpayers as a result of lower marginal rates, the switch also helps make it possible to combine the fairness objective of reinforcing effective progressivity of the tax system with the strategy of significant reduction in top marginal rates. The new rate brackets and personal credits continue to be indexed for inflation in excess of 3 percent.

As noted, the substitution of credits for certain deductions reflects the view that the rate of tax assistance for certain special expenditures should be equal across income levels. Thus the deductions for medical expenses in excess of 3 percent of income and for university tuition expenditures will be replaced by credits calculated at the first bracket (17 percent) rate. The current deduction for charitable contributions will be replaced by a credit at a rate of 17 percent on the first $250 in annual contributions and 29 percent—equal to the top marginal rate—on total contributions in excess of $250. This measure thus increases the strength of the incentive provided for charitable contributions for all taxpayers to match that currently provided by the exemption approach for top-bracket taxpayers. Deductions are retained for contributions to retirement saving.

The personal income tax changes outlined thus far would reduce personal income tax revenues by about 8 percent. This reduction is partially offset by base-broadening measures that raise revenues by about 4 percent. The most important of these in terms of revenue yield is the elimination of the $1,000 investment income deduction. An important change in tax structure terms is the sharply reduced preference for most forms of capital gains. The $500,000 lifetime exemption will be reduced to $100,000 on capital property other than farm property and shares in small business corporations. To reduce tax shelter possibilities and better match deductions with taxable income, individuals will be able to claim the exemption for taxable capital gains only to the extent the gains exceed cumulative net investment losses incurred after 1987. The fraction of capital gains included in taxable income will increase from the current 50.0 percent to 66.6 percent in 1988 and 75.0 percent in 1990.

Other base-broadening measures include reduced deductions for home offices, meals, entertainment, and automobile expenses for the self-employed; the new regime is intended to recognize a consumption element in such expenses. Certain specific tax shelter possibilities will be reduced. The government explicitly rejected, however, general restrictions on deductions for passive losses and for investment interest costs. The Canadian tax system already limits the extent to which losses arising from depreciation allowances on rental real estate and other rental properties can be deducted against other income. The new provision limiting the capital gains exemption to gains in excess of cumulative net investment losses will also provide protection against systematic exploitation of tax shelter possibilities associated with investment in appreciating assets. However, it was considered important to retain the cash flow advantages that interest deductibility provides to those investing in assets with uncertain or variable income streams.

With the narrowing in the spread between the bottom and top marginal rates, it was judged appropriate to eliminate averaging

TABLE 2. *Change in Federal-Provincial Personal Income Tax Due to Tax Reform Measures, 1988*

Income class (dollars in thousands)	Households with reduced tax		Households with increased tax		All households	
	Number affected (millions)	Average change (dollars)	Number affected (millions)	Average change (dollars)	Average change (dollars)	Change as a percent of tax
Under 15	2,800	−140	230	190	−110	−21.6
15–30	3,015	−460	245	340	−395	−12.7
30–50	2,260	−525	285	420	−415	−5.5
50–100	1,435	−735	285	795	−480	−3.1
100 and over	180	−4,165	60	8,050	−1,175	−2.3
Total	9,690	−490	1,105	865	−350	−5.5

Source: Canadian Department of Finance, *Tax Reform 1987: A Summary for Taxpayers*, pp. 30, 24, 25.

provisions. This will help simplify the tax structure. With the reduction in the corporate income tax rates for small business, it was appropriate to reduce the rate of dividend credit—which achieves approximate full integration for small, private corporations—from 33 percent to 25 percent (combined federal-provincial rate).

The combined impact of the various personal income tax measures on taxpayers of different income levels is summarized in tables 2 and 3. As shown, about 90 percent of households with incomes below $30,000 experience a reduction in tax, whereas roughly 75 percent of households with income over $100,000 have a tax decrease. On average, taxes decrease for taxpayers in all brackets, with the average decrease rising in dollar terms, but tending to fall as a percentage of tax, as income rises. There is a modest shift in the share of federal tax payable from lower- to higher-income groups.

In economic impact, the significant decrease in marginal rates facing many taxpayers may be expected to encourage a modest increase in labor supply, estimated in the range of 0.5 percent to over 1 percent.[5] The impact on marginal rates for those receiving investment income is more complex. Those with interest income above the previous

5. Canadian Department of Finance, *Tax Reform 1987: Economic and Fiscal Outlook* (Ottawa, 1987), p. 4.

TABLE 3. *Share of Federal Personal Income Taxes Paid by Income Class, 1988*

Income class (dollars in thousands)	Share of tax filers (percent)	Share of federal tax payable	
		Before tax reform (percent)	After tax reform (percent)
Under 15	46.7	1.6	1.1
15–30	28.7	25.2	23.9
30–50	18.2	38.3	38.6
50–100	5.5	22.8	23.7
100 and over	0.8	12.1	12.7
Total	100.0	100.0	100.0

Source: Canadian Department of Finance, *Tax Reform 1987: Income Tax Reform* (Ottawa, 1987), p. 37, updated for December 1987 modifications.

$1,000 exempt limit will generally experience a decline in marginal tax rates. There will usually be an increase in the rate faced on income in the form of capital gains and mixed changes in the rate faced on dividends. Very little net change in saving is expected. However, portfolio allocation will be subject to reduced distortion.

Corporate Income Tax Measures

As mentioned earlier, a first phase of corporate tax reform has already been implemented. It reduced rates and broadened the base through eliminating the inventory allowance and phasing out the general investment tax credit. The current proposals will further reduce tax rates, with the standard federal rate falling to 28 percent from 36 percent in 1986 or the 33 percent that was previously scheduled to be reached in 1989. A differential in favor of manufacturing and processing profits will continue: The rate on manufacturing profits will be phased down from 30 percent to 23 percent by 1991. There will be a single small business rate of 12 percent on the first $200,000 per year of active business income of Canadian-controlled private corporations, compared with the 1986 general rate of 15 percent and the small manufacturing rate of 10 percent.

The most important corporate base-broadening measure for revenues is the replacement of the three-year write-off currently allowed on manufacturing and processing equipment with a 25-percent declining balance rate of capital cost allowance. The change will be phased in by 1991. Reduction in capital cost allowance rates for other assets will also bring these rates closer to rates of economic depreciation. In total, reductions in capital cost allowances over the first five years provide 26 percent of the increased revenue from base broadening.

Several changes in the tax treatment of financial institutions, including tighter restrictions on allowances for reserves against potential bad debts, will bring their taxable income closer to what is usually considered economic income. A tax of 1.25 percent of the capital of large deposit-taking institutions, creditable against regular income tax, will ensure that such institutions pay some tax over the transition period. In addition, a special tax of 15 percent on investment income accruing to fund insurance liabilities of life insurance companies will lessen a bias in the current system in favor of accumulating personal saving in the form of life insurance. The various changes applicable to financial institutions provide 28 percent of the revenues from base broadening.

There are several other base-broadening measures in real estate and mining. The increased inclusion rate for capital gains applies as well to corporate gains. Corporations will be allowed to deduct only 80 percent of direct or employee expenses for meals and entertainment.

Under the Canadian tax system, a deduction is allowed to corporations for dividends received in order to prevent double taxation of dividends. There has been an increasing tendency for profitable companies, not currently in a taxable position because of tax preferences, to issue preferred shares and thus take advantage of the tax relief provided to the dividend recipient even though no tax has been paid on the underlying income. A new tax will be imposed on dividends on new issues of preferred shares, with an exemption up to $500,000 of preferred share dividends. The tax, which in general will be paid by the issuer, will be at a rate that removes the tax motivation from preferred-share financing. It will be creditable against corporate income tax and thus will not affect the relative advantages of preferred-share financing for taxable corporations.

While there is substantial base broadening, tax credits remain in place to encourage research and development and investment in lower-income provinces and prescribed slower-growth areas. The tax regimes for manufacturing and resource industries remain competitive with regimes in other countries, particularly the United States. Small business continues to benefit from lower tax rates. These special provisions reflect explicit government priorities. They mean that one would not expect the reforms to equalize fully the average tax rates in different industry sectors or the effective tax rate on new investment in different sectors. However, as shown in tables 4 and 5, base broadening is expected to reduce considerably the dispersion in such rates.

The corporate income tax changes are expected to cause a net increase in corporate tax revenue of about 8 percent over the next four years. This will offset somewhat less than half of the personal income tax cut. The changes will cause a modest increase, on average, in the cost of capital for corporate investment and thus might be expected to result in a marginally lower desired level of capital. However, the reduced variation in effective tax rates should lead to a more efficient allocation of investment.

The Sales Tax

The severe problems with the current sales tax have already been mentioned. As shown in table 6, the tax results in widely varying effective rates on different types of consumer goods, and even on similar types of goods, and thus distorts choice among consumption goods. Since it is levied at the manufacturer's level, it distorts decisions about organization of the production-distribution process. The present tax produces a bias in favor of imports; it is estimated that the effective tax rate on domestically produced goods averages one-third higher than the effective rate on competing imports, as the tax base for domestic goods tends to embody more marketing costs. Half the revenue from the tax comes from the taxation of inputs purchased by business. This can result in cascading of the impact of the tax on consumer prices. It also results in taxation of exports, which are

TABLE 4. *Average Federal Tax Rates and Taxable Income of Profitable Corporations, before and after Tax Reform*

	Before tax reform		After tax reform	
Industry	Average tax rate[a]	Percent of income taxed	Average tax rate[a]	Percent of income taxed
Agriculture, forestry, fishing	16.9	91.3	15.5	94.5
Mining	15.0	49.8	16.6	63.9
Oil and gas	21.4	67.9	20.3	75.4
Manufacturing	18.9	77.1	19.7	89.1
Construction	20.1	96.1	18.8	102.4[b]
Wholesale trade	24.5	94.7	22.6	101.0[b]
Retail trade	21.2	98.9	19.5	103.8[b]
Financial institutions, insurance, and real estate	14.5	48.7	22.4	78.0
Services	20.4	94.1	18.9	98.8
Total, all industries	18.7	72.4	19.8	84.8

Source: Canadian Department of Finance, *Tax Reform 1987: Income Tax Reform*, p. 43, updated for December 1987 modifications.

a. Tax as a percent of financial statement income.

b. Taxable income in some sectors can exceed financial statement income in a year if depreciation claimed on financial statements is greater than capital cost allowance claimed for tax purposes. This can occur when depreciation claimed for tax purposes has exceeded that deducted on financial statements in previous years as a result of accelerated write-offs.

intended to be exempt; the indirect taxation of exports is estimated at almost 0.9 percent of export sales value.

The government's objective has been to find a basis for sales taxation that will be broadly neutral across consumer goods and services; that will not tax business inputs, including capital expenditures; that will treat domestic production and imports equally; and that will eliminate the element of indirect taxation of exports. The general approach of broadening the base and lowering the rate applies with particular force to the reform of the federal sales tax.

TABLE 5. *Federal-Provincial Tax Rate on New Investment for Large, Taxpaying Corporations by Industry, before and after Tax Reform*[a]
Percent of income

Industry	Before tax reform	After tax reform
Agriculture, forestry, fishing	25.0	21.5
Manufacturing	26.2	26.1
Construction	36.7	33.2
Wholesale trade	37.8	33.8
Retail trade	37.1	32.7
Services	33.0	29.0
Oil and Gas	11.1	14.9
Mining	−15.1	8.7
Total	24.6	24.7

Source: Canadian, Department of Finance, *Tax Reform 1987: Income Tax Reform*, p. 47.

a. The values assume provinces parallel the broadening of the tax base but retain their current tax rates. Provincial tax rates are those in effect on May 1, 1987, and an average provincial rate for each sector is calculated in making the estimates.

Many administrative problems and economic distortions linked with the current tax are inherent in a system that levies a tax at the manufacturer's level. In earlier proposals for reform, the possibility of moving the tax to the wholesale level or to the retail level has been raised. Application of the tax at the wholesale level would still involve difficulties in establishing a comparable point of taxation for different goods and for the same goods passing through different distribution channels. Application at the retail level, while avoiding most of these difficulties, would still make it awkward to free all business inputs and capital equipment from tax and would be vulnerable to noncompliance.

The government has therefore proposed replacing the existing tax with a form of consumption VAT. Such a multistage sales tax would extend to the retail level and would be applied to value added in a broad range of goods and services but would exclude export sales and business investment. The tax would be supplemented with a

TABLE 6. *Effective 1987 Federal Sales Tax Rates on Selected Domestic and Imported Goods*

Item	Domestic (percent)	Imported (percent)	Ratio of tax on domestic products to tax on imports
Commodities with 12-percent statutory rate			
Luggage, purses, and wallets	5.48	5.11	1.07
Blankets, bed sheets, and towels	5.13	7.05	.73
Carpets, rugs, and mats	7.50	5.48	1.37
Household textiles	6.29	6.28	1.00
Household furniture	6.70	3.91	1.71
Small appliances	9.03	6.58	1.37
Kitchen utensils	6.14	4.59	1.34
Household air cleaning machinery	7.43	5.16	1.44
Household appliances	8.09	5.75	1.41
Hand tools	5.17	4.43	1.17
Power tools	7.62	7.95	0.96
Builder's hardware	8.10	n.a.	n.a.
Brooms and brushes	6.29	3.63	1.73
Smokers' accessories	4.51	2.39	1.88
Glassware and glass products	5.45	3.31	1.65
Garbage bags, paper plates	9.31	n.a.	n.a.
TV, radios, stereos	8.35	5.97	1.40
Electric light bulbs, lamps	5.23	3.99	1.31
Office furniture	9.20	9.68	0.95
Office and stationery supplies	5.92	5.24	1.13
Office machines and equipment	11.20	6.64	1.69
Household cleaning components	7.78	n.a.	n.a.
Tires	8.31	5.43	1.53

refundable sales tax credit under the income tax, which would be set at a level to offset the impact of the new sales tax on expenditures by low-income individuals. The incidence of the combined tax and credit would be modestly progressive through middle-income levels.

Three variants of the tax have been offered for consideration. The first, labeled the "federal goods and services tax," would be applied at a uniform rate to almost all goods and services in Canada. The

TABLE 6 *(cont'd)*

Item	Domestic (percent)	Imported (percent)	Ratio of tax on domestic products to tax on imports
Commodities with 12-percent statutory rate			
Auto parts	5.91	5.55	1.06
Recreation vehicles	8.62	5.35	1.61
Batteries	5.23	3.63	1.55
Lubricating oil and grease	8.02	6.61	1.21
Canoes, sail boats	10.35	9.02	1.15
Watches and clocks	6.29	5.05	1.24
Photographic equipment	9.70	9.62	1.01
Jewelery	4.69	2.65	1.77
Sporting equipment	7.55	4.40	1.72
Toys and game sets	8.54	4.84	1.76
Cosmetics	7.75	4.40	1.76
Average	7.26	5.48	1.33
Commodities with 8-percent statutory rate			
Builder's hardware	5.71	3.33	1.72
Paint, varnish, wallpaper[a]	6.05	3.25	1.86
Average	5.89	3.29	1.79

Source: Canadian Department of Finance, *Tax Reform 1987: Sales Tax Reform* (Ottawa, 1987), p. 17.

n.a. Not available.

a. Rate increases to 12 percent effective January 1, 1988.

common rate would mean that the base could be calculated by each firm as the difference between total sales revenues (excluding export sales) and total creditable input purchases (including capital goods). The second variant, labeled the "federal value-added tax," would be based on explicit invoicing of tax, as is done in the value-added taxes of European countries. The firm would remit the difference between tax on sales invoices and tax on purchase invoices. Explicit invoicing would allow the exemption of selected goods and services. The third variant, labeled the "national sales tax," would be an invoice-based value-added tax that would combine the new federal tax with a replacement for existing provincial retail sales taxes. The combined rate of tax would differ from province to province. This variant is currently under active discussion in the provinces.

Under any one of the variants, it is intended that the base for the tax be very broad. It would cover consumer goods, with the exception of basic groceries, prescription drugs, and certain medical devices, and most services, including the intermediation margin on financial services. Residential rentals and the resale of used residential dwellings would be exempt from the tax unless the resale takes place in the course of a business that involves the purchase, renovation, and resale of used residential dwellings. However, the tax would apply to the sale or rental of real estate for commercial use and to the sale of new residential dwellings. The level of credit and the rate of tax needed to raise the required revenues will be a function of the final decision on exclusions from the base of the tax.

An innovative aspect of the proposed sales tax is the taxation of value added by financial intermediaries. In the case of nonfinancial business, the approach generally followed under a consumption VAT is to exclude interest receipts and to provide no credit or deduction for interest payments. Such an approach clearly could not be extended to financial institutions if the intent is to tax their value added. In the case of banks and other deposit-taking institutions, the price paid by customers for the bank's services is largely in the form of the spread between interest charged on loans and interest paid on deposits, rather than in the form of explicit fees. The approach taken in the sales tax proposal is to use a separate regime for measuring the tax base of financial institutions; their value added would be measured by a subtraction approach in which the institution would include as receipts all investment income, fees, and commissions. They would be allowed to deduct interest expenses, bad debts, and purchases of inputs in the form of goods and services (including physical capital) that would have already been subject to tax.

While it is possible to obtain an appropriate measure of total value added in this way, two problems remain. First, it is in principle desirable to allow a deduction or credit for the intermediation margin "purchased" as an input by nonfinancial businesses, given that this margin is being taxed at the level of the financial institution. However, there is no direct measure of the intermediation margin attaching to a particular transaction, and any attempt to allocate an institution's overall margin to individual transactions is inevitably arbitrary. Because the impact can be expected to be small, it is proposed not to allow any notional credit on business purchases of banking services. Second, the value-added approach being adopted is intended to exempt export sales. Again, there is no direct measure of the margin on transactions with nonresidents. The approach proposed in this case is to exempt from the tax base a part of total value added given by the ratio of foreign source gross revenue (interest receipts, fees, and so on) to total gross revenues.

A similar approach is proposed for the insurance industry. The tax base would consist of premiums and investment income receipts less any interest expense and investment losses, provisions for claims, and purchases of taxed inputs. A deduction or credit will be provided on business purchases of property and casualty insurance coverage. The tax base will be reduced by a factor based on the proportion of the institution's business on risks insured outside of Canada.

With a base that is much broader than that of the existing federal sales tax, the rate could be lower than the current 12 percent and still replace the revenue from the existing tax and cover the cost of the sales tax credit. The government has stated that revenue from the new sales tax would also be used to replace personal and corporate surtaxes that are currently in effect and to provide for further personal income tax reductions for middle-income taxpayers. Final decisions on the sales tax are not expected to be made until 1988 at the earliest, and implementation, which would require considerable administrative preparation, is unlikely before 1990. In the interim, the government has proposed some broadening of the base of the existing tax, most importantly the levying of a 10-percent tax on telecommunications and cable services, excluding basic residential telephone service, and an increase in the rate applicable to tobacco and alcohol. These measures increase sales tax revenues by about 8 percent and roughly balance off the part of the personal income tax revenue reduction not offset by the corporate income tax increase.

Given the increase in gross revenues, and the fact that the tax will now apply solely to consumer expenditures, the shift to the new tax can be expected to cause a one-time increase in the level of consumer prices. It is recognized that there is a challenge to set out what will be happening to prices in such a way as to minimize any tendency for this price increase to feed back into wages.

The benefits from sales tax reform will come from the reduction in the range of distortions already discussed. Elimination of direct taxation of some capital goods and of taxation of inputs into capital goods should lower the average cost of new capital to business by substantially more than any increase resulting from the corporate tax changes. The potential allocative efficiency gains from the reductions in distortions are estimated to be larger than those from the reduction in the dispersion in effective tax rates under the corporate income tax. General equilibrium model estimates for the impact of sales tax reform range from a real income gain of the order of 0.4 percent of gross national product (GNP) for the static efficiency gains from the reduced distortion of consumer choice, to 0.6 percent of GNP when allowance is also made for the potential dynamic efficiency gains from reduced taxation of capital goods. Because of induced foreign capital inflows, potential increases in GDP are substantially larger.[6]

CONCLUSION

The significant reforms of the personal and corporate income tax outlined in this paper might to some extent be seen as a necessary periodic exercise in which special tax preferences, which have a strong tendency to accumulate over time but which outlive their usefulness, are pruned back. In the current Canadian tax reform, however, the pruning is motivated primarily by the explicit view that government should be wary of overriding the economic basis for business decisions either through the tax system or through expenditure programs and regulation. Further, the importance attached to reduced tax rates, as the best general incentive to vigorous economic performance, has put special force behind the reduction in tax preferences. Besides contributing to improved economic efficiency,

6. Bob Hamilton and John Whalley, "Efficiency and Distributional Impacts of the Tax Reform Package," in Jack Mintz and John Whalley, eds., *The Economic Impacts of Tax Reform* (Toronto: Canadian Tax Foundation, forthcoming); Canadian Department of Finance, *Tax Reform 1987: Economic and Fiscal Outlook*, p. 12; and Department of Finance estimates.

base broadening, coupled with the conversion of personal exemptions and some deductions to credits, ensures that profitable corporations and high-income individuals will be seen as paying a fair share of tax. The reform also relieves a number of lower-income individuals from personal income tax. Thus concerns about fairness are addressed. In broadening the base and lowering rates, the Canadian reforms to the personal and corporate income taxes have much in common with approaches recently adopted in many other countries.

The sales tax reform responds to pressing needs to change an out-of-date tax in a way that should offer significant benefits in economic performance. Coupled with the increased refundable sales tax credit, the reform results in a tax whose incidence is modestly progressive. A viable sales tax is considered an important part of the overall tax structure; it makes it possible to avoid the need for very high rates on any single tax base and the associated compounding of distortions and pressures for avoidance. In a world of increasing international economic integration, the sales tax, based on the destination principle, that is, exempting exports and taxing imports equivalently to domestically produced goods and services, has important additional merits. It avoids the imposition of any competitive disadvantages on domestic producers. More generally, use of the destination principle facilitates international tax harmonization.

Comment by JOHN BOSSONS

As in other countries, Canadian income tax reform has focused on tax rate reduction financed by base-broadening measures. In considerable part, this direction reflects pressures to harmonize Canadian statutory tax rates with the lower tax rates in the United States created by the U.S. Tax Reform Act of 1986. In my view, U.S. tax reform forced Canada to act, and will pressure other countries as well, to a greater extent than is now generally recognized. The structural changes introduced by the 1986 U.S. tax reforms into the taxation of U.S. firms with international operations are as important in creating this pressure as the reductions in tax rates.

In these comments, I will address four topics: the effects and directions of Canadian tax reform, the pressures for international tax harmonization introduced by the 1986 U.S. tax reforms, pressure points in the reformed income tax systems in Canada and the United States, and the effects of income tax reform on the prospects for reform of the sales tax. In both Canada and the United States, income tax reform has constrained the future policy choices of governments, increasing the likelihood that future requirements for increased revenues will be met from broad-based sales taxes. In Canada, the government proposals for sales tax reform described by David A. Dodge and John H. Sargent enhance this likelihood.

THE EFFECTS OF THE CANADIAN REFORMS

At first sight, the direction of Canada's income tax reforms is similar to that of the 1986 U.S. reforms. As in the United States, reforms include big reductions in tax rates and an offsetting reduction in investment tax incentives along with other base-broadening measures. However, the Canadian reforms differ in important respects. As Dodge and Sargent note, the potential revenue yield from base-broadening measures is lower in Canada than in the United States, partly because the Canadian system contained fewer tax preferences and special provisions before reform. To finance rate reductions in the income tax that would compare to U.S. tax rate reductions, other ways of raising revenues had to be found.

In the personal income tax, eliminating or reducing a number of concessionary allowances generated an important compensating increase in revenue. In some cases, tax credits were substituted for deductions, with the new tax credits calculated at the lowest of the new tax bracket rates. In other cases (an exemption of the first $1,000 of investment income and a universal $500 employment expense deduction), the allowances were eliminated. These modifications in concessionary allowances account for approximately two-thirds of the total personal income tax revenues raised to offset the revenue consequences of the reductions in personal tax rates. Base-broadening measures (including an increase to 75 percent in the taxable fraction of nominal capital gains) offset only 21 percent of the revenue losses from the personal income tax rate reduction.

The revenue cost of the tax rate reductions was reduced by substituting tax credits for personal exemptions. Again, the effect of the substitution was a rise in personal income taxes paid by individuals in all but the lowest of the new tax brackets. The value of the tax credit to taxpayers in the bottom bracket was increased (relative to that of the previous exemption) in order to remove low-income taxpayers from the tax rolls. The net effect of the changes in tax rates and substitution of tax credits for personal exemptions and other allowances for middle-income taxpayers was to permit marginal tax rates to be reduced without significantly changing average tax rates.

As in the U.S. reforms, the combined effect of the personal income tax changes is to reduce total revenue from the personal income tax. Again as in the United States, an increase in revenue from the corporate income tax offsets most of the net reduction in revenues from personal income tax.

Corporate base-broadening measures (some were implemented in 1986) largely fall into two categories: a reduction in investment tax incentives and higher taxes on financial institutions. Restricting the ability of companies to shift tax losses to profitable companies through flow-through shares or other financing techniques has also increased revenues. Together, the base-broadening measures raise approximately twice as much revenue from corporations as is "lost" from reductions of corporate tax rates.

The economic effects of the Canadian income tax reforms are both positive and negative. On the one hand, reducing statutory tax rates results in a significant drop in the welfare cost of remaining distortions. On the other hand, even with the drop in tax rates, the cutback of investment tax incentives results in increases in average effective tax rates on new investments in plant and equipment, enhancing existing distortions of saving and investment choices.

For most large firms, statutory tax rates will decline by about one-sixth. Using as a crude guide the Harberger rule that the welfare costs of tax distortions are proportional to the square of tax rate differentials, the reductions in statutory rates will reduce welfare costs of the remaining distortions in the tax base by 30 percent.

The lower welfare cost of remaining distortions is important.

Though the base-broadening measures reduce the dispersion of effective tax rates that affect behavioral choices, significant distortions are left in the definition of the income tax base in Canada and in the United States. Notably, reducing tax rates reduces the bias against investments in risky new investments that arises from the asymmetric treatment of gains and losses in the current U.S. and Canadian tax systems. The existing tax subsidy of debt financing is also reduced.

While the reduction in statutory tax rates results in important efficiency gains, these economic benefits are offset by the increase in effective tax rates on new investments in plant and equipment caused by reductions in capital cost allowances and the elimination of the investment tax credit. As in the United States, the net effect of the corporate tax changes in Canada has been a slight increase in average effective tax rates on new capital goods in order to finance a windfall tax reduction on existing capital. The net effect is an increase, despite the reductions in statutory rates, in the existing tax distortion of the allocation of savings between business investments and untaxed investments in owner-occupied housing.

Whether it would have been feasible in a closed economy to design a politically feasible tax reform that reduced tax rates without creating windfall gains for existing capital is a debatable issue. What is not debatable is that this issue is of only academic interest in a country such as Canada once statutory tax rates have been sharply reduced in the United States. The Canadian and U.S. economies and capital markets are closely integrated, creating substantial pressure for tax harmonization. Canada had little choice but to follow the United States in providing a windfall to existing capital. Indeed, the pressures for tax harmonization were increased by structural changes introduced by the 1986 U.S. tax reforms.

U.S. REFORM AND INTERNATIONAL TAX HARMONIZATION

The impact of the 1986 U.S. tax reforms on pressures for international tax harmonization is one of the more interesting analytic issues connected with these reforms. The impact of the 1986 reform package goes far beyond the effect of the reductions in statutory tax rates, though the rate reductions have by themselves had a powerful effect.

Structural changes in the taxation of international income of U.S. companies have increased tax harmonization pressures.

Perhaps the most interesting effect of the U.S. reforms is that they have increased the pressure to harmonize statutory as well as effective tax rates, thus greatly increasing the constraints faced by designers of tax reform in other countries. Before 1986, international tax arbitrage opportunities created by differentials in statutory tax rates were important, but their constraining effect on tax policy was diluted by the existence of other tax minimization practices open to U.S. companies with international operations. For example, the LIFO rule used under pre-1986 U.S. tax law in allocating foreign taxes to income distributed to U.S. parents permitted multinational corporations with growing foreign operations to minimize total taxes worldwide by paying dividends in alternate years, concentrating foreign deductions that were more generous than corresponding U.S. deductions in those years in which dividends were not paid.

In Canada, practices such as the yearly alternation of dividend payout and full utilization of Canadian capital cost allowances permitted U.S.-owned companies to take full advantage of lower effective tax rates on operations that resulted from investment tax incentives not allowed under U.S. tax law. In effect, the Canadian subsidiaries arranged their affairs to move Canadian taxes into the years in which they paid dividends to their U.S. parents in order to take full advantage of U.S. foreign tax credits. Because of such practices, the utilization of Canadian investment tax incentives could in many cases substitute for tax arbitrage as a means of reducing worldwide taxes.

The U.S. foreign tax credit rules introduced in 1986 have changed this situation in important ways. From a foreign viewpoint, the most important change is the requirement that all post-1986 income be pooled, with all post-1986 taxes on undistributed income being averaged together in allocating foreign taxes to newly distributed income. This change rules out the "rhythm method" of tax minimization through alternating years of dividend payout. From a U.S. viewpoint, the change was long overdue, since the U.S. Treasury had effectively been paying part of the cost of foreign tax incentives available on U.S. foreign investments. From the viewpoint of foreign governments, the change obviously increases the cost of providing investment tax incentives not implemented in U.S. tax law. Just as important, it also increases the extent to which tax arbitrage opportunities will be utilized if foreign statutory corporate tax rates exceed their U.S. counterparts.

The resultant pressures for harmonization of statutory tax rates are enhanced by other changes in U.S. tax law that interact with the changes in the foreign tax credit rules, notably the restrictions on interest deductibility and the alternative minimum corporate tax. These changes reduce the extent to which pure tax arbitrage operations (such as changing the countries in which borrowing occurs) may be utilized in responding to statutory rate differentials, thereby increasing the likelihood that jobs as well as the corporate tax base will be moved to the United States in the short run if foreign statutory tax rates are not reduced to match the new U.S. corporate tax rates.

An interesting analytic implication of the structural changes introduced by the 1986 U.S. tax reforms is that the importance of short-run behavioral responses to international tax differentials is increased. Most analyses of the effects of such differentials have focused on long-term equilibrium adjustments. From a policymaking viewpoint in foreign countries, the U.S. tax changes have made short-run analyses more relevant. The interesting behavioral adjustments in the short run (besides tax arbitrage that may change the international distribution of taxable income without changing "real" operations) are equilibrium changes in the location of production by multinational firms given their current endowment of fixed capital in different countries.

The pressures for tax harmonization imply that it is increasingly costly for the foreign tax treatment of corporations to diverge in important respects from the U.S. corporate tax system. The pressure points within the reformed U.S. tax system thus tend to be exported. While the defects in the Canadian reforms are to some extent homegrown, the most important defects are at least in part attributable to constraints imposed by pressures to harmonize the Canadian corporate tax with its U.S. counterpart.

PRESSURE POINTS IN THE REFORMED SYSTEM

Two key potential sources of future pressure could change the reformed income tax system in both Canada and the United States: inflation and the government deficit. The first results from the failure to take advantage of tax reform to introduce measures (such as those advanced in the initial 1985 U.S. Treasury reform proposals) to index the income tax base for inflation. The second occurs because the income tax reforms were designed in both countries to be approximately revenue neutral in the short run, leaving the revenue shortfall underlying the significant structural deficits in both countries to be dealt with in the future. The income tax reforms are probably not viable in the long run without an increase in indirect taxes.

In both countries, the effects of the failure to index the income tax base are not serious at current levels of inflation. However, the moves in the opposite direction in capital gains taxation (increasing the taxable fraction of nominal capital gains to 75 percent in Canada and 100 percent in the United States) are almost certainly not sustainable if inflation revives even just to high single-digit levels. Because of the political importance of capital gains taxation as part of the total reform package, reversing the capital gains tax changes would almost certainly lead to increases in the top statutory tax rates and so back to pressures to reduce effective tax rates by reintroducing tax preferences. Similarly, the other distortions that would be reintroduced by a revival of inflation would also create pressures for the reintroduction of offsetting corporate tax incentives.

This is not the place to discuss the feasibility of comprehensive indexation of the income tax system, other than to note that most of the implementation difficulties in the United States arise from transitional problems on long-term debt contracts. These problems are minimized by introducing indexation when inflation is low. In Canada, the indexation issue is more difficult because of the tight integration of U.S. and Canadian capital markets. In a small, open economy such as Canada's, the impact of inflation on equilibrium nominal interest rates is primarily determined by the U.S. tax structure. This makes it difficult to introduce comprehensive indexation in Canada so long as the U.S. tax system is unindexed.

Nevertheless, even without comprehensive indexation, it would have been possible (and remains possible) to index capital gains for inflation, as has been done in the recent Australian tax reforms. Although indexation of the capital gains tax base is clearly a "second best" reform when nominal interest is deductible in full, it is better than retreating to partial inclusion of nominal capital gains.

On the pressure points arising from revenue needs, little need be said other than noting the critical importance of the tax rate reductions in the reform packages in both countries. In Canada, political pressures to match reductions in U.S. personal income tax rates exacerbate the constraints imposed by the virtual necessity of harmonizing Canadian and U.S. statutory corporate tax rates. These constraints increase the importance of reforming Canadian sales taxation. As in the United States, the most important potential source of additional tax revenue in Canada is a value-added tax.

SALES TAX REFORM IN CANADA

The biggest difference between the tax reform package announced by the Canadian government and the 1986 U.S. tax reforms is that the Canadian package includes the planned introduction of a value-added tax. The principal motivation for the proposed value-added tax is not to raise revenue but to replace an existing federal sales tax on manufactured goods that is arbitrary, inefficient, and difficult to administer.

Though the income tax reforms are about to be legislated, it is uncertain whether the sales tax reforms proposed by the Canadian government will be implemented. The federal government is attempting to negotiate an agreement with provincial governments to implement an even more ambitious sales tax reform in which a national value-added tax would replace existing provincial retail sales taxes as well as the federal manufacturers' sales tax. If this goal can be achieved, the sales tax reform would have substantial economic benefits, resulting in a sales tax system that would be much more neutral. (A large part of provincial sales tax revenue arises from the taxation of business inputs rather than final goods.)

Even without achieving the ambitious goal of reforming provincial as well as federal sales taxes, the replacement of the existing federal tax on manufactured goods by a value-added tax would result in significant welfare gains in Canada. From an international perspective, the most important implication of this reform is that border tax adjustments would be harmonized with normal international practice. The current manufacturers' sales tax imposes the equivalent of a 3-percent tax penalty on net Canadian exports, which would be removed by the proposed reform. The proposed value-added tax would conform to the European norm of taxing imports and exempting exports.

Besides replacing the existing federal sales tax, the proposed value-added tax would also be used to make up the revenue shortfall in the income tax resulting from the proposed reductions in personal and corporate tax rates. The resultant change in the tax mix is not substantial, but the direction of the change is significant. Moreover, sales tax reform provides a basis for a further change in this direction.

CONCLUSION

The tax reform package proposed by the Canadian government is substantial. In part, these reforms respond to the pressures created by the reductions in statutory income tax rates in the United States introduced by the 1986 U.S. tax reforms. However, as in the United Kingdom, the Canadian tax reforms also reflect the ideological goals of the Canadian government. The income tax reforms on balance result in a more neutral tax system, even though average effective tax rates on new investment are somewhat increased. The proposed sales tax reforms would greatly increase the efficiency of indirect taxation.

Canadian tax reform would not have been so substantial were it not for the economic and political pressures created by the 1986 U.S. tax reform. The pressures for international tax harmonization created by the U.S. reforms will grow as the full effects of the U.S. reforms become appreciated by foreign governments.

Denmark

The tax debate in Denmark over the past ten years has focused on the income tax system. The substantial deficit in the government budget and in the current account of the balance of payments has contributed to an increase in the tax burden. Economic sanctions to contain the trend in domestic spending during this period have frequently been in the form of excises, but the income taxes have also shown an upward trend during the period. Almost all quarters agree that the overall tax burden is extremely heavy. At the same time this burden cannot be reduced until the deficit is reversed.

It nevertheless proved possible to implement a reform of the Danish income tax system. On June 19, 1985, the parties in power (the Social Democrats and the Radical Liberal party) agreed on a tax reform to take effect in fiscal year 1987.

The object of the reform was to discourage tax speculation, encourage private saving, lower the marginal rate of taxation, improve the conditions of families with children, and provide a more equitable distribution of the tax burden by making allowances for low-income taxpayers.

The main elements of the tax reform were the following:
—Reduction of personal taxation
—Reduction of taxation of capital income
—Restrictions of allowances
—A special taxation scheme for private business activities
—Taxation of gains on financial claims
—Taxation of companies
—Taxation of foundations and charitable organizations

A transitional arrangement applies to individuals, so that the fiscal consequences of the changed taxation of interest and other deductions will become fully effective only gradually. The transitional arrangement is structured so that the tax reform will not be fully operative until 1992.

The tax reform has not generally reduced the tax burden. As is true in several other countries, Denmark's tax reform involves a rearrangement of the tax burden. It is a question of easing personal taxation and raising taxation of companies and foundations. The changes thus involve an increase in the taxable base, achieved by restricting tax allowances and by taxing incomes that were heretofore tax free.

PERSONAL TAXATION

The tax reform modifies the former principles of personal taxation. The new rules governing personal taxation and the new business tax constitute the most significant aspects of the tax reform. Basically the taxable income is to be calculated along the same lines as before. Certain allowances, however, have been abolished or restricted.

The essential difference, compared with the former rule, is that, besides the general taxable income, personal income and capital income are to be determined separately and taxed at different rates. Taxable income is made up as follows:

$$
\begin{array}{l}
\text{Personal income} \\
+ \text{Capital income} \\
\underline{- \text{Assessment allowance}} \\
= \text{Taxable income}
\end{array}
$$

This breakdown of the taxable base is something new and essential for the new personal tax system.

Taxable income is taxed proportionately at approximately a 50-percent rate, which goes to the national government and local authority collectively. It is not possible to give an exact rate for the whole country as the local rate varies from one place to another. The local councils may fix the local rate at their discretion.

Furthermore, an additional income tax is payable to the national government at the rate of 6 percent and 12 percent of the part of the personal income exceeding certain basic allowances. In this way the marginal tax on personal income may run as high as 68 percent $(50 + 6 + 12)$.

Similarly, under certain conditions an additional income tax of 6 percent on net capital income is payable to the national government. The marginal tax on capital income thus amounts to approximately

56 percent (50 + 6). Interest payments or other negative capital income normally have a tax value of only approximately 50 percent.

Personal Income

Personal income is all income that is included in taxable income and is not capital income, that is, all types of income not expressly classified as capital income are included in personal income.

However, the expenses that are deductible from personal income are subject to severe restrictions. Apart from expenses relating to independent business activities, only premiums and contributions to tax-privileged pension schemes are deductible from personal income. Thus contributions to pension schemes have a tax value of up to 68 percent.

Other assessment allowances, however, are deductible only from taxable income, which means that the tax value of these allowances is only about 50 percent.

Examples of income to be included in personal income are pay, pensions, and profits from independent business activities. Examples of amounts deductible from personal income would be premiums for and contributions to pension schemes, deficits from independent business activities, fiscal depreciation, and appropriations.

Persons engaged in independent business activities may choose to be taxed under a special business arrangement. For self-employed persons taking advantage of this arrangement, the taxable income of the business is subject to tax. The net profit of independent businesses allows for the deduction of all expenses, including interest payments, that is, the interest paid by the business has the "full tax value" for the owner.

Persons engaged in business and not using the special business arrangement may deduct all working expenses in connection with the business, except interest paid. Such interest payments are included in the statement of the owner's capital income, which means that they have a tax value of only about 50 percent.

Capital Income

Capital income comprises the total net amount of capital earnings. Incomes to be included as capital income are interest receipts, dividends from joint-stock companies, taxable gains on financial claims, taxable share profits, profits on freehold dwellings, and capital returns on own business under the business arrangement. The deductions from capital income are interest payments, deductible losses on financial claims, deficits on freehold dwellings, safe-deposit box rent, safe custody fees, and the like.

Restriction of Allowances

The tax reform has imposed certain restrictions on tax allowances. The major change is that the personal allowances are deducted from taxable income and not from personal income. Thus the tax value of the allowances has been reduced to approximately 50 percent. However, this formula does not apply to premiums for and contributions to pension schemes, which are deductible from personal income and therefore come off the top of the income.

Other allowances have also been restricted. For example, wage-earner expenses for the extra cost of food when working overtime, work clothes, specialist literature, and other costs may only be deducted to the extent they exceed Kr 3,000. Similarly, entertainment expenses are deductible only to the extent of 25 percent of actual expenses.

Under the former rules the right to deduct current contributions to charitable societies, foundations, and religious organizations was unlimited. In the future, a deduction will be allowed only for foundations and religious organizations approved by the taxation authorities. Moreover, the category of institutions that may receive approval has been considerably narrowed. Approval is allowed only for religious organizations, charitable institutions organized for humanitarian purposes, and organizations devoted to research or protection of the natural environment. Such contributions may be deducted only to the extent that the amount does not exceed 15 percent of personal income plus capital income.

Grant to Families with Children

As part of the tax reform the Inland Revenue authorities will provide an annual grant to families of Kr 5,000 (in 1987, only Kr 2,500) for all children under the age of 18 and residing in Denmark.

The amount, which will be adjustable once a year, is tax free and independent of the child's and parents' income.

Personal Allowances

The assessed taxes are reduced by the tax value of personal allowances. These are fixed as follows:

Type of allowance	1987 Kr
General personal allowance	
The national government	27,100
Local authorities and county boroughs and the Church	21,200
Pensioners	
Single pensioners	46,500
Married pensioners	26,200
Unmarried persons under the age of 18	18,800

ASSESSMENT OF PERSONAL INCOME TAX

The assessment of tax is still based on taxable income. As before, taxable income is used for assessing the local authority and county borough taxes, as is the national income tax, which is levied at a 22-percent rate. For an average district, the total local authority and county borough taxes amount to approximately 28 percent of taxable income.

The national government then assesses two surtaxes. The first is assessed at the rate of 12 percent on personal income exceeding Kr 200,000. The second is assessed at the rate of 6 percent on the sum of net capital income and personal income after deduction of a basic amount of Kr 130,000. Any basic amount not utilized may be transferred to the other spouse for the purpose of assessing this 6-percent tax. If one spouse has a negative capital income and the other a positive capital income, the negative income is deducted from the positive income in assessing the 6-percent tax for the spouse having the positive capital income. The amounts of Kr 200,000 and Kr 130,000 respectively are adjustable once a year.

Example of Tax Assessment

The following example illustrates the calculation of tax liabilities for a family with both spouses reporting personal income and capital income or loss. For purposes of this illustration, the amounts of income of each spouse are as follows. A rate of 28 percent for local authorities and county borough taxes is used in the computations.

Type of income	Spouse one Kr	Spouse two Kr
Personal income	350,000	210,000
Capital income	−40,000	60,000
Assessment allowances	−20,000	−70,000
Taxable income	290,000	200,000

The tax is assessed as follows:

Spouse one		Amount Kr
Tax on taxable income:		
National government: 22% of Kr 290,000		63,800
Local authorities: 28% of Kr 290,000		81,200
Tax on personal income exceeding Kr 200,000		
12% of Kr (350,000–200,000)		18,000
Tax on personal income and capital income		
6% of Kr (350,000–130,000)		13,200
Total tax		176,000
Personal allowance:		
22% of Kr 27,100	5,962	
28% of Kr 21,200	5,936	−11,898
Total tax		164,302

Spouse two		
Tax on taxable income:		
National government: 22% of Kr 200,000		44,000
Local authorities and the Church: 28% of Kr 200,000		56,000
Tax on personal income exceeding Kr 200,000		
12% of Kr (210,000–200,000)		1,200
Tax on personal income and capital income		
6% of Kr (210,000 + 60,000 − 40,000 − 130,000)		6,000
Total tax		107,200
Personal allowance:		
22% of Kr 27,100	5,962	
28% of Kr 21,200	5,936	−11,898
Total tax		95,302

Tax Ceiling

The former tax ceiling has been lowered from 73 percent to 68 percent and will have significance where the local authority and county borough taxes exceed 28 percent. The tax ceiling is a marginal tax ceiling. If the tax rates taken together exceed 68 percent, the tax on the marginal krone cannot exceed 68 percent. In practice, the tax ceiling provision will only affect persons whose personal income exceeds Kr 200,000.

CAPITAL TAX

The capital tax (or net wealth tax) is not affected by the tax reform. This tax is still payable at the rate of 2.2 percent on the part of the taxable assets exceeding an index-tied basic amount, fixed for 1987 at Kr 1,278,700.

If the total income taxes and the capital tax after deduction of the tax value of the personal allowance exceed 78 percent of taxable income, total taxes are reduced by an amount up to the capital tax. Consequently, the total tax on taxable income and personal income may exceed 78 percent of taxable income.

TAXATION OF PRIVATE BUSINESS ACTIVITIES

The tax reform also introduced a special tax on self-employed persons' business activities. The arrangement permits the owner to be taxed on an equal footing with joint-stock companies and private companies. Any accumulated profit is therefore subject only to a provisional business tax of 50 percent.

Another objective of the arrangement is to ensure that self-employed persons may deduct in full interest payments incurred in connection with the business activities.

A final objective is to place investment in a private business on an equal footing with, for example, returns on investment in bonds. This aim is achieved by taxing part of business profits as capital income at the rate of approximately 50 percent.

Guiding Principles

The business arrangement may be used by persons engaged in independent business activities. Both persons with full and limited tax liability may take advantage of the arrangement.

The arrangement is voluntary, and it is even possible to decide year by year whether to use it or not. If the business arrangement is not elected, the profit or deficit of the business together with its interest earnings and payments are taxed along the same lines as individuals. In that case interest payments are deductible only at the rate of 50 percent.

Taxation of Business Profits

Business profits are divided into return on capital and a remaining surplus. The owner of the business may either withdraw the surplus or let it accumulate wholly or in part in the business. If the surplus is withdrawn, the amount is included in the owner's personal income. That amount will thus be subject to taxation up to 68 percent. If the owner chooses to let the surplus accumulate in the business, it is taxable at a provisional business rate of only 50 percent.

When any accumulated business profit is later withdrawn, it is included in the owner's personal income. When assessing the owner's final tax, the previously paid business tax is deducted as a credit against the personal tax.

The capital income of the business is computed as a return on the capital invested by the owner in the business. The interest rate applied is a market rate computed by the Copenhagen stock exchange. The computation of return on capital serves only to decide how much of the actual return on the business is to be taxed as capital income.

When the owner ceases to use the business arrangement, any provisionally taxed profit is included in his personal income for the fiscal year following the year of termination.

TAXATION OF GAINS ON FINANCIAL CLAIMS

As of fiscal year 1986, the treatment of profits and losses on claims and debts was drastically revised, mainly to ensure that bonds, mortgages, and other financial claims would be issued at a market rate of interest. Should the nominal interest of the claim fail to satisfy the requirement of a minimum rate fixed at the time of issue, the gains are taxed as capital income. However, losses are not deductible.

Gains and losses on claims and debts for parties taxable by virtue of being in this business, such as banks, stockbrokers, and finance companies, remain liable to tax as before.

The minimum rate of interest is fixed six months at a time but may be changed in case of significant fluctuations of the market rate. It is computed by the Copenhagen stock exchange on the basis of the market rate applying to bonds. The minimum rate is currently 10 percent per annum and will for the time being apply to the end of 1987. Since the tax reform became effective, the minimum rate of interest has been as follows:

January 1 to April 1, 1986:	9 percent
April 2 to June 30, 1986:	7 percent
July 1 to December 31, 1986:	8 percent
Beginning January 1, 1987:	10 percent

TAXATION OF COMPANIES

As part of financing the tax reform, the rate of company taxation was increased from 40 percent to 50 percent. The agreement on the tax reform also includes the abolition of double taxation of dividends, but this action will not become effective until January 1, 1990. Legislation on this subject has not yet been enacted.

A committee appointed by the minister of Inland Revenue has submitted a proposal for abolishing double taxation. However, the political parties behind the tax reform have not yet agreed on the technical details. In this context, the treatment of foreign investors must be worked out. In addition, evasion or tax reductions by disguising other payments from companies as dividends must be prevented. The objective is to simplify the overall taxation of dividends as much as possible.

TAXATION OF FOUNDATIONS AND ASSOCIATIONS

The tax reform has meant a substantial extension of taxes to foundations and charitable organizations.

Foundations and associations were previously subject to taxation. However, the liability to pay tax was confined to income earned by business activities. Foundations and associations were thus exempt from tax on noncommercial activities such as interest, gains on securities, subscriptions, contributions, donations, and capital gains.

A guiding principle of the tax reform is that foundations and associations should be taxed like joint-stock companies, that is, at the rate of 50 percent of taxable income. Basically, foundations and associations are required to calculate taxable income along the same lines as joint-stock companies. This means that all income must be included in their taxable income. There are exceptions, however, so that foundations and associations will be taxed primarily on their interest, dividends, and capital gains.

Besides the general deductions from income, for example, with respect to expenses, foundations may deduct apportionments to charitable or other public-welfare purposes. Furthermore, a foundation is allowed to deduct apportionments for other purposes if the beneficiary is liable to tax in Denmark. Finally, a foundation may deduct funds set aside to preserve its capital, up to a maximum of 25 percent of apportionments made for charitable or public-welfare purposes.

REARRANGEMENT OF TAXATION UNDER THE TAX REFORM

One of the political objectives of the tax reform was that it should be revenue neutral. Financing of the personal tax reliefs has been accomplished by broadening the tax base and increasing company taxation (table 1).

The new tax base for individuals provides less tax value for the allowances than the previous tax. The assessment based on personal income without allowances, which applies to interest and other property income, is expected to reduce tax speculation and personal borrowing. But the surtaxes of 6.0 percent and 12.0 percent will have very little significance for revenue. As shown in table 2, the surtaxes account for only 5.5 percent of the total personal income taxes.

The rearrangement of taxation under the tax reform means tax relief for some persons and increases for others. Persons with small allowances will receive tax reductions, whereas persons with substantial allowances will be taxed more heavily. The children's grant

TABLE 1. *Financing of the Tax Reform, 1987*

Tax change	Amount (billions of Kr)
Tax rates for persons	−5.4
Allowances for families with children	−3.8
Abolition of double taxation of dividends	−0.7
Total tax reduction	−9.9
Financed by:	
Restructuring of allowances, including allowance for entertainment	4.1
Foundations and associations	
Increased company taxation	6.0
Taxation of capital gains	
Control measures, exodus of taxpayers	0.8
Total tax increase	10.9
Surplus (government and local authorities)	1.0
Addendum:	
Personal income taxes	−5.8
Companies, foundations, and other establishments	6.8
Surplus	1.0

naturally benefits families with children. Table 3 illustrates these changes. The figures apply to 1991, which is the last year of the five-year transition period.

THE TAX BURDEN IN DENMARK

The tax burden in Denmark is heavy—50 percent of the GDP in 1986 at market prices. The Danish tax burden is among the heaviest in the international community. Moreover, the personal income tax accounts for a relatively high percentage of total taxes—approximately 47 percent in Denmark compared with an average of about 30 percent in other OECD countries in 1983—largely because social security contributions are modest. Such contributions are regarded as social contributions in the other OECD countries and are much heavier than in Denmark.

TABLE 2. *Taxable Base after the Tax Reform, 1987*

Type of income	Amount (billions of Kr)
Gross income on the tax return	551
Assessment allowances	−131
Taxable (net) income	420
Personal allowances	−108
Basis for assessment of general income tax of 50 percent	312
Basis for assessment of 6-percent surtax[a]	482
Basis for assessment of 12-percent surtax[b]	470
Revenue	
General income tax (3.4 million persons)	158.8
6-percent tax (1.4 million persons)	5.4
12-percent tax (0.5 million persons)	3.9
Total	168.1

a. Personal income plus net capital income taxable at 6-percent rate on amounts over Kr 130,000 (Kr 260,000 for married couples).

b. Personal income taxable at 12-percent rate on amounts over Kr 200,000.

CONCLUSION

The Danish tax reform will narrow the gap between the highest and lowest income tax rates. Formerly, the gap was as high as seventy-three percentage points. For example, the gains made both by persons and foundations on bonds were tax free. Foundations' interest earnings and dividends were likewise tax free. By contrast, the top marginal rate on labor income was 73 percent. Moreover, company taxation was only 40 percent, whereas the lowest tax rate applying to persons was at least 50 percent.

The tax reform will narrow the gap between the lowest and highest tax rates to eighteen percentage points. Moreover, most of the population will not be paying any surtax, so that they will be subject to a flat tax.

The reduction in the spread of the marginal tax rates will reduce

TABLE 3. *Examples of Tax Changes under the Tax Reform, 1991*

Examples		Single person (Kr)	Husband and wife[a] (Kr)
Taxpayer with low allowance (Kr)			
Pay	150,000		
Interest allowance	5,000	− 2,300	− 4,700
Other allowances	5,000		
Pay	250,000		
Interest allowance	20,000	− 4,500	− 12,800
Other allowances	5,000		
Tax "speculator" (Kr)			
Pay	500,000		
Interest allowance	250,000	40,000[b]	31,000[c]
Other allowances	25,000		

a. Husband and wife are both employed, no children.
b. For 1987 the transitional tax will be Kr 24,600.
c. For 1987 the transitional tax will be Kr 15,700.

the incentive to engage in tax speculation. Other elements of the tax reform will also reduce speculation. For example, the taxable base is divided into personal income and capital income. Since capital income will be taxed at a proportional rate, there will be considerably reduced possibilities for speculating in the type of income that is easiest to move around. Second, foundations are liable to tax, just as other taxable entities. This removes the possibility of speculating by establishing foundations. Third, tax-free gains on financial claims are considerably restricted. Fourth, the new business tax applies the same rules to all forms of business organizations. Consequently, there is no longer any need to operate as a corporation for tax reasons.

The most consistent solution to most of the problems surrounding tax speculation is proportional taxation of all types of income. This reduces the distorting effect of the tax system on saving and investment and improves the allocation of resources. The Danish tax reform has taken a long step in that direction.

Finally, the tax reform is the result of a compromise among six political parties. Four of the parties are in power, and the other two are in opposition. Under the circumstances, further progress will be difficult.

Comment by ROBERT KOCH-NIELSEN

A recent newspaper article about Denmark and its tax laws concluded as follows:

> The Danes apparently never understood what capitalism is about. Their Viking forefathers got wealthy by robbing abroad. Today Denmark maintains its wealth by borrowing abroad. The principle is really the same: The Danes like wealth but they do not create it.

To understand the Danish tax reform, it is necessary to have in mind that borrowing and interest payments are important not only to the Danish economy but also to the Danish taxpayers. To put it another way, no change in Danish tax law could reasonably be called a tax reform unless it instituted a different way of dealing with borrowing and interest payments.

Two stated objectives of the recent Danish tax reform are to reduce tax arbitrage and to encourage private saving. The Act on Taxation of Financial Claims has solved the arbitrage problem in a simple way. Before the act went into effect, interest-bearing instruments were issued at a discount by reducing the nominal interest rate substantially below the market rate. When the security was redeemed at par, the taxpayer received tax-free income equal to the difference between par and the discounted purchase price. This was equivalent to the treatment of an investment made through a loan with tax-deductible interest. This type of tax avoidance has now been closed by a new rule that requires interest rates on interest-bearing securities to be equal to the market rate when they are issued.

The main element in the reform is the Act on Personal Taxation. This act divides taxable income into personal income and capital income and imposes a surtax of 6 percent on capital income and a surtax of up to 18 percent on personal income. Why personal income is taxed at a higher rate than capital income is a mystery. One would think that earned income would be taxed more favorably than unearned income. Future tax speculators will probably devote much time and effort to transferring income from the personal category to the capital category.

Another notable feature of the act is the transition rule for taxation of captial income. This rule, which has no termination date, allows taxpayers to transfer Kr 25,000 a year to be taxed as capital income (at a rate of 50 percent rather than 56 percent). Thus many people with high capital income will only be able to take advantage of the lower rate on capital income for a fraction of that income.

Like the tax reforms in other countries, the Danish reform broadens the tax base. Unlike them, it raises rather than lowers the corporate tax rate. The increase, from 40 percent to 50 percent, will almost surely worsen the competitiveness of Danish business and make it harder for Denmark to attract foreign investments.

The tax base has been broadened by taxing foundations and associations. However, foundations may deduct charitable and welfare distributions in their calculation of taxable income. Other distributions are also deductible, but only if the beneficiary is liable to tax. This means that foundations are, in effect, taxable on any income they do not distribute for charitable or welfare purposes.

The base-broadening objective has also been promoted by the new legislation dealing with emigration. According to this legislation, the value of certain tax-related assets that are taken out of the country will be considered as a deemed sale at the time of emigration.

A special feature of the tax reform is the Business Arrangement Act, which is designed for businesses that cannot be incorporated, such as farming, medicine, and law. The act is a consequence of the limitations on the deduction for interest payments. It limits the tax on income that is retained in the business to 50 percent—significantly below the personal income tax ceiling of 68 percent or, if net wealth tax is included, 78 percent. It also permits interest expenses to be deducted from the capital income of the enterprise. Although the act is complicated, it has been welcomed by the business community.

The primary effect of the Danish tax reform is to redistribute the tax burden. With inflation and interest rates down, the tax reform appears to be successful. Ordinary taxpayers are now benefiting from the tax reduction and are beginning to understand that saving money and earning interest are preferable to borrowing money and paying interest.

France

Many, if not all, industrialized countries have recently experienced reforms of their tax system. However, the scope and magnitude of the changes differ greatly from one country to another. Some have introduced major modifications in the structure of the overall tax system (implementation of a value-added tax (VAT) or tax similar to VAT, for example). Others have moved tax rates slightly or corrected for inflation to reduce or eliminate the fiscal drag or have improved the treatment of families, as Germany did recently. France chose a middle way: no upheaval of the tax system, but a removal of some of the main shortcomings of that system.

Tax reform may be influenced by several factors. First, an analysis of the existing tax system may lead public authorities to one of two conclusions: either the tax system needs to be completely overhauled, or it simply needs small changes. The existing tax system has to be judged according to various criteria, including economic efficiency, equity, simplicity, and fairness. Because the results of this examination will differ, the pressure for tax reform may vary considerably from one country to another. Second, the implementation of a tax reform may be delayed or made impossible by prevailing political conditions. Often, a pure tax reform, that is, one that is budget neutral, leads to a situation where some are better off while others are worse off. If the tax reform is considered generally desirable, it is because society as a whole is supposedly better off. As people whose situation worsens generally complain while people whose situation improves rarely congratulate the government, and as the benefits of reforming the tax system for the society as a whole need time to be fully realized, political conditions play a big role in the implementation of such a reform.

This paper first focuses on the main characteristics of the present tax system in France, highlighting its shortcomings but also its good qualities, which should not be ignored. That overview will provide some indications of the possible room for tax reform. We then describe how in recent years the French government has dealt with tax issues. Finally, we discuss the prospects for further changes in the tax system, giving full consideration to political and international constraints. In particular, we examine the constraints tied to the unification of the European market.

CHARACTERISTICS OF THE FRENCH TAX SYSTEM

Compared with the average of other industrialized countries of comparable size, the French tax system may be characterized by three main elements:

—A high level of overall taxation

—High (compulsory) social security contributions

—High indirect taxation and relatively low but distorting direct taxation, stricto sensu.

Overall Tax Burden

France's overall tax burden is one of the heaviest among industrialized countries, especially among big industrialized countries. Total tax revenues represent 45 percent of gross domestic product (GDP). This ratio is higher than in the United States, Japan, Germany, the United Kingdom, Italy, and Canada; only some countries of smaller size show higher ratios.

The tax ratio (ratio of taxes and compulsory social contributions to GDP) increased dramatically during the second half of the 1970s and the first half of the 1980s—from about 37.5 percent of GDP to the current 45.0 percent. The reasons for such an increase may be summed up as follows. Before the first oil shock, growth rates used to be high in France, in the range of 5 percent to 6 percent annually. Under these conditions, substantial increases in real public expenditures could be afforded easily with the tax ratio remaining steady and no public deficit. Output decelerated after the first oil shock, and again after the second oil shock; as public expenditures did not decelerate accordingly (on the contrary, there was pressure for accelerating some expenditures, for example, unemployment benefits), the tax ratio had to rise in order to prevent the emergence of growing deficits.

As a matter of fact, French fiscal policy was fairly orthodox until the beginning of the 1980s. In 1980 the budget ran a surplus of 0.2 percent of GDP, while there were deficits of 2.9 percent in Germany, 1.3 percent in the United States, 3.5 percent in the United Kingdom, and 4.4 percent in Japan. In 1985, however, the deficits were 2.6 percent in France, 1.1 percent in Germany, 3.4 percent in the United States, 2.7 percent in the United Kingdom, and 0.8 percent in Japan.

Social Security Contributions

The French social security system has reached a high level of development. French workers benefit from good protection against illness and a decrease of their income due to old age or unemployment, compensated in a large measure by the public social security system. In addition, family grants are rather attractive.

The counterpart of that protection may naturally be found in the high level of contributions, which are the main source of revenue for social security funds and which are based principally on gross wages, and secondarily on self-employment income. For an employee with an average wage, employer contributions now amount to 40.6 percent of gross wages and employee contributions to 16.8 percent, or a total of 57.4 percent. High and growing social security contributions during the last fifteen years explain a large share of the high tax ratio.

The social security contribution burden is assumed to be borne both by employers and employees, the first bearing a higher but, since 1983, declining share. This characteristic of the French system does not really matter in a long-term view: as firms pay the whole cost of labor and workers earn a net of contributions wage, the institutional gross wage will move to the right position for the labor market to clear in response to any shift from one sort of contribution to the other. However, in the short run, a shift from one side to the other may well have macroeconomic effects, through demand and cost channels.

Whether social security contributions should be considered "pure" taxes or a part of the wage is an interesting theoretical issue. In the French case, an analysis of the way contributions are levied and benefits provided (see appendix 1) leads to the conclusion that social security contributions ought to be considered mainly as distorting taxes.

In France social security contributions are rather regressive; however, that feature is more than offset by a highly progressive income tax.

Indirect Taxation

Mainly through the VAT, indirect taxation provides more than one-half of central government receipts in France (the yield of the VAT alone represents nearly 9 percent of GDP).

The VAT is levied on a rather broad base, with most goods and services included in it. It may be also considered only slightly distortionary, although departures from the theoretical consumption tax may be found, including the following:

—The multiplicity of rates, ranging (except for second-order details) from 5.5 percent to 33.3 percent

—The incomplete deductibility of the VAT on goods used for intermediate consumption or for investment, such as cars, fuel, and products made by VAT-exempted sectors

The excise taxes on alcohol and tobacco are rather small by international standards. On the other hand, excise taxes on oil are high.

Direct Taxation

Central government direct taxation, that is, income tax and corporate tax, does not yield much compared with other countries: 6 percent of GDP for individual income tax and 2 percent for corporate income tax.

The discrepancy between top marginal rates, in excess of 70 percent in previous years if all taxes on income are taken into account, and the low yield of income tax deserves to be analyzed. Several factors are responsible for this feature. First, the high progressivity of the tax schedule leads to average rates that are much lower than the marginal rates. In other words, a large share of the tax base bears low rates in comparison with the top marginal rates (table 1).

Second, the tax base is reduced, for several reasons:

—The share of taxable wages in GDP is relatively low, due to the deductibility of the high social security contributions, which are levied primarily on labor income;

TABLE 1. *Marginal Individual Income Tax Rates, 1986–88*
Percent

Taxable income[a] (1987 francs)	1986	1987	1988
0–16,560	0	0	0
16,561–17,320	5	5	5.0
17,321–20,530	10	10	9.6
20,531–32,460	15	15	14.4
32,461–41,730	20	20	18.2
41,731–52,410	25	25	24.0
52,411–63,420	30	30	28.8
63,421–73,170	35	35	33.6
73,171–121,920	40	40	38.4
121,921–167,670	45	45	43.2
167,671–198,330	50	50	49.0
198,331–225,610	55	55	53.9
225,611–255,710	60 ⎤ 58	56.8	
255,711 and over	65 ⎦		

a. The tax in the current year is based on the previous year's income.

—A general deduction of 28 percent (up to a ceiling) is applied to wages for the calculation of taxable income;

—Tax is calculated on a "consumption unit" basis rather than on a family basis, a provision that may be considered necessary because of the high progressivity of the tax schedule; however, the treatment of families is much more favorable than in most other countries;

—Interest is mostly taxed at a special flat low tax rate, perhaps as a consequence of historically high inflation; and

—The "traditional" deductions, exemptions, and rebates exist in France, though perhaps on a smaller scale than in other industrialized countries.

The result of this situation is a tremendous concentration of the tax burden: half of the potential taxpayers do not pay any income tax, a large share of the rest pay little income tax, and the top 5 percent of taxpayers pay 50 percent of the income tax.

France's corporate tax principles do not differ fundamentally from those of other countries. The tax rate (50 percent from the 1960s to 1985) has recently been reduced. The tax base is not defined in a particularly tight or loose manner in comparison with other countries. The problem of reforming corporate tax will be examined further.

Local Taxation

At the local level, tax receipts may be divided into two groups of comparable size:
—Taxes paid by households based on the rental value of land and buildings; and
—The notorious "professional tax," based on the use of labor and capital, the latter being taxed implicitly at higher rates than the former (the tax base being the total of 18 percent of gross wages but the whole of estimated capital costs).
The professional tax was implemented in the 1970s to substitute for the old specific professional tax. This experiment with an actual though small-sized tax reform was particularly unpleasant for the public authorities of that time.

CHANGES IN THE TAX SYSTEM SINCE 1970

During the 1970s tax policy was characterized by the need to face growing public expenditures and the preeminence of redistributive considerations. These features were reinforced in the early 1980s. However, the effect of taxes on economic efficiency became a matter of concern in 1984, and measures were implemented to limit the tax burden and remove tax provisions that were considered particularly unfavorable to economic efficiency. That policy was accelerated in 1986.

The 1970s: Focus on Distribution

The 1970s saw a trend toward an increase in the tax ratio in order to pay for increases in social security and other public expenditures without accumulating public debt. The rise in the tax burden consisted mostly in increases of social security contributions, and particularly, for a while, of those assumed to be paid by employers. The progressivity of the tax system was reinforced during this period, with the side effect of increasing tax revenue somewhat. This was accomplished, for example, through the removal of most of the ceilings used previously for the calculation of social security contributions and the implementation of a ceiling limiting the deduction granted to wage earners in the calculation of the income tax base.

At that time, tax policy was a matter of partisan concern to a high degree, and, notwithstanding the measures just discussed, the opposition on the left argued that the tax system was not progressive enough; in other words, the tax burden was too heavy on the poor and too light on the rich.

The Early 1980s: Reinforcing Redistribution

Accordingly, when the left coalition government took power in 1981, the trend toward more progressivity was reinforced. The top marginal income tax rate was increased from 60 percent to 65 percent, and progressive additional taxes on the base of a highly progressive income tax were implemented. Special taxes were assessed on various expenditures by business firms that could be considered to benefit the managers or the executive staff.

The most striking example of the goals pursued by tax policy at the beginning of the 1980s is found in the implementation of a tax on "large fortunes." The French tax system did not previously include direct taxes on capital or wealth. Nevertheless, wealth used to be taxed rather heavily, sometimes several times, when it took the form of land and buildings (at the local level), when it passed from one generation to another whatever its form, and when the owner received income from it.

The implementation of any wealth tax without reforming taxes on capital income and bequests would have added distortions to a complex system. As the actual tax was designed to apply only to the richest people, and as during the process of parliamentary debate many exemptions were accepted, the potential shortcomings of a wealth tax were reinforced by the very narrow base. Despite the high rates (up to 1.5 percent each year), the tax finally produced very little revenue (about 0.1 percent of GDP). It was removed by the right coalition government in 1986.

1983–84: Emphasis on Efficiency

At the same time as the redistributive potential of the tax system was addressed, the shortcomings of a high tax burden and high marginal rates became more and more obvious, especially in the context of growing international competition.

It was decided in 1984 that the tax burden should be reduced, and a cut of 1 percent of GDP was planned for 1985. About one-quarter of the decrease consisted of the removal of a proportional income tax previously implemented for social security financing; another quarter of rebates on income tax; another quarter of rebates on professional tax, those rebates being borne by the central government budget; and the final quarter of various small-sized measures. This plan led only to a stabilization of the tax ratio, tax revenue and GDP being imperfectly controlled by the government and subject to random shocks.

Throughout this period, the efficiency losses that might arise not only from a high tax burden but also from high marginal tax rates even in low-yielding taxes became a matter of concern. However, in 1985 there was no consensus for a reduction in the marginal income tax rates, for that tax seemed to be a symbol of the redistributive role of the whole tax system. Improving economic efficiency could be more easily experimented with through the corporate tax, as the public had become more aware of the need for maintaining the profitability of business enterprise.

Accordingly, the government decided in 1985 (starting from 1986) to reduce the corporate tax rate from 50 percent to 45 percent. As a result of the debate, it had become clear that rate reduction was preferred to any special investment tax subsidy, such as acceleration of depreciation allowances. The choice was made on the ground that tax subsidies would have introduced a bias into managers' decisions, contrary to the goal of a neutral tax system.

The argument nevertheless was not brought to its logical conclusion, as the reduction in the corporate tax rate was planned to be applied only to undistributed profits. The idea was to favor investment more directly. Not enough consideration was given to the consequences of differential treatment of distributed and undistributed profits, especially in a context in which distributed profits were still taxed more than undistributed profits (because of partial double taxation through the corporate and individual income taxes). A bias against efficiency-improving reallocation of capital among firms was thus reinforced. Finally, the implementation of the measure posed practical problems. The tax rate reduction was thus extended to distributed profits by the new government at the beginning of 1986, before the measure became effective.

1986–88: More Efficiency without Forgetting Equity

The new government formed after the 1986 elections decided to make a further and more significant reduction of the overall tax burden and to correct the main sources of possible distortions in order to reduce the efficiency losses resulting from the tax system.

More than 70 billion francs of tax cuts have been implemented or planned for the period 1986–88. The measures have been designed to promote efficiency while taking into account considerations of equity. The most significant are the following:

—The reduction in corporate tax to 45 percent was extended to the whole of profits, and this decrease will be followed by a further reduction in 1988 to 42 percent. The tax rate cut has the side effect of further reducing the double taxation of distributed profits, as the tax credit granted for purposes of the individual income tax is a share of the dividends and not a share of the corporate tax.

—More neutrality in corporate taxation was achieved through an improvement of the loss carryback system and of the taxation of firm groups.

—A special tax on certain firms' expenditures was reduced and then removed as of 1988.

—Cuts in the professional tax were implemented.

—The top marginal rates of income tax were reduced from 65.0 percent to 58.0 percent and 56.8 percent; tax cuts from 3.0 percent to 11.0 percent, depending on the tax paid, have been implemented.

—To introduce more equity for families, the tax exemption for married couples was increased. Although this measure may be desirable on social grounds, it has the defect of reducing the tax base and the number of taxpayers.

—More equity for families and greater neutrality for the financing decisions of business were implemented by the unification of the tax-exempt ceilings for interest and dividends and the calculation of the ceiling according to the number of adults in the family.

—A special law on savings was enacted. The main provisions of this law are an increase in the tax-exempt ceilings, the removal of a pretax on interest, and deferred and reduced taxation of savings set aside for retirement.

—The low-yielding and high-distorting tax on "large fortunes" was removed.

—The VAT rate on cars, far from the European average, was lowered from 33.3 percent to 28.0 percent; telecommunications were included in the VAT base, so that firms may deduct the tax on the use of such service; and deductions were allowed for the VAT on fuel used by professional transporters.

PROSPECTS FOR FURTHER REFORM

As a result of many years of fiscal discipline in the 1960s and 1970s, the share of public debt in GDP in France is low by international standards. However, the expansionary policies in the early 1980s have led from a near-to-balanced position to a significant public deficit (3 percent of GDP). Though the deficit has since been stabilized and then reduced, the decline in inflation tends to increase the ratio of debt to GDP. Meanwhile, real interest rates in excess of output growth make it increasingly necessary to reduce the deficit in order to prevent the emergence of a constantly rising debt. Reducing the deficit may thus be considered a major economic policy target.

Under these conditions, room for reducing the tax burden depends heavily on the ability to cut public expenditures. Everyone knows how difficult such an exercise is in practice. A high degree of political will, as well as great tenacity of purpose, is necessary.

Financing Social Security

The French are said to be very attached to their social security system, perhaps partly as a result of the apparent disassociation in the past of the generous benefits from the burden of financing. Social expenditures have been increasing faster than output growth as a result of factors that seem relatively inelastic, the most important being the following:

—Part of health expenditure is virtually free of charge for the consumer, so that the demand for such goods and services is nearly insensitive to prices;

—The population is aging, with a double effect on social expenditures. First, and directly, pension benefits rise rapidly. Pension schemes, which are usually unfunded and do not equalize the present values of contributions and benefits, cannot finance such increases with stable contribution rates. Second, and indirectly, health expenditures are stimulated because such expenditures usually rise with age.

In practice, rules to regulate the growth of expenditures have been implemented at various times, but with only modest success and at high political cost. Accordingly, most of the adjustment measures were based on increases in contribution rates.

The system will be balanced in the long run only when public opinion becomes fully aware of the direct relationship between benefits and tax burdens, which is not the case currently. A step in the direction of promoting transparency has been taken by making compulsory (from 1989) wage statements that will include all contributions paid by employers and employees. For a transitional period, it will not be possible to avoid increases in contribution rates or in proportional taxes on income for social security funds, increasing the tax ratio accordingly.

European Market Unification

Currently, tax systems differ greatly among member countries of the European Community (EC). The departures of the French tax system from the average of other EC countries are mainly the following:

—Relatively high level of overall taxation

—High VAT tax rates and yields; moreover, the tax base is broader in France as a result of the nondeductibility of VAT on various inputs used by firms, such as cars and fuel, in contradiction to VAT principles and on the presumption of a major private use of such items for private purposes

—Excise taxes of moderate size, resulting from low taxation of alcohol and tobacco

—High social security contributions and low direct taxation

If goods may be considered as free traded at the intermediate rather than at the final consumption level, European mobility of services, labor, and capital is far from perfect. The ultimate goal of the unification of the EC market may be defined as the disappearance of borders of any sort. That raises several questions:

—Should indirect taxes be harmonized at the European level?

—Should both the tax base and tax rates be harmonized?

—Is the harmonization of indirect taxes more urgent than the harmonization of the rest of the tax system?

—May the harmonization of indirect taxation be considered independently from the harmonization of the whole tax system (some argue that a nonharmonized system would create fewer distortions than a partly harmonized system)?

Answering those questions is far from easy, as may be seen in appendix 2. Common sense suggests that a convergence of tax systems would alleviate the problem of unifying markets. This convergence, however, may conflict with various countries' internal tax policy goals, or produce large shocks. In addition, the average EC system may be judged nonoptimal: For example, France may argue that such a high-yielding, low-distorting, and generally equitable tax as VAT should play a larger role in modern tax systems. The extent to which harmonization should be carried out and the aspects of the system that should be addressed first are now being considered by the government.

Social Security Receipts

As stated earlier, social security will probably require increased receipts in the coming years, making reduction of the overall tax burden more difficult. The need for transparency suggests that social security receipts should be earmarked rather than transferred from the central government budget. Under these conditions, the tax policy problem is to raise additional receipts. One possible way is to increase traditional contribution rates. Another is to find a broader base in order to limit the distortions. Looking for a broader base is a traditional theoretical response, but it has rarely been implemented.

As a matter of fact, the present base of contributions is rather broad: it includes labor earnings and all self-employed income (capital and labor income cannot be distinguished in this case). A hypothetical broader base would include the rest of capital income and retirement income. Including capital income in the social security base raises two problems: its relatively low share in net national product leads to only a slight increase in the base, while the risk of worsening a still-complex and sometimes highly distortionary system of capital taxation increases. Taxation of retirement income is economically equivalent to a decrease in benefit rates, though it may be considered easier to implement from a political point of view. However, the practical problem of substituting an income base for a wage and nonwage earnings base is that the former is eroded by traditional exemptions, deductions, and so on. Accordingly, it ultimately may be narrower than the latter.

However, there is now in France an interesting debate on the specific question of family allowances. Contributions to finance these allowances are based on gross wages, with a rate of 9 percent up to a ceiling corresponding approximately to the average wage. Since, as a matter of fact, this is a pure redistribution, the resulting relative increase of the cost of labor in the lowest part of the wage distribution seems highly questionable, especially in a country where youth unemployment is very high. Several alternatives have been considered for the financing of family allowances, though all of them raise practical difficulties. However, a broader tax base to finance family allowances should be considered, taking into account both equity and efficiency.

Corporate Tax

Depreciation allowances for tax purposes are calculated according to expected life durations of investment goods that are usually shorter than the actual durations. Moreover, most industrial equipment may be depreciated according to a double-declining balance system. These two factors more or less compensate for the erosion of allowances due to inflation, if the rate of inflation is relatively low. This is presently the case and should continue in the future, the stance of current economic policy being resolutely anti-inflationary. Under such conditions, reducing the tax rate will unambiguously reduce distortions. In fact, there is a risk that special measures designed to accelerate depreciation allowances would reinforce the existing distortions in the taxation of profits.

If there were room to reduce the yield of the corporate tax, that room should be used for reducing the tax rate. Investment would thus be stimulated, the rate would tend to join the lowest in the industrialized world (the 42-percent rate in force in 1988 still being competitive), and discrimination against distributed profits would be reduced. The individual income tax credit is half of the dividend; a reduction of the corporate tax rate to 33.3 percent would thus entirely eliminate double taxation of dividends.

Income Tax

The present government plans to continue to lower the marginal tax rates, especially those in excess of 50 percent. It is not desirable to reduce the still-narrow tax base, particularly since other taxes such as social security contributions or the VAT are paid starting from the first franc of wage or consumption. On the contrary, economic efficiency would require a much broader base. However, broadening the income tax base seems to be extremely difficult to implement for political reasons. The income tax is a symbol of the whole system despite its low share in public receipts.

In the longer run, the issue of integrating the high-yielding, slightly regressive social contributions and the low-yielding, highly progressive income tax deserves to be addressed.

Indirect Taxes

As stated earlier, the unification of the European market will exert pressure to harmonize VAT bases and rates. Harmonizing the VAT base is desirable to a certain extent (although the argument that cars and fuel bought by firms may be used for private consumption purposes is valid to a degree) and is limited only by fiscal considerations. Harmonizing VAT rates is desirable too, should the reduced rate not be too low.

The EC commission proposals are oriented toward a two-rate structure: a normal one and a reduced one for some essential items.

As the rate structure in France is presently highly complicated and as the rates are generally opposite to those resulting from Ramsey's recommended rules, welfare gains would be realized following a harmonization of the European rate structure.[1] Such welfare gains will probably not be offset by any significant equity losses, as VAT average rates on consumption do not depend significantly on the level of personal income, despite the multiplicity of rates. The only limit to improving economic efficiency and preserving tax receipts will lie in the political difficulties of agreeing on a reduced rate that is high relative to the standard rate. There is no serious impediment to having different reduced rates among countries, since the items in question (mainly food) offer little room for cross-border arbitrage.

If harmonized, excise taxes on oil should be lowered and taxes on tobacco and alcohol increased. The latter measure is theoretically justified because the costs imposed on society by consumers of those items in our system of nearly free-of-charge health care expenditures greatly exceeds present tax levels. However, harmonization among those products would generate large changes in relative prices.

Local Taxes

The problem of local government financing should be mentioned because of its relationship to local government responsibility. Local receipts in France depend heavily on central government subsidies. Some of these subsidies are paid because they substitute for local taxes that were eliminated to make room for central government taxes. For instance, when the VAT was introduced, a local tax on wages was removed.

More recently, the introduction of the professional tax to replace another specific local tax has led to massive internal transfers within the corporate sector, constraining the central government to pay that part of the burden that is in excess of a national level or a national rate of increase considered bearable. When cuts in professional taxes were decided at the central level, those cuts were to be borne by the state budget. Accordingly, one may say that the central government pays a significant share of the professional tax, and perhaps a higher

1. F. P. Ramsey, "A Contribution to the Theory of Taxation," *Economic Journal*, vol. 37 (March 1927), pp. 47–61.

share in marginal terms. The (political) opportunity cost of local receipts may have decreased for those reasons, and that may raise a problem of consistency at a time when the central government strives to keep its receipts and deficit under strict control.

APPENDIX 1: SHOULD SOCIAL SECURITY CONTRIBUTIONS BE CONSIDERED TAXES?

To address this issue, non-lump-sum taxes should be considered distortionary since they change the relative price of goods in a broad sense. When placed in the whole system of public finance, taxes distort to the extent that the expenditures they finance are distributed according to criteria differing from those on which taxes are levied. In other words, if a tax is used to provide a social benefit granted in the same way the tax is levied (for example, proportional to income), the overall system is not distortionary. French social security contributions will be examined in the light of these considerations.

Health Care

If contributions were calculated as an insurance premium related to the risk of illness, they would not be considered pure taxes. The only distortions of the system would arise from the extent to which the compulsory level of health expenditures does not necessarily coincide with individual tastes. In fact, social security contributions for health care are proportional to wage levels, and expenditures depend only on the illness risk. Under those conditions, health care contributions must be regarded as distortionary taxes.

Old Age

Compulsory pension schemes would lead to relatively minor distortions if the contributions based on wages were directly related to future pensions. Furthermore, with perfect financial markets, one could imagine that people wishing lower pensions could discount the excess of future pensions and use the cash to pay the excess contributions. Nevertheless, in practice financial markets have not reached such a degree of refinement. Pension schemes do not conform perfectly to theoretical norms, as benefits are not equal to contributions in present terms and as provision is made for maximum and minimum benefits. In addition, unfunded private pension schemes are no longer generally balanced at the aggregate level in present value terms, so that a nonnegligible uncertainty surrounds the present value of future benefits for contributing workers. For these reasons, old-age contributions should be considered mainly as taxes.

Unemployment

Unemployment contributions are also far from insurance premiums. Contributions depend on wages regardless of risk (the unemployment rate ranging from nil to more than 25 percent according to socio-professional groups), and benefits are partly proportional, partly lump sum, but above all related to risk.

Family

The contributions are a purely proportional tax (up to a ceiling), with benefits tied to demographic criteria. Moreover, as part of family grants are means tested, the distortionary effect is reinforced.

APPENDIX 2: ISSUES RELATED TO THE UNIFICATION OF THE EUROPEAN MARKET

At present, and despite its name, the value-added tax is merely a tax on final consumption. The mechanism that secures this characteristic is the zero rate on exports, while imports are subject to the same tax as domestically produced products. This mechanism is generally considered as contributing to neutrality, insofar as VAT does not affect the international competitive price structure. However, this argument has been criticized on the ground that other taxes are also incorporated in the pricemaking decision. Removing some but not all taxes from the pricemaking decision might thus worsen the distortions and induce a welfare decreasing bias in international specialization.

The harmonized VAT should normally remain a consumption tax in principle. The removal of borders would not change anything for the distribution of intermediate-stage goods (intermediate being defined in a broad sense to include goods transferred before the retail sales stage), as the VAT on those goods would be reimbursed to industrial and commercial firms. Thus the two main problems that arise from the removal of borders are the following:

—Firm A from country A buying a product from firm B from country B will seek a reimbursement from the treasury of country A of a tax previously received by the treasury of country B. How will country A's treasury be reimbursed by country B's treasury in practice?

—Some items will be sold at differing prices to final consumers across borders, as before-tax prices will tend to equalize and the VAT rates may differ from one country to another. To what extent will such departures among prices be bearable? Transportation costs and consumers' habits will intervene in this issue.

The extent to which the VAT and excise tax rates should be aligned with European standards—to prevent the emergence of large cross-border purchases and thus (ex post) reduced public receipts—will determine the magnitude of the overall (ex ante) loss of indirect tax receipts. It will also determine the magnitude of the changes in relative prices, some items being currently taxed too much or not enough according to European standards.

Some have proposed to solve these problems by taxing value-added rather than final consumption. As a matter of fact, these problems are not solved by such mechanisms; rather, they are replaced by the general problems raised by differences in the overall tax systems.

If not on consumption, taxes are levied, from an economic point of view, on production factors or on the production process. Improved mobility of factors within the EC will reduce differences in rates of remuneration for labor and capital, assuming production is taxed to the same extent as under a VAT. In particular, if capital becomes fully mobile among countries, differences in the taxation of savings and capital would present excellent opportunities for arbitrage and could quickly become unbearable.

Finally, mention should be made of the VAT base harmonization problem. At present, the nondeductibility of cars and fuel produces a competitive handicap for the firms concerned. The removal of borders would not change that handicap. However, stronger competition that might arise from market unification will exert pressure for the reduction of such disparities among countries.

Comment by PIERRE-ANDRE CHIAPPORI

The paper presented by Jean-Claude Milleron and Didier Maillard gives an exhaustive description of the French tax system, including compulsory social contributions, and explains the recent reforms. In my comments I shall first concentrate on two difficulties facing the public sector: the deficit of social security funds and the harmonization of tax systems within the European Community. I shall then briefly discuss two issues that appear central to the tax reform controversies in France: the link between marginal taxation and efficiency on the one hand, and the issue of equity and redistribution on the other.

As indicated by the authors, financing social security will be one of the toughest economic problems faced by the next government, whatever its political complexion. First, demographic trends are unambiguous: the dependency ratio in the French population will increase until the end of the century. Second, the growth rate of health expenditures, even corrected for demographic effects, has consistently outstripped GNP growth. Such rapid health expenditure growth is a direct consequence of the social security financing mechanism. In the French system, people pay a compulsory contribution independent of their consumption of health care; in return, most health services are free of charge. A strong pressure for improvement of medical services from both physicians and the public also encourages rapid growth of expenditures.

I doubt that any solution can be found, short of a complete overhaul of the system itself. The view expressed in the paper, that expenditures could be controlled if the public were "fully aware of the direct relationship between benefits and tax burdens," seems overly optimistic. In fact, this is a pure free-rider problem. Even if people know that aggregate contributions and expenditures are closely related, they still have no incentive to cut their own consumption, since doing so would not reduce their own tax bills. Incidentally, it has been recently suggested that public health insurance could and should be deregulated—that is, that private insurance firms should be allowed to compete with the public sector. The proposal appears highly controversial.

A second problem stems from tax system discrepancies between

France and other EC countries. The authors indicated that the VAT yield is much higher, and income tax much lower, in France than elsewhere in the EC. So the harmonization of VAT rates—an apparently urgent measure—would probably require a dramatic increase in the direct tax burden. Because income tax rates are already high, and in fact are currently being reduced, it would probably be necessary to broaden the income tax base and tax people who are not now taxed. The political cost of such a reform is likely to be high; clearly, people are extremely sensitive to direct taxation, though it plays only a minor role in the French system.

Both problems must be considered from a more general point of view. A principal argument in favor of reforming the tax system, especially of reducing the income tax, is the efficiency loss due to high marginal rates. A principal counterargument is the redistributive function of the tax-benefit system. Both arguments merit further discussion.

Table 1 shows the effective marginal rate of a sample of French wage earners. The computation of marginal rates includes income tax and main family benefits; it does not include social security contributions or housing or unemployment benefits. The average marginal rate is either 16 percent or 20 percent, depending on how the marginal rate is defined.[1] Only 0.5 percent of households in the sample are taxed at the maximum income tax rate, 58 percent; their average gross income is 728,000 francs, or approximately $125,000. However, 1.5 percent of the households—all middle- or lower-income—face marginal rates over 60 percent, essentially because of means-tested benefits. Some benefits may even result in effective marginal rates exceeding 100 percent—an apparently major source of inefficiency. And because social security contributions are either entirely proportional, or proportional up to a ceiling, the resulting marginal rates, which should be added to those in table 1, are higher for low incomes. These results suggest an important conclusion. Clearly, for the tax-benefit system to play a redistributive role, part of the population must face "high" marginal rates, at least as compared with their average rates. If redistribution is achieved by the income

1. If all incomes were increased by the same amount, the marginal rate would be 16 percent; if all incomes were increased by the same percentage, the marginal rate would be 20 percent.

TABLE 1. *Distribution of a Sample of Wage Earners by Effective Marginal Tax Rates under Frances's Tax-Benefit System, 1987*
Percent except where noted

Effective marginal rates[a]	Population	Average gross income (thousands of francs)
0	13.1	60
0.1–5.0	2.0	73
5.0–8.0	5.0	83
8.0–10.0	19.6	100
10.0–13.3	11.8	132
13.3–16.7	14.4	146
16.7–20.0	9.4	156
20.0–23.3	3.9	156
23.3–26.7	6.2	167
26.7–30.0	7.3	279
30.0–40.0	5.0	259
40.0–55.0	0.3	626
55.0–60.0	0.5	728
60.0–70.0	0.2	70
70.0–90.0	1.3	150

Source: Calculated by author on the basis of a sample of 2,000 wage earners.

a. Includes income tax and family benefits. Excludes social security contributions, housing, and unemployment benefits.

tax, the high rates will apply to wealthy households; if redistribution is based on means-tested benefits, only low-income households will be concerned—at the risk of creating a "poverty trap."

A different, potentially important cause of inefficiency is the complexity of the French tax-benefit system. For example, tax allowances are provided to musicians, bus drivers, clockmakers, and pipemakers in Saint Claude (Jura). In 1981 a discontinuous structure of surtaxes was applied; after 1983 the surtaxes were transformed into tax cuts. As a consequence, some marginal rates may exceed 100 percent. The more than fifteen types of national family benefits are supplemented by numerous local subsidies. The complexity of the benefit structure actually contributes to poverty: many low-income households are simply unaware of benefits for which they could apply. Simplifications are clearly needed.

The French tax system is not now strongly redistributive. The main progressive tax, the income tax, represents only 10 percent of overall taxation; the remaining 90 percent is levied through proportional (VAT) or regressive (social security) taxes. The weight of nonprogressive taxes, moreover, is likely to increase; for instance, a 1-percent supplementary contribution based on all incomes will soon be implemented to cover the social security deficit.

Even the French income tax, though globally progressive, incorporates regressive components, the most important of which is the income-splitting or "quotient" mechanism for the taxation of the family. Taxable income is divided by the number of "parts" in the family: one for each adult and one or one-half for each child. The tax is calculated on the basis of income per part, and the resulting figure multiplied by the number of parts. The effect is to reduce the progressivity of the schedule: the higher the gross income, the bigger the tax break. The quotient is usually supported on the ground that it redistributes from small to large families, thus encouraging fertility. But even this effect is ambiguous. Large families gain only insofar as their gross income is high enough for splitting to be important. Hence, the joint distribution of income and family size is crucial. Replacing the quotient by an increase in family benefits would result in a transfer from rich to poor, but also from small to large families (see table 2). In other words, the quotient is not beneficial to large families, but rather to wealthy large families.

In two recent studies, Atkinson, Bourguignon, and Chiappori showed that replacing the French tax-benefit system by a British-style one would unambiguously reduce inequality.[2] They also found that the large difference in yield between French and British income

2. A. B. Atkinson, F. Bourguignon, and P. A. Chiappori, "The French Tax-Benefit System and a Comparison with the British System," in A. B. Atkinson and H. Sutherland, eds., *Tax Benefit Models* (London School of Economics, Suntory Toyota Centre for Research in Economics and Related Disciplines, forthcoming); and A. B. Atkinson, F. Bourguignon, and P. A. Chiappori, "What Do We Learn from International Comparisons of Tax Systems?" forthcoming in *European Economic Review*.

TABLE 2. *Effect of Replacing the Quotient System by Increased Family Benefits, 1987*

Percentile	Average gross income (thousands of francs)	Average family size[a]	Average change in net income (thousands of francs)
Population by range of gross income			
0–10	42	2.29	15.8
11–20	67	2.69	18.2
21–30	80	2.61	13.1
31–40	93	2.65	9.9
41–50	110	2.55	3.3
51–60	124	2.50	0.8
61–70	143	2.46	−5.8
71–80	168	2.51	−10.8
81–90	206	2.62	−15.7
91–95	267	2.73	−21.9
96–98	364	2.77	−33.1
99–100	685	2.83	−48.6
Population by family size			
0–10	92	1.00	0
11–20	120	1.70	−7.2
21–30	156	2.00	−11.6
31–40	139	2.30	−10.9
41–50	156	2.50	−12.3
51–60	152	2.60	−10.9
61–70 / 71–80	153	3.00	−3.6
81–90	142	3.40	14.3
91–95	135	3.71	28.7
96–98	113	4.34	51.6
99–100	65	5.61	105.3

Source: See table 1.

a. Adult = 1; child = 0.5.

taxes was essentially due to the quotient mechanism. Reducing the role of the quotient, neutrality being secured by appropriate increases of the VAT and family benefits, could simultaneously strengthen the redistributive properties of the system and reduce the difference between the tax system of France and other EC countries.

ADALBERT UELNER & THOMAS MENCK

Germany

Germany's taxation is based on direct taxes (including individual and corporate income taxes, a tax on net wealth, and a municipal trade tax [Gewerbesteuer]), a general consumption value-added tax, and several excise taxes. Social security is financed by specific contributions to a system providing, among other things, unemployment and sickness insurance as well as old-age pensions. In 1985, 35.0 percent of total revenues came from direct taxes, 25.6 percent from indirect taxes, and 36.5 percent from social security contributions. In this respect the German tax system is close to the average of the countries in the Organization for Economic Cooperation and Development (OECD).

This paper reflects the state of the government's plan for reform as of November 1, 1987, and deals only with reforms of the tax system. The system of social security will also be overhauled in the Federal Republic of Germany during the next several years.

HISTORY OF TAX REFORM IN THE FEDERAL REPUBLIC OF GERMANY

During the last decades, the German tax system has been continuously reshaped and adapted to changing economic conditions. Since 1966 more than one hundred major changes have been made, ranging from complete reforms of specific taxes to improvements in technical details. Some highlights are the introduction of a value-added tax (1968) and its overall adaptation to regulations of the European Community (1977); continuous efforts to adapt personal income tax to changing conditions and demographic requirements; and full integration of the corporate and personal income taxes through the split rate and credit system (1976).

In the autumn of 1982, the federal government announced a tax policy program set out in the form of a three-stage plan to reshape the tax system to encourage growth and to make productive activity more rewarding. In the first two stages enterprises were relieved by a reduction of the nonprofit-related tax burden and by improvements in the loss carryback and special depreciation allowances. The third stage, providing for a reduction of personal income tax, blended into the current ambitious project of a thorough reshaping of income taxes.

INTERNATIONAL ASPECTS

The Federal Republic of Germany is internationally open, and its economy is highly interdependent with the world economy. It must, therefore, keep in line with international developments in shaping its tax laws. Thus its general consumption tax is embedded in the common value-added tax of the countries in the European Community (EC) and its system of direct taxation is coordinated internationally by a network of treaties for the avoidance of double taxation. Economic developments and tax reforms in other countries tend, furthermore, to affect German tax policies as a consequence of international interdependence. Thus the recent U.S. tax reform was and is carefully studied by German tax politicians.

TAX REFORM TODAY

The German government has undertaken a thorough reform of direct taxes in three steps scheduled to take effect in 1986, 1988, and 1990. According to present laws, the reform will reduce the direct tax burden by some DM 50 billion and eliminate existing tax preferences by some DM 19 billion, thus compensating in part for the planned reductions. The fact that the reform does not aim at revenue neutrality reflects the success of the tight budget policy pursued since 1982.

The 1988 and 1990 steps of the reform were worked out by the coalition parties and the government in a two-step decisionmaking process. The tax rate reductions were planned in spring 1987, and concrete decisions about the elimination of tax preferences were taken in the autumn of the same year. The overall reform package will be presented to Parliament in the first half of 1988. It is possible that certain changes in the projected reform will still be made as a lively process of discussion is currently under way in the Federal Republic of Germany.

As in other countries government spending grew continuously in Germany over almost two decades. Taxes rose along with expenditure: the ratio of tax receipts to gross domestic product (GDP) increased from 31.6 percent in 1965 to 38.0 percent in 1980 and declined only slightly to 37.7 percent in 1984.

Curbing Government Expenditures

Since the present coalition government took office in the autumn of 1982, the foremost goal of German fiscal policy has been to curb this growth. In a first phase, the aim was to cut back the dangerously high public-sector deficits and, at the same time, to prepare the ground for a substantial reduction in the tax burden.

This policy has achieved notable successes since 1982. From 1982 to 1985 the ratio of public spending to GDP was brought down from 49.4 percent to 47.2 percent. The share of public-sector deficits in gross national product (GNP), standing at 3.7 percent in 1981, was reduced to 1.2 percent by 1986. These policies provided elbow room for tax reductions, which have been used to the full. Between 1983 and 1985 the trade tax (a municipal tax on commercial and industrial profits) and the net worth tax, were reduced and the depreciation allowances were improved (tax reductions amounting to DM 8 billion, or roughly 0.5 percent of GNP). The 1986–88 Tax Reduction Law provided income tax cuts of some DM 11 billion for 1986, or about 0.6 percent of GNP.

The Goals for Reform in 1988 and 1990

The German tax reform now under way is continuing with this endeavor. For 1988 the 1986–88 Tax Reduction Law provides for further cuts in the personal income tax amounting to some DM 8.5 billion. The government coalition has agreed that this relief should now be stepped up by DM 5.2 billion (the so-called Louvre agreement of February 1987) by bringing forward the reductions planned for 1990 to 1988. This includes the increase of the basic personal allowance, reductions in the tax rates, an increase in the education allowance, and an increase in the special depreciation allowance for small and medium-sized firms. The total tax relief in 1988 will thus amount to some DM 13.7 billion, or 0.65 percent of GNP.

For 1990 the coalition has agreed on further tax reform, amounting to DM 39.2 billion. The objective of this reform is to bring about extensive improvements in the German income tax system, that is, in the tax rates as well as in the tax base. It also incorporates specific relief measures for the business sector, including a reduction of the corporation tax rate on retained profits from 56 percent to 50 percent and additional increases in depreciation allowances for small and medium-sized firms. The net relief for taxpayers will amount to DM 20 billion, or roughly 0.85 percent of GNP.

The Budgetary Consequences

The balance between the aggregate tax reductions in the 1990 reform of DM 39 billion and the net relief of DM 20 billion amounts to DM 19 billion. This is to be made up largely from the broadening of the tax base, that is, from a reduction of numerous tax preferences. It will serve to simplify the tax system and make it more equitable, thus also improving the economic effectiveness of the system as a whole. The planned net relief of DM 20 billion will be funded by maintaining stringent limits on public spending, largely by refraining from adding new entitlements in the next two years. The growth of federal government expenditure will be held below 3 percent in the coming years and will thus remain below the growth of nominal GNP.

TECHNICAL DESCRIPTION OF TAX REFORM

The current reform will require many changes in the tax law. The main features and their impact on revenue are shown in tables 1 and 2. The following discussion highlights the major features of the reform.

Individual Tax Rate Structure

One of the problems besetting the tax systems of many countries is the impact of high marginal income tax rates on broad strata of

TABLE 1. *Tax Reductions in the Proposed Tax Reform, 1990*

Changes in tax law	Amount (billions of DM)
Increase in the basic personal allowance	5.6
Lowering of the tax entry rate by three percentage points to 19 percent; reduction in the spread of the lower proportional zone	6.7
Introduction of a linear-progressive tax schedule	20.7
Reduction of the top marginal rate by three percentage points to 53 percent plus bringing forward the starting point of the upper proportional zone	1.0
Increase in the child allowance	2.0
Increase in other family-related allowances (household allowance, allowance for the support of dependents, education allowance); introduction of an allowance for the home care of invalids in particularly serious cases	0.3
Improved advance deduction of provident expenses	0.6
Reduction of the corporation tax rate on retained profits by six percentage points to 50 percent	2.3
Total revenue reduction	39.2

their populations. While progressivity as such is still regarded as a necessity, the general rise of mass incomes and inflationary tendencies has, under unchanged tax rates, led to implausibly high marginal rates even for average earners. The U.S. tax reform, dramatically reducing progressivity to a two-rate system with its modest rates, has been widely discussed in the Federal Republic of Germany. For several reasons this scheme was deemed inapplicable to Germany at this time, but some reductions will be made in the high marginal tax rates.

Figure 1 shows the marginal rates in the old and in the new schedule. The lowering of the entry tax rate and the top marginal tax rate will reduce the overall tax burden. The tax reduction will

TABLE 2. *Tax Preferences to Be Eliminated under the Proposed Tax Reform, 1990*

Changes in tax law	Amount, 1990 (billions of DM)
Business preferences[a]	3.0
Preferences of wage and salary[b]	4.0
Measures to improve equality of taxation[c]	7.0
Changes with respect to private expenses	1.3
Cuts in regional incentives	2.8
Total additional revenue	18.1

a. Elimination of certain special depreciation allowances, tax-deductible reserves (future anniversary expenses, global value, adjustments of banks), and special rules for foreign investment (Auslandsinvestitions gesetz); cuts in the deductibility of certain expenses (for example, cost of business entertainment, privately used cars); and abolition of special rules for small enterprises in the field of value-added tax.

b. Changes in general and standard deductions for expenses; limitation of existing exemptions for certain overtime pay; and termination or limitation of exemption for certain fringe benefits (for example, certain provident payments and allowances for meals).

c. Ten-percent witholding tax on interest (with exceptions), generalized liability to pay interest on tax claims, and termination of certain depreciation allowances in the private sector.

amount to an average of 9.9 percent for all taxpayers; for the lowest bracket, it is 12.4 percent; for the highest bracket, it is 3.3 percent.

Broadening the Tax Base and Improving Tax Equity

In the U.S. tax reform, the reduction of tax rates had its counterpart in broadening the tax base. Germany's tax reform will follow this line. The changes extend over a wide field, correcting several deficiencies that had crept into Germany's tax system. The major items are the introduction of a new 10-percent withholding tax on interest that covers almost 25 percent of the envisaged additional revenue; broadening of the tax base of commercial and industrial profits by, among other things, cuts in special depreciation allowances and in

FIGURE 1. *Individual Income Tax Rates in Germany, 1985, 1988, 1990*

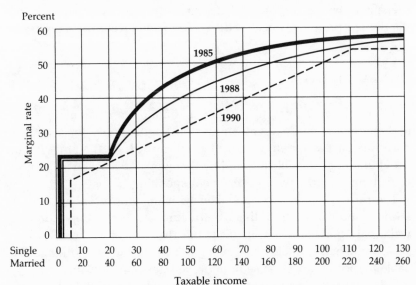

regional incentives (almost 33 percent of additional revenue); and limitations of tax benefits with respect to salaries and wages, mainly fringe benefits, and the deduction of certain professional and personal expenses. The overall goal is to require adequate sacrifices from all who benefit from the reform.

Corporate Income Tax

During the last decades, the normal rate of corporate income tax and the top marginal income tax rates have never drifted far apart in Germany. This is a safeguard for neutrality of taxation. Therefore the current income tax rate on retained profits of 56 percent has been reduced to 50 percent.

International Aspects

From an international point of view, two developments are of interest. First, certain German rules regarding foreign investment have been terminated. Second, negotiations on double-tax treaties with respect to withholding tax on dividends will be undertaken as the spread between the corporate income tax rates for retained and distributed profits has been reduced from 20 percent to 16 percent.

EVALUATION

The tax reform is intended to give a stimulus to economic growth and employment. Competitiveness and tax neutrality for economic decisions have been improved. The reform will, on the other hand, avoid unacceptable deficit spending that would defeat the major goal of curbing the growth of government spending.

The reform has been undertaken with the aim of enhancing the fairness and simplicity of the tax structure and promoting economic welfare. Important achievements in this respect will be the following:

—About half a million taxpayers will in the future no longer be liable to income tax because of improved general allowances.

—The future structure of tax rates combined with a balanced broadening of the tax base will improve the system's fairness.

—Deep cuts in tax preferences and in deductible expenses will make the application of the system simple and contribute to its fairness as well.

With all this, the taxes that must be accepted by the German population will remain high. The relative weight of direct and indirect taxes, the sharing of tax burden between businesses and households, and the distribution of taxation between the national and local levels of government will remain issues for debate.

Germany's tax policies seem to be correlated with the idea of reform: since the beginning of this century demands for improvement and change in the tax law have never ceased. Repeatedly they formed a chorus pleading for fundamental reforms. The basic values at the core of these demands have been more or less the same: fairness and justice, simplicity, and economic efficiency. Statements about the basic goals of tax reform made in the twenties and the eighties have a similar ring and often use identical words. Almost as soon as tax legislators have reacted to such demands, they have had to face new complaints and new proposals for tax changes. Thus the tax law seems to be an everlasting building site rather than a completed building. This has given rise to the idea of a "permanent reform," which will permit the tax system to adjust to changing demographic, economic, and cultural requirements of the country. The reform now under way contributes to that effort, but we will have to wait until the year 2000 to see whether we have achieved this objective.

Comment by GEROLD KRAUSE-JUNK

The gross volume of the German three-step tax cut in 1986, 1988, and 1990 will be about DM 70 billion and the net volume DM 50 billion, at income level 1990. It is the largest tax cut in the history of the Republic, in absolute terms as well as in relation to GNP (2 percent) or to the overall tax yield (9 percent).[1] Still, there is some debate about whether the Treasury has given up real revenues or has merely returned what it acquired "secretly" as a result of the impact of inflation and economic growth on a progressive tax system. The answer to that question depends on which public revenues one is looking at. The overall tax-to-GNP ratio in 1985 was no larger than in 1975, the year of the last large tax cut. This is true if one considers taxes only. But if one includes social security contributions, tax ratios as a percentage of GNP have risen somewhat. The ratio of taxes to GNP would have increased if endogenous pressures (due to the progressive income tax rates) had not been compensated for with deductions and allowances. The benefits of these, however, generally do not reach all taxpayers. It is no surprise, then, that some people feel it is time for a "rebate," while the government rather enjoys acting the part of Santa Claus.

Leaving aside the question of whether it is a real tax cut or an adjustment for inflation and economic growth, it is true that the Social Democratic opposition and the trade unions are very much

1. This is not an all-time record if one considers tax cuts in 1986, 1988, and 1990 separately. But most people view the three-step reform as a unit.

against the reform.[2] Maybe this response is simply a natural reaction to a program put forth by a conservative government. While opponents clearly don't like the reform because of its general structure, they also fight it with fiscal and macroeconomic arguments.

The long-term finance plan of the federal budget shows, indeed, a certain increase of the budget deficits, beginning in 1986. This would end a phase of substantial budget consolidation that has taken place since the coalition government came to office in 1982.

It is not surprising that the public, remembering the political fight about public deficits in the late seventies, realizes how the leading parties have switched their arguments. Now the Social Democratic opposition is concerned about the solidity of public budget financing, and the conservative government sees no reason to be worried.

As always in these matters, it is hard to tell right from wrong. The opposition correctly points out that the tax reform might be a drawback for the consolidation process, all the more because substantial budget risks have not been accounted for in long-term planning: inevitable demands from the European Community, tremendous finance gaps in the social security system (in the early nineties), and further subsidies to steel, coal, and airplane industries.

On the other hand, the government has two arguments in favor of the reform. It can emphasize the changed quality of the deficits, as—compared with the early eighties—the ratios of the deficits to GNP or to the overall federal public expenditures have declined.[3] The government can also claim that tax-reform induced deficits—as distinguished from public-spending induced deficits—are apt to be self-financing because of their beneficial effects on economic growth.

The last point leads to the much more important question of what kind of macroeconomic effects the tax cut might induce. The opposition view is that the tax cut is unfavorable to economic development and employment because it goes along with a strict limitation of federal expenditures. That argument implicitly assumes that without

2. Except for an increase in the standard deduction, the trade unions want to abolish the 1988 and 1990 steps of the tax reform altogether.

3. According to the German Council of Economic Advisors, public deficits were already back to normal (that is, the long-term average) by 1985. The council, therefore, would really not object to any deficit increase beginning in 1985 with a rate not larger than the GNP growth rate.

a tax cut, public expenditures would be higher. Public investments, that, for whatever reason, are both more appreciated and more flexible than other expenditures, are especially endangered.

There is some support in the data for that kind of reasoning. Moreover, the government considers (relative) expenditure cuts the main source to finance the tax cut. One might even suspect the tax cut to function as the major instrument to set further limits to the federal budget. (That, of course, would only work with a government that is very involved in an antideficit philosophy.) The opposition, therefore, might be right about how it sees the impact of the tax cut on federal (and general) public expenditures.

But is it also right in its analysis of the effects of public expenditure restrictions on economic development? This, of course, is economic theory's most controversial topic. On the one hand, limiting public expenditures, and thus setting more market forces into operation, is considered a major remedy for an economy shaken by low growth and high unemployment rates. This is the reason why the coalition government has been—successfully—engaged in lowering the expenditure to GNP ratio since it took office.

On the other hand, there still is some support for the Keynesian view that public demand has to give some impulse to the overall performance of an economy and that the tax cut fails to do so because of its negative effects on public, and its rather dubious effects, on private expenditures. There is at this time, however, at least one reason to see it the other way round. The actual German unemployment rate (9 percent) is considered mainly structural, meaning, among other things, that there is just not enough real capital to employ more workers.

From that point of view, the effects (including announcement effects) of the tax cut on private real investment are crucial, and these effects are anybody's guess. Investments might be induced for the following reasons:

—Disposable private income is substantially increased, in all likelihood increasing private saving and private consumption;

—Income (and profit) tax rates are lowered, and therefore net returns on investments are increased; and

—There is a substantial shift from the share of direct to the share of indirect taxes. (Indirect taxes are considered more favorable for investors. The value-added tax (VAT) does not fall on investments and does not discriminate against national production because of the rebate on exports.)

However, hopes for substantial tax relief for investment income were high, and potential investors might be disappointed because of the following:

—The 3-percent cut in the highest marginal income tax rate (from 56 percent to 53 percent) is less than what was considered necessary;[4]

—The shift to indirect taxes is smaller than expected as up to now no indirect tax increase has been announced; and

—Contrary to some announcements, the 1990s tax reform might turn out to be the last one for a long time. Therefore, no change seems to be in sight for the trade tax and the net-worth tax, both candidates for major improvements.

In spite of the record tax relief, it might turn out to be too little and too late. The government already has reshuffled the timetable and raised the 1988 tax cut by DM 5.2 billion that was originally included in the 1990s total. That was done to comply with international commitments to promote economic growth ("Treaty of Louvre"). Recently, the five leading German institutes for economic research urged the government to advance the final reform step from 1990 to 1989. The government will not do it. It would be amusing indeed if the final tax cut of the German tax reform, strongly inspired by the 1986 U.S. tax reform, will be made effective just when the United States raises its tax rates again.

THE NEW INCOME TAX RATE STRUCTURE

The volume and structure of the tax relief are, of course, closely connected. Especially the structure of the new income tax rates, the so-called linear progression, could hardly be introduced if there were

4. West Germany is considered to have the highest capital cost among the leading OECD countries, particularly because of taxation. Mervyn A. King and Don Fullerton, eds., *The Taxation of Income from Capital: A Comparative Study of the United States, the United Kingdom, Sweden, and West Germany* (University of Chicago Press, 1984), pp. 295–302.

not a substantial overall tax relief.[5] There is, nonetheless, controversy about the new income tax rates.

The opposition compares the absolute tax reliefs of high- and low-income people, for example, a millionaire and a shop girl, and claims utmost unfairness.[6] The government emphasizes that the largest losses of tax receipts occur in the lower- and middle-income groups and that the decrease of the top marginal income tax bracket will cost only DM 1 billion. Both arguments somehow miss the point, as they neglect necessary relativity. But how would a methodologically proper analysis of fairness of reform look? What, for example, is a distributionally neutral tax relief? There is no simple answer.

One possible notion of neutrality is a proportional tax relief for all taxpayers. Comparing the 1990 rates with the proportionally reduced (by 25 percent, roughly the average tax reduction) 1985 average tax rates, one observes a more than proportional relief in the very low- and middle-income classes, both for good reasons (table 1). The very low had to be granted a tax-free minimum subsistence and the middle-income group had so far suffered most of the sharp progression. But this measure of neutrality does not take into account changes in income after tax.

A second possible notion of neutrality is a proportional increase of income after tax. Table 2 compares the net and gross income ratios, using the 1985 and 1990 rate structures corrected by a 25-percent tax relief, which amounts roughly to an average increase of 6 percent in net income.[7]

A comparison of tables 1 and 2 shows clearly that some of the taxpayers who enjoy a more than proportional tax relief still gain less

5. The notion of linear progression stirs some curiosity outside Germany. It means that the marginal tax rates increase linearly with taxable income. (The second derivative of the marginal tax rate is zero.) Naturally, the average tax rates within that bracket increase with declining rates. (The second derivative of the average tax rates is negative.)

6. Obviously, tax reduction for the top income is the big political issue. People with little income and little absolute amounts of tax reliefs are not the only ones who feel treated unfairly; even people with large tax absolute and relative reliefs consider themselves losers.

7. The ratio of taxable income to net national product is assumed to be 0.482.

TABLE 1. *Actual and Proportional Tax Relief, 1985 and 1990*

Taxable income[a] (DM) (1)	Effective tax rate[a] (percent)			Difference (column 4 − column 3)
	1985 (2)	1990 (3)	1985[b] (4)	
5,616	5.5	0.0	4.1	+4.1
8,100	10.6	5.8	7.9	+2.1
10,000	12.7	8.4	9.6	+1.2
13,000	14.9	11.1	11.2	+0.1
20,000	17.5	14.7	13.1	−1.6
30,000	21.9	17.9	16.4	−1.5
40,000	26.3	20.2	19.7	−0.5
45,000	28.3	21.2	21.3	+0.1
50,000	30.2	22.2	22.6	+0.4
70,000	35.9	25.8	26.9	+1.1
90,000	39.8	29.1	29.8	+0.7
110,000	43.1	32.4	32.3	−0.1
130,000	44.6	35.4	33.4	−2.0
150,000	46.1	37.8	34.6	−3.2
200,000	48.6	41.6	36.4	−5.2
500,000	53.0	48.4	39.8	−8.6

a. For a single taxpayer with no children.

b. Tax liability according to the 1985 tax schedule is corrected by minus 25 percent, roughly the average decrease of tax revenue caused by the reform of tax rates, 1986, 1988, and 1990.

than proportionally in net income. It is hard to tell which of these notions gives a more satisfactory picture of neutrality or whether a neutral tax relief according to either one of these notions would be a fair one.

Both notions of neutrality, however, miss important aspects of the reform. They don't take into account the fact that one of the main reasons for reform was to correct for internal shifts of the tax burden caused by inflation and economic growth. Nor do they take into account the fact that a substantial tax cut generally confines the distributional potential.

The following measure tries to overcome both deficiencies. I define α as a measure of distributional effort as follows:

$$\alpha_i = \frac{D_i^g - D_i^n}{D_i^g - D_i^m}$$

with

$$D_i^g = \frac{Y_i^g}{\overline{Y^g}} \left[\begin{array}{l} \text{taxable income of the i-th taxpayer over} \\ \text{average taxable income} \end{array} \right]$$

$$D_i^n = \frac{Y_i^n}{\overline{Y^n}} = \left[\begin{array}{l} \text{income after tax of the i-th taxpayer} \\ \text{over average income after tax} \end{array} \right]$$

$$D_i^m = \left[\frac{Y_i^n}{\overline{Y^n}} \right]^m = \left[\begin{array}{l} D_i^n, \text{ if taxes from the i-th and the} \\ \text{average income recipient are distributed} \\ \text{in the most egalitarian way possible.} \end{array} \right]$$

Note that for a proportional tax $\alpha = 0$, and for a tax borne solely by high-income earners (which is the most egalitarian way to distribute it) $\alpha = 1$.

Table 3 presents some values of $\alpha(Y_i)$ for the 1975 and 1990 tax rates. To take care of the general income increase during that period, the αs for 1975 and 1990 are compared at different income levels. The distributional effect seems to have declined slightly in 1990, except with respect to the very low- and the very high-income brackets. This again allows one to interpret the German tax reform as removing some distributional strain from the middle class. My notion of distributional effect, of course, far from solves the problem of a fair tax reform. Again, actual tax rates are related to historical ones, and I do not want to suggest that old tax rates were good tax rates or that economic and social development has not changed the sense of fairness.

Reform of tax rates is to be judged not only by the actual redistribution of the tax burden currently, but perhaps even more critically by what it does to the future distribution. It is here, where the new so-called linear progression within the direct progression range (DM 8,153 to DM 120,042) is most appreciated. Linear progression is considered a much more durable solution, as the distribution of the tax burden is believed to be less affected by inflation and growth. But this interpretation is valid only in relation to the range of very steep progression in the old income tax schedule. If one considers the total range of direct progression, one has to realize that the reform schedule, much like the old one, must lift the marginal

TABLE 2. *Actual and Proportional Increase in Net Income after Tax, 1985 and 1990*

Taxable income (DM) (1)	Income after tax divided by taxable income[a] (percent)			Difference (column 3 − column 4) (DM)
	1985 (2)	1990 (3)	1985[b] (4)	
5,616	94.5	100.0	100.2	−0.2
8,100	89.4	94.2	94.8	−0.6
10,000	87.3	91.6	92.5	−0.9
20,000	82.5	85.3	87.5	−2.2
30,000	78.2	82.1	82.9	−0.7
33,000	76.8	81.4	81.4	0.0
40,000	73.7	79.8	78.1	+1.7
50,000	69.8	77.8	74.0	+3.8
70,000	64.1	74.2	67.9	+6.3
90,000	60.2	70.9	63.9	+7.0
110,000	56.9	67.6	60.3	+7.3
130,000	55.4	64.6	58.7	+5.9
150,000	53.9	62.2	57.1	+5.1
200,000	51.4	58.4	54.5	+3.9
500,000	47.0	51.6	49.8	+1.8

a. For a single taxpayer with no children.

b. Income after tax in 1985 is raised by 6 percent, which is equivalent to the estimated increase resulting from the 25-percent tax cut in 1990.

tax rates thirty-four percentage points within an income range of about DM 110,000. The direct progression range is very small indeed and therefore the new schedule, too, will not end the need for periodic tax rate adjustments.[8] (I leave aside whether adjustments are not something the politicians rather like.)

Linear progression also gets some credit for improving incentives (in a crucial range) and adhering better to the ability-to-pay principle. Both arguments are difficult to evaluate because one really knows little about the relationship between income on the one hand and

8. Estimates are that tax rate adjustments might be necessary again as early as the mid-1990s.

TABLE 3. *Distributional Effects of the Income Tax, 1975 and 1990*

1975[a]		1990[a]		
Taxable income (DM) (1)	α_i (2)	Taxable income (DM) (3)	α_i (4)	Difference (column 4 − column 2)
2,925	1.00	5,616	1.00	0.00
4,219	0.72	8,100	0.73	+0.01
5,208	0.58	10,000	0.59	+0.01
9,375	0.30	18,000	0.30	0.00
10,417	0.26	20,000	0.24	−0.02
15,625	0.18	30,000	0.12	−0.06
20,833	0.18	40,000	0.11	−0.07
22,063	n.a.	42,244	n.a.	n.a.
26,042	0.20	50,000	0.13	−0.07
31,250	0.23	60,000	0.14	−0.09
41,667	0.28	80,000	0.22	−0.06
52,083	0.37	100,000	0.32	−0.05
62,500	0.43	120,000	0.40	−0.03
72,917	0.48	140,000	0.47	−0.01
78,125	0.50	150,000	0.50	−0.00

n.a. Not available.
a. For a single taxpayer with no children.

incentives and ability to pay on the other. Still, one has to concede that incentives might be impaired not only by high marginal tax rates, but also by a high rate of change of marginal tax rates. One could imagine that such an effect would be destructive to a society if it occurred exactly within that range where social mobility is supposed to take place and puts, so to say, a barrier between low and high income. This kind of reasoning, however, is rather speculative.

BROADENING THE INCOME TAX BASE

The government is willing to finance a substantial part of the gross tax relief, namely DM 20 billion, by cutting tax expenditures. In

October 1987 it decided to terminate a list of about fifty single items. If that plan is implemented, long-time public demands and often-set targets would be fulfilled. But there is still quite a way to go, and there is not a single measure against which interest groups are not prepared to protest.

Actually, there are at least two reasons why affected taxpayers find it difficult to go along. There is, first, the phenomenon that anyone, as much as he or she might generally oppose tax expenditures, finds those that affect himself quite all right. And, second, nobody is willing to accept that his or her tax expenditures should be cut as long as others remain untouched.

One finds among the expiring tax expenditures some that even the government does not consider expenditures as such, for example, the employees' allowance and the Christmas allowance (which is really just another name for an employees' allowance). Actually, the abolition affects only those who can claim expenses in employment of more than DM 920 a year, but it does not make sense to hurt those who claim more than average expenses because they probably are the mobile ones, that is, have a characteristic for which, in a situation of unemployment, they rather deserve a bonus. Besides, since, in the future, employment expenses lead to tax relief only when they exceed DM 2,000, there will be no great incentive to look for work that might be expensive to reach.

Other tax rules to be changed are considered tax expenditures proper, for example, the Berlin subsidies or depreciation allowances for investments that favor environmental protection. But it is doubtful that their raison d'être is dispensable. Finally, there are expenditures on the expiring list that were not considered as such by the taxpayers affected. Examples include reserves for the purpose of anniversary bonuses to employees and tax-free employer contributions to canteen meals (up to DM 1.50 per meal). Actually, one might ask whether benefits such as these—comparable to provisions of proper working rooms, parking lots, sanitary installations, and so on—should be taxable.

Considering these problems, affected taxpayers feel entitled to doubt the fairness of the reform if they find many public subsidies (and tax expenditures) completely untouched. Of course, there is no common opinion on which public expenditures and tax rules have to be counted as subsidies. But the quantitative estimates exceed by far what now is to be abolished. The government itself reports some

DM 30 billion federal subsidies, or a total of DM 68 billion if one includes states and communities. The independent Institute for World Economy in Kiel estimates public subsidies at about DM 120 billion, and the trade unions even suggest a number of DM 210 billion.

Why, the affected taxpayers ask themselves, has agriculture, that "cask without bottom," been left out completely? Why do capital gains remain practically tax free in the taxation of private households? Why should private housing keep its preferential treatment? Of course, there is a ready answer: because politicians try to avoid clashes with politically potent groups. But this answer may be too simple because the planned measures do, in fact, touch the interests of politically powerful groups. Surely, one cannot blame the government for not having cut all subsidies at once. It has made a remarkable start from which, it is hoped, it will continue.

CORPORATION TAX AND WITHHOLDING TAX

As part of the tax reform, two taxes that are closely connected with the income tax are to be changed, namely, the corporation tax and the withholding tax. Of course, these changes are also heavily debated.

As far as the corporation tax is concerned, there is no question that its base should be broadened in somewhat the same way as the personal income tax, even if at least one of the measures (the 80-percent rule for deduction of entertainment expenses) does not conform with the principle of taxation of corporation profits. The corporation as such hardly enjoys the feast.

There is also wide agreement that the corporation tax rate has to be lowered when the top personal income tax rate goes down. But there is a remarkable difference in the amount of the decrease. Whereas the top marginal income tax rate decreases only by three percentage points, the decline in the top corporate tax rate is to be twice as much. Thus the equality of the two rates is to be eliminated. The obvious reason is that the government wanted to ease the taxation of firms substantially but could not overcome severe political opposition against a corresponding reduction in the top personal income tax rate.

Still, the decision is wrong. It abolishes two important improvements of the 1977 corporate tax reform: tax neutrality with respect to the legal status of a firm and tax neutrality with respect to the disposition of profits. The new rate structure violates neutrality, even if one takes into consideration that the average income tax rate also is lowered substantially and—up to the very high income—lies well under the marginal rate. Allocational decisions are taken with respect to the marginal rates.

Along with income tax reform two important changes in the withholding tax on income from capital are to come: a 10-percent withholding tax on interest payments, which, until now have been free of withholding tax, and a new 10-percent tax on some life insurance returns.

Withholding of tax on general interest payments is essentially a means to enforce existing Treasury claims. Further, it is not really an additional tax burden, because for nationals the withholding tax is deductible against the income tax and for foreigners a rebate of the withholding tax is generally granted if a tax treaty exists. If there is no tax treaty, foreigners can generally deduct the withholding tax from their national income tax. In fact, the withholding tax is a burden only to those people who evade their income tax.

Unlike other types of income, however, tax evasion with respect to interest payments seems to be not the exception but the rule. It is so prevalent that quite a protest arose about the new tax, even deploring its distributional effects as burdensome as if especially low-income people were, so to speak, entitled (maybe from a long-term practice) to evade income tax on interest income. (Actually, it is not widely known that interest received above a basic allowance must be properly declared, even for people in the lowest income-tax bracket.)

Now is the increased withholding tax about to bring forth greater tax honesty, since the tax could give the Treasury at least the 10-percent share? It is not easy to answer the question.

—Many observers see a danger that money assets, invested so far in Germany, will be transferred abroad. Of course, most of Europe imposes a withholding tax on interest payments, so a transfer would pay only if the foreign net interest rates exceed the German ones. But that could well be the case, at least to begin with. Soon after the reform German interest rates might go up, so the state as a major debtor might eventually lose more than it gains.

—Some taxpayers may interpret the 10-percent withholding tax payment as sufficient compliance with their tax liability. Therefore, some people who have properly declared in the past might not do so after the introduction of the withholding tax.

—There is to be an exemption, with legal notice, of saving accounts (for social reasons). That may be interpreted to mean that these kinds of capital returns are income-tax free. Consequently, people may reshuffle their portfolios in favor of saving accounts (not a generally favorable shift by itself) and so evade income tax.

—Low-income taxpayers can obtain a personal exemption from the withholding tax. (They have to apply for it at the revenue office.) Conceivably, many taxpayers will misunderstand that exemption and may relate it to their total income tax liability.

In sum, expectations that the new withholding tax is going to result in more honesty from the taxpayers are probably too high. So one might ask whether the tax is worth the considerable administrative cost. These costs are especially annoying to foreigners, who get a complete rebate anyhow. It may, however, be the case that many foreigners will not apply for a rebate because for one reason or another they want to stay unnamed. Then, of course, the German Treasury realizes a net gain.

The second withholding tax reform, the 10-percent tax on certain life insurance returns, is of a different quality, as these returns had previously been income-tax free. The new withholding tax levies a definite additional tax burden.

There are two possible ways to look at this reform. On the one hand, it narrows a very annoying tax loophole, as capital returns from life insurance (with a minimum period of twelve years) are income-tax free. On the other hand, one can regard these kinds of returns as a special type of capital gains. (The selling price of the life insurance policy exceeds the buying price.) That leads to the question of why only life insurance gains, and not all kinds of capital gains, are taxed.

THE MAKING OF THE REFORM

The tax reform was carried out in a remarkable way. Early in 1987, soon after the general elections and even before the new coalition government (actually the old one) was formed, an income tax cut of about DM 50 billion to take place in 1990 was announced. It would be the third of a three-stage tax reform, with cuts in 1986, 1988, and

1990. The bulk of the cut was to be financed by limiting public expenditure growth—with the exception of some DM 19 million, to be financed by closing loopholes (and, possibly, by small increases in some special consumption taxes). The decision about loopholes to be eliminated was postponed until autumn 1987, that is, three-quarters of a year later. Thus who would pay the bill was anybody's guess. Many politicians and business executives deplored the tax situation, which was even blamed for the unsatisfactory developments in the economy.

Another thing happened. Tax cuts and, of course, the individual benefits announced for 1990, were regarded, as, so to say, a new base. Any future tax increase, even if it would only offset part of the original gain, was regarded as an additional burden. Rumors went wild. So when the government finally announced its plans, they came partly as a relief—nobody was severely hit—but partly as a burden to be resisted strongly. Seldom has a government that cut taxes by so much received so little praise. It is a common opinion that the government played its handful of aces extremely badly. But did it really?

One might argue that this was the only possible way to play the game. If the government had tried—as many professional economists and scientists proposed—to present the tax reform in one piece, it might never have succeeded. Any attempt to broaden the tax base would have met formidable resistance, and not much would have been left over to be used to finance the intended tax rate reduction. What the government did, therefore, was to put itself under considerable constraint—comparable, possibly, to the Gramm-Rudman legislation in the United States. The objective was set, and the government could not abandon it without losing face and, possibly, the next elections. It had to come up with a finance plan and it did. But that procedure did not look exactly like a vote-maximizing strategy, which according to Rose's "law of inertia" is performed best by doing nothing.[9] One must acknowledge that politicians sometimes are better statesmen than professional economists assume, or, maybe, economists are just not good politicians.

9. Richard Rose, "Maximizing Tax Revenue while Minimizing Political Costs," *Journal of Public Policy*, vol. 5 (August 1985), pp. 289–320.

ALDO CARDARELLI & MICHELE DEL GIUDICE

Italy

In 1987, the Italian government adopted several short-term measures
to increase tax collection and proposed structural changes to improve
the tax system. This report consists of two parts: a summary of the
legislation already enacted and a discussion of the plans for long-
term tax reform.

SHORT-TERM MEASURES

The short-term measures were introduced by two Council of Ministers'
decrees in August and September, 1987. They were converted into
an act by Parliament according to the rules set forth by Italy's
constitution on November 21, 1987. These measures were dictated
by Italy's economic situation, which, at the time, required restraint
of domestic demand and reductions in public expenditures.

In early 1987, domestic demand increased, particularly that related
to consumption. A reduction in foreign demand also occurred. A
major factor in the increase in domestic demand was a rise in public
expenditures. Because of these developments, the current account of
the balance of payments deteriorated, and the exchange value of the
lira—which was also affected by an increase in the price of oil—
declined. The government action was intended to stop the decline
in the value of the lira and to prevent an increase in the rate of
inflation.

The government accelerated the payments of withholding taxes on
interest, premiums, and other income paid to depositors in credit
institutions and banks and of corporate income taxes. It also raised
the value-added tax (VAT) on motor vehicles, furniture, electrical
appliances, and audio-visual and photo-optical goods for the period
from the date of the decree until December 31, 1987. This special tax
applied only to goods that were subject to the normal 18-percent

VAT rate; items subject to the reduced 2-percent and 9-percent rates were not affected. Finally, the government increased the excise taxes and corresponding border taxes on gasoline and other oil products beginning in 1988.

STRUCTURAL TAX POLICY

The government's structural tax policy focuses mainly on income taxes, which have increased sharply in Italy because of the progressivity of the tax rates and the failure to adjust them for inflation. In fact, the real tax burden has increased even after January 1, 1986, when the most recent adjustments to the tax rates were made. In 1987 income taxes accounted for about 58.6 percent of central government tax revenues, and indirect taxes accounted for the remaining 41.4 percent.

The income tax amendments enacted by the government include the following:

—Adjustment of personal income tax (IRPEF) rates and of the deductions relating to the personal circumstances of the taxpayer;

—Revaluation of the assets of enterprises for inflation;

—Taxation of capital gains and modification of carryforwards of losses in the case of company mergers;

—Acceleration of payments by corporations on account of the corporate income tax (IRPEG) and the local income tax (ILOR), as well as the withholding tax at source on interest; and

—Liberalization of reserves for bad debts on securities issued by foreign countries.

Personal Income Tax Rates and Tax Credits

The adjustments recommended by the present government start from a bill submitted to the previous Parliament that amended the tax rate schedule and revised the tax credit for dependent spouses. (Allowances for family status are in the form of tax credits in Italy.) This bill reduced the tax rates in all brackets and increased the tax credit for dependent spouses. The revised bill modified the proposed rate changes, advantaged lower-income brackets ranging between 11

TABLE 1. *Individual Income Tax Rates in Italy, 1987 and 1988*
Percent

Taxable income (millions of lire)	1987	1988	
		Rates previously proposed	Revised rates
0–6	12	11	11
6–11	22	22	22
11–12	27	26	22
12–28	27	26	26
28–30	34	26	26
30–50	34	33	33
50–60	41	33	33
60–100	41	40	40
100–150	48	40	45
150–300	53	45	50
300–600	58	50	55
600 and over	62	56	60

and 12 million lire, added to the increase in the dependent spouse credit, and raised the deduction for employment income.

The 1987 tax rates range from 12 percent to 62 percent (table 1). The rates proposed for 1988 and later years by the previous government ranged from 11 percent to 56 percent; the rates proposed by the new government range from 11 percent to 60 percent. The number of tax brackets will remain unchanged. Thus the new rates are more progressive than those previously proposed.

The dependent spouse credit, which was formerly 360,000 lire, would have been raised by the previous proposal to 420,000. The new bill made this change for 1987 and then raised it to 462,000 lire in 1988 and 504,000 lire beginning in 1989. In addition, the income ceiling for entitlement to the allowances for dependents would be raised from 3 million to 4 million lire.

Finally, the bill increased the tax credit for employment income from 492,000 lire to 516,000 lire in 1988 and 540,000 lire beginning in

1989. An additional tax credit of 228,000 lire would be allowed for those with employment income up to 11 million lire.

Revaluation of Assets

Since the end of World War II, there have been periodic adjustments for inflation of the value of business assets for tax purposes. The adjustments are needed to determine the depreciation allowances of business enterprises and taxable profits on the sale of assets.

The last revaluation applied to assets purchased before January 1, 1983. The new bill revalued assets for the increase in prices from 1983 through 1987. However, it limited the reduction of taxes resulting from asset revaluation to 25 percent of the taxes otherwise due.

Capital Gains and Loss Carryforwards

Capital gains from the sale of business participations were taxable under prior law if they exceeded 2 percent of the capital of the corporation for shares quoted on the stock exchange and 10 percent for other shares; for noncorporate enterprises, such gains were taxable if the share of the business transferred exceeded 25 percent of its capital. The new bill reduced these percentages to 1, 5, and 10 percent, respectively, beginning in 1988. Firms engaged in the arts or professions, commercial enterprises, partnerships, and businesses conducted by disabled persons are exempt from this tax. The purpose of this provision is to curb tax avoidance by individuals who cash in accumulated profits in a business enterprise by selling their shares in the enterprise.

Under prior law, a limit was imposed on the losses that corporations participating in a merger could deduct from the profits of the merged corporation. This limit was the value of net assets of the merged corporations eighteen months before the merger. Parliament suspended the loss carryforward limit for mergers carried out before January 1, 1988, among corporations that were controlled by the surviving company for at least two years or from the date of incorporation, as well as among corporations controlled by the same company. The government achieved the objective of these provisions more effectively by introducing more objective criteria for loss limitations for mergers.

Current Payment

Three changes to speed up tax collections were made in 1988. First, corporate tax payments (both for the national and local taxes—IRPEG and ILOR) were increased from 92 percent to 98 percent of the tax due. Second, banks were required to pay to the government at least 50 percent of the withholding taxes remitted in the previous period. Third, withholding taxes on interest were increased from 25 percent to 30 percent.

Bad Debt Reserves

Under prior rules, deductions for allocations to bad debt reserves could not exceed 0.5 percent of total liabilities and 0.2 percent when the total reserve reached 2.0 percent of total liabilities. No deduction was allowed when the total reserve reached 5.0 percent. These limits are not adequate for reserves on foreign loans to a number of developing countries. Other countries permit their banks to set aside much larger reserves for such loans. For example, U.S. banks may set aside reserves of more than 20 percent for such loans, and Swiss banks are allowed to set aside more than 30 percent. The new bill increased the annual deduction for bad debt reserves of banks to 10 percent of foreign loans until the total reserve on these loans reaches 30 percent.

Indirect Taxation

The VAT rates for motor vehicles will be increased beginning January 1, 1988. In addition, the government has extended until the end of 1990 the rule that the VAT for motor vehicles, and for fuels and lubricants for such vehicles, is not deductible if not used in the ordinary business operation of an enterprise. The purpose of this provision is to encourage reduced consumption of fuel and lubricants.

Revenue Effect

The reductions in the personal income tax rates and the increases in the family status tax credits amounted to an estimated 5,470 billion lire in 1988. However, the restrictions on the revaluation of assets of business enterprises increased tax liabilities by 3,000 billion lire, and the speedup of corporate tax payments and withholding taxes increased receipts by 3,950 billion lire. The changes in the value-added tax raised revenue by a total of 1,764 billion lire in 1988.

Because of these changes, the ratio of indirect to total tax revenues will increase somewhat. For the year 1988, indirect taxes will account for an estimated 43.1 percent compared with 41.4 percent in 1987.

PROSPECTS FOR TAX REFORM

There is considerable interest in further tax reform in Italy. The view is widespread, at least among academics, that there is an urgent need to broaden the income tax base and to simplify the tax system. There is also agreement that the local tax system should be completely overhauled.

In 1988 the government intends to concentrate on simplifying the taxes on real property and on reforming the local tax system. Under the current system, real estate is subjected to several indirect taxes arising whenever any transfer occurs (purchase and sale, inheritance, gift). At the same time, income from real estate constitutes a part of the taxable base subject to direct taxes. A new tax is being developed to replace many of these taxes. The levy, which would be paid once a year at a low proportional rate (0.20 percent to 0.30 percent of real estate value), would be assessed and charged at a local level.

Reform of the real property tax will be the first step toward a complete overhaul of the local tax system. By January of 1989 the government expects to introduce a real autonomous system for local government. Besides the present wide administrative autonomy, these reforms will provide fiscal autonomy for local administrative bodies, including those responsible for tax collection and expenditure. This reform should reduce the public deficit and have a positive effect on Italy's economy.

Comment by EMILIO GERELLI
LUIGI BERNARDI

A brilliant economist, Sylos Labini, once said that Italy is like a centaur, half man and half horse, so when it is in trouble one never knows whether to call a physician or a veterinarian. This is why, to comment on the Cardarelli–del Giudice paper, we first of all must distinguish between two groups of countries according to their tax and economic structures. Following Musgrave's theory of tax structure development, we can classify as "advanced" those countries where the progressive income tax has been in existence for a long time, tax administration is efficient, and taxpayers are by and large honest. Disregarding the nearly opposite case of immature countries, let us consider here the case of what have been called "intermediate" countries. Such countries make up a significant part of the Western economies, and centaur-like Italy is a case in point.

In an intermediate country, tax exclusions and preferences granted to lagging sections of the economy as well as to capital income in general open the way to tax "erosion." Examples in Italy are incomes from agriculture, which are substantially exempt; interest on public debt, which for personal income taxpayers is subject only to proportional taxation;[1] and capital gains, which are excluded from the tax base.

As a consequence the tax burden of an intermediate country is often concentrated at the lower end of the income scale. For example, in Italy almost 70 percent of net income tax is paid by employed workers with low to average incomes. For this reason, large deductions are granted to low-income workers, and tax evasion is prevalent among those in the higher-income brackets. The average man is squeezed (table 1).

Italy demonstrates another characteristic of the intermediate country: a truly general and progressive income tax was not introduced until 1974. The immaturity of the system allows considerable evasion

1. In fact, taxation of capital income is chaotic since there are twelve different regimes.

TABLE 1. *Individual Income Tax in Italy: Evasion, Avoidance, Exemptions, 1984*
Thousands of billions of lire unless otherwise specified

Item	Total income[a]	Declared income[b]		Evasion[c]		Avoidance[d]		Exemptions[e]	
		Amount	Percent	Amount	Percent	Amount	Percent	Amount	Percent
Land rents	14,500	1,500	10.3	100	0.7	12,200	84.1	700	4.8
Building rents	37,500	10,300	27.5	10,700	28.5	12,800	34.1	3,700	9.9
Capital income	72,500	1,500	2.0	n.a.	n.a.	71,000	98.0	n.a.	n.a.
Employed work and pensions	352,800	247,900	70.3	22,400	6.3	42,400	12.0	40,100	11.4
Nonemployed work and individual firms	169,500	63,200	37.3	47,500	28.0	58,800	34.7	n.a.	n.a.
Total	646,800	324,400	50.2	80,700	12.4	197,200	30.5	44,500	6.9

Source: L. Bernardi and A. Marenzi, "Il sistema tributario, alcune evidenze por un intervento sugli imponibili," in Banca d'Italia, *Ricerce quantitative e basi statistiche per la politica economica* (Rome, 1987).

n.a. Not available.

a. Total income of households (as estimated in the national accounts), which should be taxed if there were no evasion and avoidance.

b. Income declared on tax returns.

c. Evasion equals total income less avoidance, exemptions, and declared income.

d. Avoidance is any kind of income that the tax law excludes from the income tax base (for example, interest on bank deposits that are subject to a proportional tax) or for which a "normal" figure that underestimates the actual amount is allowed (for instance, land and building rents). Estimates of avoidance so defined are based on the relevant national accounts data.

e. Exemptions reported on tax returns.

(about 40 percent of declared incomes) apart from the area of employed work, where the pay-as-you-earn mechanism works wonders. This evasion can continue, of course, because the tax-collecting capabilities of the public administration are modest at best.

Given this profile, it is obvious that attempts at reform can create unanticipated problems in intermediate tax systems; they run the danger of pushing the economy from bad to worse. The fiscal changes described in the paper by Cardarelli and del Giudice are a case in point. Briefly, the outcry of employed workers and trade union members that they were paying too much led the government to propose lowering progressive income tax rates. To compensate for the loss of yield, an increase of the tax on value added, which had been rather lagging in recent years, was introduced. But in the fall of 1987 the whole program was canceled, allegedly as an aftermath of Black Monday, October 19, on Wall Street, but in reality because the increase in VAT rates proved inflationary at a time when inflation seems again on the rise.

Recent history also demonstrates that in intermediate countries tax changes are difficult to implement. For instance, all countries entering the European Community (EC) must apply a value-added tax. France, whose tax system is considered "mature," introduced it even before the founding of the EC for competitive reasons (to take advantage of the investment deduction) and sold the idea to the rest of Europe. Germany changed its "Umstatzsteuer" rather swiftly, but among the EC latecomers only the United Kingdom had a fairly satisfactory purchase tax that paved the way for the VAT. (However, the elimination of changes in purchase tax rates may have brought about some loss in the efficiency of demand management.)

By contrast in the southern European "intermediate" countries the VAT has occasioned great pain and requests for delays. Italy, in particular, though one of the founding EC partners in the Treaty of Rome, had to be in effect physically coerced into changing its tax policy in the early 1970s, when the EC Commission punished Italy for its long delays by progressively reducing border refunds connected to the old tax on gross sales. This tough attitude by the EC, the appropriate bitter medicine, convinced Italy to undertake major tax reform, thus creating a shining moment of legislative tax maturity. I am fairly sure that without it, Italians would still have proportional taxes on income, a multistage tax on gross sales, and so forth.

TABLE 2. *Model Simulation of Comprehensive Tax Reform in Italy: Marginal and Average Rates by Income Brackets, 1987*
Percent

Income bracket	Marginal rates		Average rates	
(millions of lire)	1987 law	Comprehensive reform	1987 law	Comprehensive reform
0–6	12	12	12	12
6–11	22	22	16.5	16.5
11–28	27	25	22.9	21.7
28–50	34	25	27.8	23.1
50–100	41	25	34.4	24.1
100–150	48	25	38.9	24.4
150–300	53	25	46.0	24.7
300–600	58	25 ⎫	52.0	24.8
600 and over	62	25 ⎭		

Source: L. Bernardi, "The Reform of Personal Income Taxation: The Case of 'Intermediate' Systems," paper presented to the Athens meeting of the Institut International de Finances Publiques, August 26–30, 1986.

For these reasons, structural tax reform in intermediate countries looks rather like wishful thinking. Utopianism is, however, a powerful force, and we therefore report in table 2 the results of a model simulation, performed by Luigi Bernardi, applying the comprehensive income tax reform concept (that is, broaden the tax base and flatten the rates) to the Italian income tax system.[2]

One conclusion of the study is that the characteristics and effects of comprehensive tax reform are rather different in intermediate systems compared with advanced systems. The characteristics are different because in the intermediate country the base is widened by reducing the evasion and erosion typical of several broad categories of income. It is not obtained, as in the United States, by eliminating special tax preferences that are available to individuals who report their incomes accurately.

2. See L. Bernardi, "The Reform of Personal Income Taxation: The Case of 'Intermediate' Systems," paper presented to the Athens meeting of the Institut International de Finances Publiques, August 26–30, 1986.

The effects of comprehensive tax reform are different because, the yield being equal, a general lowering in both average and marginal rates takes place in the more advanced countries. Furthermore, there is a redistribution of the tax burden that seems to hit high incomes.

The objectives of tax reform are also different in the advanced and intermediate countries. Let us summarize them in three points.

First, the allocative effects. We think that in Italy today the disincentives of personal tax on the supply side are rather low. However, the comprehensive approach could have two principal, contrasting effects. The positive effect would consist of the reduction of current rates and future burden on the income of employed workers. This outcome in turn would reduce the pressure on wages and production costs. The other effect would be negative: a rise in the taxation of incomes that today benefit from erosion and evasion, in particular earnings from agriculture and financial activity.

Second, the equity problems. Broadening the base by reducing evasion and erosion would promote greater horizontal equity. But this improvement in equity would be reflected in more equal tax burdens among different categories of income recipients (because of the elimination of erosion and evasion) rather than among different individuals who may belong to the same category (due to fewer tax deductions). Furthermore, vertical equity might be affected by the rise in the tax burden on higher incomes. In practice, it is difficult to separate the distributive modifications resulting from improvements in the two aspects of equity—horizontal and vertical equity.

Third, the administrative considerations. Even here we see that the results would be different from those that have taken place in the advanced countries. In the intermediate country, the tax office is characteristically overburdened and ineffectual. On the one hand, it would greatly benefit from the simplification that might be achieved by comprehensive reform. Yet on the other hand, tax collectors would be newly charged with reducing evasion and with assessing types of income exempt up until the change.

Political acceptance of comprehensive reform in Italy would also face serious obstacles. Although it would not achieve the degree of improvement in horizontal equity of the more advanced countries, comprehensive reform would involve favoring some groups and hammering others. The latter—that is, agriculture, financial markets, self-employed workers, and small firms—are politically very cohesive and influential.

Let us conclude on this point with a last observation. Certainly comprehensive reform has many merits, but it always involves some sacrifice: that is, redistributive "fine-tuning" and an allocative function of a selective nature. There are good reasons for believing that these objectives of income tax today may have to be reconsidered. This, however, is more true for the advanced countries than for the intermediate ones, where broader problems of distribution and development are still important. For these countries, what may be needed are other adequate tools of economic policy.

Personal income taxation must, of course, be coordinated with corporate taxation, since in the end all taxation falls on individuals. In Italy the connection is made explicit by a tax credit for personal income taxation equal to the full amount of the corporate tax paid on distributed income. Applying the comprehensive reform approach would, however, be inconsistent, as we have seen, with such loopholes as the accelerated depreciation provisions now in force in Italy. While this loophole is prized by those who benefit from it, in fact someone has to pay for its costs; that is, accelerated depreciation reduces the tax yield and must be compensated for in some other way. Concerning its alleged impact on employment, investment, and so forth, accelerated depreciation probably favors capital intensive firms and industries and therefore—if the level of tax yield is given—it must burden other production activities.

However, no step is being taken in Italy to abolish this or other special provisions. On the contrary, accelerated depreciation would be made more valuable by the revaluation of historic asset costs to take into account inflation described in the Cardarelli–del Giudice paper. This government proposal has been criticized as being too favorable to business. Final judgment is difficult because inflation affects various income categories differently. I feel, however, that the proposal was in line with the accepted *"vérité des prix "* (real income) philosophy. From the distributional viewpoint it was probably justified by the simultaneous reduction of personal income tax rates and by the increase of indirect taxation falling in the first instance on business and reducing demand if shifted forward.

Another existing loophole is the failure to tax capital gains. Great debates took place a few months ago between proponents of such taxation from the leftist parties and the finance minister, who stated that for practical reasons the proposal had no possibility of being implemented.

At the end of the day we must conclude that the intermediate country is probably doomed to tax "bricolage" and must give up more ambitious architectural schemes. Nevertheless, for Italy and similar European countries, some hopes for change can be pinned on outside help from the EC, which, as we have seen, was decisive in catalyzing the 1974 Italian reform. If everything works out as planned, by 1991 the internal EC market should be a fact. The community could then consider the further step of harmonizing direct taxation in Europe. This step, however, would be linked to an increase of the EC budget to permit expenditure policies that would compensate for the greater constraints caused by EC harmonization of direct taxation. I also hope that harmonization is not mistaken for the simplistic idea of complete uniformity, since equity means dealing with different countries in a different though coordinated way.

Could the few countries with advanced tax systems influence those with intermediate or developing systems to make a tax-mature community? This is the hope of the struggling intermediate country.

ATSUSHI NAGANO

Japan

On September 19, 1987, Japan's Diet approved a set of bills that introduced important changes in the tax system. The recently adopted legislation deals mainly with direct taxes and is only part of the overall review of the tax system that Japan is undertaking.

In this paper, I will describe the economic and social background of the movement for tax reform in Japan. I will also explain the recently approved tax revision and the future direction of the reform effort.

CHANGES IN THE SOCIETY AND THE ECONOMY

The basic structure of the current tax system was established in 1950 when Japan had hardly recovered from the damages of World War II. Since then, the Japanese society and its economy have undergone drastic changes, including the transformation of its industrial structure, higher income levels accompanied by equalization of the income distribution, diversification of consumer outlays, and internationalization of economic activities.

Despite occasional revisions in the past forty years, the Japanese tax system has failed to keep up with the new circumstances brought about by the changes, creating a number of distortions in the system. For example, a tax system relying mainly on direct taxes, particularly on the highly progressive individual income tax, was required by society in the 1950s, when there were large differences between the rich and the poor and a redistribution of income through the tax system was necessary. In 1985, however, the richest one-fifth of households earned only 2.9 times more than the poorest one-fifth, compared with 1950 when the richest fifth earned 5.8 times more than the poorest. With a far more equal income distribution, the need for a highly progressive tax system today is not as great as it was earlier.

Because of the steep progressivity of individual income tax, the work incentives of wage earners, who now account for about 80 percent of taxpayers, may be discouraged. Their earnings go up gradually with seniority, while their household expenses increase, particularly in their forties and fifties when spending for their children's education or for the purchase of a residence is concentrated. In addition, because their income is relatively high, they bear a heavy tax burden. Thus much of their salary increase is offset by increases in tax and other expenses. This situation leads middle-income earners to feel that their tax burden is too heavy. Under these circumstances, it is necessary to reduce the progressivity of the income tax, especially as it applies to middle-income earners.

As for the corporation income tax, the tax rates have been raised several times since 1970, mainly to finance the individual income tax reductions. The effective corporate tax rate, measuring the combined burden of national and local taxes, which remained around 45 percent during the 1960s and 1970s, has now risen to more than 50 percent. After recent reductions the marginal U.S. corporate rate dropped sharply from 51 percent to 39 percent. In Japan, the effective rate remains at a high level, though it declined a bit in April 1987, from 52.92 percent to 51.55 percent following the expiration of earlier temporary rate increases.

In the present world, the domestic economies are so closely interrelated that Japan cannot be immune to the international environment. Large differences in tax burdens among countries are likely to produce distortions not only in international trade but also in the domestic economy. Active corporations may consider avoiding heavy tax burdens by moving their place of business to countries where taxes are lower. Such a development could make the Japanese economy less dynamic, if not actually depressed.

An outstanding feature of Japan's indirect tax system is that its tax base is limited to a certain number of selected items. This situation contrasts with the general consumption tax, either on a national or local level, in other countries. Moreover, Japan's indirect tax system has failed to keep pace with the rapid change in consumption patterns. However, it is not easy politically to introduce a new indirect tax or to extend the application of existing indirect taxes to newly emergent consumer goods. Consequently, the percentage of indirect taxes in the total tax revenue has been decreasing for years. The difficulty of adding new items to the list of taxable items has led to a heavy tax burden on those items currently taxable, particularly liquor and motor vehicles, and this state of affairs is criticized abroad. A fundamental review of the indirect tax system is therefore required.

The rapid aging of the population is the most challenging problem for Japan today. It is estimated that in 2020, the ratio of the population over 65 years of age to the population in the working ages between 20 and 64 years will be 1 to 2.3, while that ratio in 1985 was 1 to 5.9. In 2020, 23.6 percent of the Japanese population will be over 65 years old, while the figure will be 15.4 percent for the United States and 21.2 percent for West Germany.

This rapid aging of the population requires large increases in social security expenditures. If Japan is to finance these expenditures with the present tax structure, the resulting tax burden on individuals and corporations would become unbearable. To cope with the issue of an aging population, the tax system must be based on the principle that all members of society should share the tax burden equally. Wage earners and corporations should not be burdened unfairly.

REVIEW OF THE TAX SYSTEM

In September 1985, then Prime Minister Yasushiro Nakasone requested the tax advisory commission to review the current tax system and make suggestions to establish a new one adapted to the challenges of the twenty-first century. After an intensive, wide-ranging examination, the commission submitted "The Report on the Overall Review of the Tax System" in October 1986. The report was guided by the basic principles of equity, fairness, simplicity, taxpayer's choice, and economic efficiency. It also stressed economic neutrality and the international aspects of taxation. The reforms proposed by the commission include, among others, alleviating the individual income tax burden and replacing the current excise taxes with a new type of indirect tax on consumption.

In December 1986, the tax commission published "The Report on the Fiscal Year 1987 Tax Reform," which outlined the concrete steps that should be taken to implement its report. In accordance with these recommendations, the government's fiscal year 1987 tax reform proposals consisted of the following points:

—Reduction and rationalization of the income tax burden, especially for middle-income earners

—Reduction of the corporation tax rates

—Introduction of the sales tax in place of the current excise taxes

—Review of the tax-exempt saving system

This proposal faced strong opposition in the Diet and failed to get approval during the December 1986–May 1987 season (except for a few amendments relative, for instance, to prolongation of some expiring special measures). The issue of overall tax reform was then taken up by the ad hoc committee of the Lower House composed of members of both the Liberal Democratic party and the opposition parties, which was set up in May to follow the mediation offered by the Speaker.

The committee submitted an interim report at the end of July 1987. The government, taking the report into consideration, introduced tax revision bills to the Diet, proposing measures urgently needed to cope with the changing domestic and external situation. These measures include reduction of the income tax burden, reform of the tax-exempt saving system, and a review of the taxation on land. In September 1987, the Diet adopted the proposed legislation with some amendments.

THE SEPTEMBER 1987 REVISIONS

Individual income tax burdens were reduced by expanding the range of taxable income to which the minimum rate applies and by reducing the rate of graduation in the higher tax brackets (table 1). This reduction in tax burdens, particularly for middle-income earners, is expected to contribute to the expansion of domestic demand.

Review of Tax Rates

In detail, the minimum rate of 10.5 percent is applied to taxable income of not more than ¥1.5 million (corresponding to an annual salary of about ¥4.77 million for a wage earner with a spouse and two children), instead of not more than ¥0.5 million (annual salary

TABLE 1. *Individual Income Tax Rates, before and after Revision, 1987*

Taxable income before revision (thousands of yen)	Rate (percent)	Taxable income after revision (thousands of yen)	Rate (percent)
500	10.5	1,500	10.5
501–1,200	12.0	1,501–2,000	12.0
1,201–2,000	14.0	2,001–3,000	16.0
2,001–3,000	17.0	3,001–5,000	20.0
3,001–4,000	21.0	5,001–6,000	25.0
4,001–6,000	25.0	6,001–8,000	30.0
6,001–8,000	30.0	8,001–10,000	35.0
8,001–10,000	35.0	10,001–12,000	40.0
10,001–12,000	40.0	12,001–15,000	45.0
12,001–15,000	45.0	15,001–30,000	50.0
15,001–20,000	50.0	30,001–50,000	55.0
20,001–30,000	55.0	50,001 and over	60.0
30,001–50,000	60.0		
50,001–80,000	65.0		
80,000 and over	70.0		

of about ¥3.15 million). Consequently, about two-thirds of wage earners will be taxed at the rate of only 10.5 percent. In addition, the local inhabitants tax, or local income tax, was reduced and personal exemptions were increased.

The income tax reduction will cost about ¥1,540 billion. To compensate for the loss, offsetting revenues were obtained through the reform of the tax-exempt saving systems.

Special Deduction for Spouse

The Japanese individual income tax allows a self-employed person to reduce his tax by paying salary to his spouse and other members of his family for their contribution to the business. For wage earners, however, there is no way to split income for tax purposes, even though spouses may be contributing to family earnings by working at home. This situation gave rise to the criticism that an imbalance existed between the tax burdens of wage earners and the self-employed. To correct this imbalance, a special deduction for spouses was created. A person whose spouse's income is below a certain amount is allowed to deduct from the total income of the couple ¥165,000, besides the ordinary deduction for a spouse of ¥330,000.

The Tax-Exempt Saving System

The tax-exempt system for small savings, or "Maruyu," has been modified to cover only the saving of those truly in need of social assistance, such as the elderly (more than 65 years old), fatherless families, and physically handicapped persons. The former tax-exempt saving system to promote the build-up of employees' assets, or "Zaikei," will be applicable only to savings made for the acquisition of a house or for pension purposes. Apart from these exemptions, interest payments will be subject to a withholding tax at the rate of 20 percent, without being aggregated with other types of income.

The reasons for this reform were as follows:

—More than 70 percent of personal saving enjoyed the tax exemption, and therefore a huge amount of interest income (¥ 13.5 trillion) was excluded from the tax base. This brought about an imbalance in the taxation of interest income and other categories of income, such as employment income, business income, and corporation income.

—Higher-income earners benefited more from the tax-exempt saving system than did average-income earners with less savings.

—In view of Japan's huge capital accumulation and high savings rate, the policy of intentionally giving preference to savings in general was not only unnecessary anymore but was also sometimes criticized abroad.

Not a few misuses of tax exemptions were found. As an alternative way of implementing the reform, some people advocated that the tax-exempt saving system should be maintained as it was and that misuses of the system should be checked through the introduction of a taxpayer identification number system. Such an alternative is inappropriate because, although taxpayer identification numbers could be useful in checking the misuse of the tax-exempt saving system, they would not solve the other problems just mentioned. In addition, the identification number system would not provide sufficient revenues to pay for the large income tax cut that was being contemplated.

Land Taxes

To discourage land speculation, "super short-term" land transactions or certain land sales done within two years from acquisition will be taxed more heavily than ordinary short-term sales. To create positive effects on land supply, the application of reduced taxes on long-term transactions was extended to sales made more than five years after acquisition (rather than the previous ten years). In addition, the burden of the registration and license tax on land registration will be temporarily increased by 50 percent.

Taxation of Securities

Taxation on capital gains from the sale of stock will be reinforced by extending the definition of "continuous sales" for which capital gains are taxable. Additionally, the securities transactions tax and the Bourse tax were reviewed in view of the internationalization of financial markets and taking account of balance of burden among different securities.

Implications for Households and the Economy

The income tax cut amounts to ¥ 1.5 trillion ($11 billion) in fiscal year 1987. In fiscal year 1988, the reduction of the local inhabitants tax amounting to ¥ 600 million ($5 billion) on a full-year basis will take effect. The income tax cuts are expected to have favorable effects on domestic demand.

According to an estimate of the Ministry of Finance, the income tax cut will reduce the overall income tax burden, including the taxation of interest income, by 11.6 percent for an average household of a married couple with two children.

THE FUTURE OF TAX REFORM

On October 16, the government and the ruling Liberal Democratic party jointly approved "The Guidelines on the Overall Reform of the Tax System." These guidelines state that the 1987 tax revision has effectively opened the door to tax reform, but that Japan is still only partway through. The guidelines reiterate the necessity of an overall tax reform to promote economic dynamism, as well as to build a firm basis for a society with an aging population. The guidelines emphasize first that the taxpayers' perception of inequality must be wiped out and second, that taxes should be shared more broadly in order to reduce the average tax burden.

The guidelines call for the expeditious conclusion of tax reform to establish a stabler tax system that will build on a balanced set of tax bases, namely, income, consumption, and property. The guidelines refer to four main areas for review:

—Personal income tax, giving consideration to middle-income earners' tax burden and with a view to ensuring taxpayers' confidence in equity

—Corporate tax, taking account of internationalization of activities

—General consumption tax to replace the current item-by-item excise taxes

—Property tax, including inheritance tax and capital gains tax

Comment by KEIMEI KAIZUKA

Tax reform in Japan finally escaped from a political muddle over tax policy in the Diet in September 1987. The tax reform, based on the Fundamental Proposal for Tax Reform prepared by the Tax Advisory Commission of the government and modified by the Tax Committee of the Liberal Democratic party, got into trouble chiefly because of strong opposition to adopting a value-added tax (VAT)—a variant of the sales tax. Even though the Liberal Democratic party has a large majority in the Diet, the original tax reform was shelved, and a partial revision of the personal income tax was substituted. This revision could be favorably interpreted as one component of the proposed reform. Nevertheless, the state and the direction of tax reform in Japan have been confused by the shelving of the Fundamental Proposal. This comment tries to clarify the problems of the current tax system, evaluate the Fundamental Proposal, and offer a perspective on the direction of future tax reform in Japan.

PROBLEMS OF THE TAX SYSTEM

The tax system in postwar Japan was originally based on the recommendations of the Shoup mission in 1949. These recommendations, reflecting the mainstream of tax theory in the United States in the 1940s, were derived from the idea of comprehensive income taxation. The recommendations were the dominant influence on how the Japanese thought about taxation, even though the actual tax system has substantially diverged from them. The main divergences can be summarized as follows:

—The comprehensiveness of personal income taxation has broken down as a result of the tax exemptions accorded to most property income (for example, the exemption of capital gains from sale of securities, the exemption of small amounts of property income, and the lower tax rate on other property income).

—Numerous tax preferences have also been incorporated in the corporate income tax (mainly for promotion of export and encouragement of business saving and investment), although this tendency has been reversed in the 1980s. The consistency between the corporate income and personal income taxes, which was suggested by the Shoup mission, has also been weakened through the adoption of differential rates between dividend and retained profit. These preferences and differential rates have added to the complexity of the corporate income tax.

—Several measures (for example, the special treatment of unincorporated businesses as quasi corporations) have favored unincorporated over incorporated enterprises and were major causes of horizontal inequities in the personal income tax.

—Progressivity in the personal income tax was steepened in the 1960s and 1970s from eight brackets, with tax rates ranging from 20 percent to 55 percent, to nineteen brackets, with rates ranging from 10 percent to 75 percent. The maximum rate, including local income taxes, rose to 93 percent.

These divergences from the original plans have converted the Japanese income tax virtually to a highly progressive tax on wages. In certain conditions, a wage tax is equivalent to a consumption tax; in effect, therefore, the Japanese personal income tax has diverged considerably from a comprehensive income tax and instead has been approaching a consumption tax.

As a result of these divergences, the tax system faces various problems. The inequities of a very low tax on income from financial assets and horizontal inequities from the favorable treatment of unincorporated business have frequently been mentioned as weak points in the tax system, and there has been popular support for correcting them. Since the early 1980s the heavy burden on corporate income and the distortions of the present income tax system have emerged as issues. In the 1950s and 1960s the corporate income tax included numerous tax incentives so that the effective tax rate on corporations was not as high as the statutory rates suggested. Since the middle of the 1970s, several tax incentives in the corporate income tax have been curtailed, and the basic tax rate has been raised slightly. However, in several Western countries, especially in the United States and the United Kingdom, such tax incentives were maintained during this period. Therefore, the effective corporate tax rate has been higher in Japan than in other Western countries, and reduction of the corporate tax burden has gained support. Supply-sider arguments have strengthened the unfavorable attitude toward these high tax rates and the distortions they created.

THE FUNDAMENTAL PROPOSAL

As explained in Nagano's paper, there are four major recommendations in the Fundamental Proposal: reduction of the burden of the personal income tax mainly through simplification of the rate structure (six brackets, with rates ranging from 10 percent to 50 percent); the abolition of tax exemption for small savers (through the adoption of a 20-percent withholding tax); reduction of the basic tax rate on corporate income (from 42.0 percent to 37.5 percent); and introduction of a variant of the VAT.

Does this package solve the problems in Japan's tax system satisfactorily? At least it is possible to say that each change responded to a specific problem. The simplification of the personal tax rate structure contributes to moderating excessive progressivity, and the reduction in the rate on corporate income tax will help to reduce the distortions in corporate business decisions. The introduction of a VAT can be justified as an improvement in horizontal equity because the burden is spread evenly among all consumers, irrespective of whether they are wage earners or businessmen. The abolition of the tax exemption for small savers would improve the distribution of the tax burden because the exemption has been abused extensively by wealthy people as a result of inadequate enforcement of the limitation on the maximum amount of saving eligible for the tax exemption.

Even though the Fundamental Proposal would resolve these issues, it is difficult to say whether it would resolve them in a consistent manner. To evaluate the consistency of the proposal, it is necessary to see whether it conforms to the basic criteria of equity, neutrality, and simplicity.

Choice of Tax Base

Any real reform must choose an appropriate tax base for the tax system (income or consumption). The Fundamental Proposal chose a mix of the income tax and a general consumption tax because relying on one or the other tax base distorts the allocation of resources and causes inequalities in the tax burdens of taxpayers. A mix of tax bases could be justified when different economic decisions are equally responsive to each tax (that is, they have the same elasticity to the tax rates), but it is difficult to accept this rationale.

The proposed mix of tax bases has obvious shortcomings. Those who support the comprehensive income tax favor the abolition of the tax exemption for small savers (because interest income should be included in an income tax base), although they are not very happy about the adoption of a separate flat withholding tax rate. However, they do not approve of the VAT proposal because of its regressivity. Those who support an expenditure tax favor the adoption of a VAT (because it is a consumption tax), although they recognize that the tax burden on poor people should somehow be adjusted by tax credits or by direct grants. I favor adopting a VAT. I also believe that the abolition of the tax exemption for small savers is unnecessary because it is a move in the opposite direction from an expenditure tax.

Neutrality

The proposal aimed to reduce tax distortions by cutting the number of personal income tax brackets and lowering the corporate income tax rate. However, it introduced a new distortion. Adopting a separate withholding tax on interest income and eliminating tax-exempt saving accounts produce a distinct nonneutrality in the portfolio selection of savers and investors. As already mentioned, the tax system exempts the tax on the capital gains from sales of financial assets, and the proposal retains this exemption. In contrast with the 1950s and 1960s, Japan's financial markets absorb huge volumes of domestic saving as well as funds from foreign countries. Tokyo has become one of the world's major financial centers. Foreign investors and Japanese institutional investors are sensitive to differences in rates of return among various financial assets. Even average Japanese savers accumulate sizable assets and are very concerned with the choices in their portfolios. Differences in after-tax rates of return on deposits and securities created by tax rules will inevitably generate shifts from deposits to bonds and securities. The resulting distortions in portfolio choice could have a harmful effect on the efficiency of the financial system.

Another distortion caused by the proposal is the introduction of a special deduction for spouses. This measure was included along with the abolition of tax-exempt saving accounts in the revised tax reform enacted in September 1987. As explained in Nagano's paper, the special deduction for spouses was introduced mainly to moderate the horizontal inequity between wage earners and individual entrepreneurs. However, it produces a distortion in the work incentives of spouses by discouraging their participation in the labor force. It would have been better to reduce horizontal inequity between wage earners and entrepreneurs by curtailing income splitting between entrepreneurs and other family members.

Simplicity and Tax Administration

Simplicity was also an important objective in the fundamental tax reform. Simplicity diminishes compliance costs for taxpayers and also improves efficiency in tax administration. It is sometimes argued that a reduction in the number of personal income tax brackets contributes to tax simplicity. This argument is not wrong, but it is not persuasive. The contribution of a smaller number of brackets toward simplification is small when compared with the simplification that might be achieved by curtailing tax preferences. Take the case of compliance costs for taxpayers who prepare their own tax returns. The simplification through the elimination of such provisions as the deduction of interest payments, the complicated deduction for aged people, and the special treatment of capital gains would greatly reduce compliance costs by shortening the time required to prepare tax returns and reducing the need to pay tax advisers. In contrast, the reduction of compliance costs by diminishing the number of tax brackets is insignificant.

From the standpoint of tax administration, the most important feature of the Fundamental Proposal is its greater reliance on withholding. The tax system already relies heavily on withholding. Income taxes of all wage earners, except part-time workers, are collected almost entirely through withholding by employers; only a small percentage of wage earners self-assess their tax and report and pay directly to the tax offices. Collection of the tax on property income depends almost exclusively on the withholding method, and the Fundamental Proposal as well as the September 1987 tax reform strengthens this dependency. Now a separate tax rate will be applied to interest income (at 20 percent) through withholding. This decision diverges from the idea of comprehensive taxation. Formerly, in spite of widespread abuse of the tax exemption for small savers, at least some taxpayers were taxed on their interest income at marginal tax rates that applied to their total income including interest income.

Admittedly, the withholding tax on interest income is an efficient way of collecting taxes. However, in spite of the greater efficiency in tax administration, dependence on a separate withholding tax, especially in the taxation of property income, reduces tax equity.

The effect of separate interest withholding on international financial flow needs to be mentioned. Recently, most major countries abolished their withholding taxes on interest income of nonresidents. However, the Japanese tax system retains withholding on interest from bonds that are issued in foreign markets; there is also separate withholding on interest on domestically issued bonds. Thus reliance on withholding for taxing income from securities will distort international financial flows and hamper the further development of Tokyo's financial center.

THE FUTURE

As explained in Nagano's paper, after the Fundamental Proposal was shelved, the Diet accepted a partial revision of the personal income tax without introducing the VAT and without reducing the corporate income tax. My earlier comments, especially those about the adoption of the separate withholding tax on interest income, apply to the recent revision of the personal income tax. Even though it is not easy to judge the future direction of tax reform—particularly of the continued political muddle over tax policy—I will offer a perspective on possible reform developments.

One direction is to follow the lines of the Fundamental Proposal. The additional reforms needed to complete the proposal are the introduction of a VAT, more flattening of the personal income tax rate structure, and a reduction in the corporate income tax rate. Another direction is to remedy the shortcomings of the personal income tax by adopting a unified numbering system for reporting financial transactions of taxpayers and by taxing capital gains from the sales of securities, proposals that are supported by the left-wing parties and by proponents of comprehensive income taxation. A third direction would be to adopt a VAT that would be earmarked for specific social expenditures, for example, expenditures needed to finance the subsidized portion of the government's compulsory pension system. This proposal is said to be supported by the new Prime Minister Noboru Takeshita.

For full implementation of the Fundamental Proposal, the additional reforms would consist mainly of regressive measures when compared with the comprehensive income tax approach. It is difficult to give enthusiastic support to regressive taxation even though I would prefer to introduce a graduated expenditure tax and would also be sympathetic toward adopting a consumption tax. Strengthening the personal income tax through stricter monitoring of financial flows among taxpayers would certainly be justified on equity grounds. However, full taxation of capital gains will not be sufficient to finance the expansion of social expenditures in Japan's rapidly aging society. Finally, even though the idea of earmarking is novel and perhaps politically acceptable, earmarked taxes—even if used to expand social programs—cannot be justified on the basis of tax theory.

In brief, because of the continued political sensitivity of tax policy, a new consensus will be required. Further progress on tax reform will take more time than originally expected.

Netherlands

Criticism of the complexity of the Dutch tax system as a whole has intensified over the past ten to fifteen years. Disapproval has focused particularly on the income tax, whether deducted at the source or paid by assessment, because of both the high rates and the complexity of the system. Although legislation introducing complexities was broadly accepted at the time of passage, over the years it has proved difficult to stop the process of further complicating the system. Lately, however, a major simplification seems within reach.

This presentation concentrates on the wage and income tax, but also touches on other taxes, including the corporate income tax. The pending tax reform in the Netherlands is a microbased more than a macrobased reform, changing the technique of income tax collection more than the distribution of the tax burden.

From a population of approximately 14 million, 2 million (over 14 percent) are wage earners, liable solely for income tax deducted at source. This means that they do not need to file tax returns. An additional 5 million people (almost 36 percent of the population) complete annual tax returns. A recent survey has revealed that three out of four people in the latter category are unable to fill in their tax forms without assistance. We should point out that a large number of those who are not required to complete tax returns barely comprehend the difference between their gross pay and their net pay. Investigations showed that people seldom have any real awareness of the actual tax burden.

If we believe that simplicity contributes to the acceptance of taxation in society—and we do—then simplification is of the utmost importance in order to uphold the grand old lady, as the income tax is sometimes called.

The extent to which the regulations are clear and comprehensible is probably determined in part by cultural factors. There is a fair amount of variance among different countries in regard to the degree of necessary form-filling, the number of articles in the law books, and so on. The reaction on the part of the taxpaying public seems remarkably uniform: everything is too complicated. There are no internationally recognized objective criteria for measuring complexity. The conclusion that everything is too complicated could be due to such factors as the actual scope of legislation, the comprehensibility of the legislative structure, the extent to which general principles are subject to unnecessary explanation, or the extent to which specific exceptions are embodied in the legislation. It could, however, be simply psychological: the degree to which a particular law is perceived as complex.

CAUSES OF COMPLEXITY

Any inquiry into what caused the increased complexity of Dutch tax legislation invites pointing a finger at the many refinements that income tax has undergone. The first version of the Income Tax Act dated from 1893, and new laws were passed in 1914, 1941, and 1964. These were followers without U-turns or sudden shocks. A number of these legislative refinements were connected with efforts to achieve a distribution of the tax burden among the population that was politically and socially acceptable. Some stem from the use of taxation as a means of attaining objectives other than the collection of general revenue for financing government expenditure. In the 1970s and early 1980s income tax was one of the instruments used by the government for the redistribution of income. At that time socioeconomic policy was based on the idea that lower-income groups ought to benefit more than higher-income groups from increased prosperity. A tax structure based on heavily progressive rates of income tax led to a significant paring down of net income differences. The general feeling now is that differences in net income may have become too small, and there is evidence of pressure to move in the opposite direction.

Another reason for the income tax law's complexity is the large number of provisions that were designed to close down perceived loopholes. The Dutch tax system, particularly as it developed after the Second World War, rested on the premise that taxpayers were reasonably mature, law-abiding citizens. Under a system designed with such individuals in mind, tax authorities usually can perform their task of inspection satisfactorily at an administrative level. Under such circumstances even complex regulations and a higher burden of taxation need not necessarily cause problems. In practice, however, it became increasingly clear that the type of taxpayer the government had in mind when devising the system was an idealized figure, and repercussions in the form of fraud and tax evasion have been particularly noticeable since the early 1970s. However, the government's response—closing legislative loopholes—has not made tax law any simpler until now.

The process of refining has been further accelerated by the fact that taxation and the impact of taxation have become matters of great importance to society as a whole. There also is a link between complexity and levels of taxation. The higher the taxes, the greater the pressure for refinements.[1] It is interesting to note that high taxation is described as complex even if, viewed objectively, it is not complex but merely high.

Legislation on two-income households introduced several years ago appears to have brought this process to a head. The aim of the legislation was to reflect the different views in society and bring the tax system into line with the different forms of cohabitation in the Netherlands. There are, for example, separate tax thresholds for families with one wage earner, with two wage earners, and for single persons and single parents. This, in itself simple fairness, has possibly been carried too far if looked at from the point of view that legislation should also be comprehensible. This legislation was, technically speaking, a success. However, it, and the public debate centered on it, proved to be the straw that broke the camel's back. The clamor for simplification of the tax system became universal and led to extensive political pressure on the government to take decisive action. The fact that there is pressure for action only on income tax implies, in our opinion, that other taxes, including the corporate income tax,

---

1. One of the refinements, the inflation correction, which is an automatic adjustment of the widths of tax brackets and certain provisions, proves that refinements are not always complicated. In the period 1982–87 this provision prevented an approximately 15-percent increase in wage and income tax.

are not perceived as too complex.[2] The corporate income tax in the Netherlands is considered quite simple, with few special provisions and a moderate rate of 42 percent.

THE GOVERNMENT'S RESPONSE

The government's hesitation was easy to understand, given the fact that attempts to simplify the system in the past had led to more and more regulation of even greater complexity. This time, however, the government opted for a different approach. Realizing that simplifying the tax system was a major operation that could not succeed without broadly based social and political support, the government set up a committee of tax experts. Although they were not politicians, the political background of the committee members ensured that the three main political parties, the Christian Democrats, the Socialists, and the Liberals, were equally represented.

Within a short time (a little more than six months) the committee—with technical support from the Ministry of Finance—issued its report, outlining a number of practical proposals for simplifying the tax system. The report met with widespread political approval. The present administration adopted its main points and amplified them in its interim statement. The main points are as follows:

—There would be one fixed rate at 40 percent over a large range of income up to approximately 50,000 guilders. About 80 percent of taxpayers are in this bracket.

—Income tax would be combined with the general social security contributions.

—Wage taxes would, as far as possible, be the final levy, paring down the number of tax returns to be filed.

—Certain deductions and other schemes would be streamlined.

PUBLIC SUPPORT

The government statement on the simplification of the tax system is currently the focus of a "great debate." Parliamentary hearings have

2. The Dutch tax system has no major taxation outside the taxes of the central government.

been held, reports have been issued by the Equal Rights Council, and both platforms have been composed of representatives of both sides of industry. Much attention is being devoted in the debate to the socioeconomic effects of the proposals. The consideration given to their consequences for income distribution is greater still. The implications for the different income groups, for example, have been portrayed in great detail. Although these procedures inhibit rapid progress, they appear in the Netherlands to be essential in achieving a general social consensus. Taking into account that it took a century to reach the present degree of complexity, achieving a major simplification within four years is still a good result. Implementation of the new system is expected in 1990.

INTEGRATION

The technical reform includes what we term partial integration, which combines tax on income with social security contributions. It is a partial integration because, for example, the financing funds for social security remain separated from the budget, with their own rules including certain insurance aspects. To the taxpayer and premium payer the difference should be made visible by printing not only the total sum to be paid but also those parts that are tax and those that are social security premiums.

In the Netherlands income tax and social security contributions are levied according to slightly different principles. Tax paid on income is progressive and based on the principle of taxable income. The social security contribution, on the other hand, is a fixed percentage of income. As the latter is largely the same as taxable income, the influence of the income tax system is felt on social security contributions. The base for social security is roughly the same as taxable income increased by the amount paid as social security contributions, which are deducted from the levy base for income tax purposes. Although income for social security purposes is derived from taxable income, the connection between the two is unclear to many people. Their understanding of the combined burden of tax and social security contributions is further complicated by the fact that the two are levied separately.

In the past, when social security contributions were on a much smaller scale, the separate levying of tax and social security contributions hardly caused any problems. By now, however, the initially low burden of contributions has soared so high that for many taxpayers social security contributions outstrip their income tax liabilities. This situation is illustrated by the fact that in 1960 the burden of social security contributions was about 9.1 percent of national income; by 1987 this figure had risen to 22.1 percent. The incomprehensibility of the system as a whole leads to discontent and puts pressure on the separate income tax and social security contributions.

THE CONSEQUENCES OF INTEGRATION: THE COMPENSATORY RISE IN GROSS SALARY

The gist of the committee's proposal is that certain social security contributions, currently payable by the employer, will in the future be paid by the employee. To avoid a fall in income, the employee's gross salary will be increased by the amount of the contributions to be paid by the employee and currently paid by the employer. This is termed the compensatory rise in gross salary of the "grossing up process." The labor costs for the employer will remain the same.

In theory, the transfer in contributions and compensatory rise in gross salary would entail no more than a simple one-time adjustment of pay, which may total more than 5 percent of GNP. However, a number of potential problems have loomed large in the public debate and have been particularly apparent in the reports that have been received in response to requests for advice on the issue. Among the problems, to which attention has been drawn chiefly by employer and employee organizations, are the possible effects of the measures on labor costs and the adjustments to which they will necessarily lead in the base figures for calculating pensions.

As a result of these expressed concerns, an interim solution has been worked out for a key element in the proposals for simplifying the tax system: grossing up will take place over a two-year period, giving more time to implement the proposals as a whole. This example proves that a merely technical reform can be necessary to prepare the field for further simplification or other reforms, even when the work to be done absorbs a major part of the ability of government, administration, and polities to prepare and implement changes in the tax system.

RATE OF TAXATION

Other important elements in the proposals for simplifying the system relate to tax rate structure and tax base. While in a strictly theoretical sense there is little connection between levels of taxation and simplifying tax legislation, there is an interplay between high rates of taxation and an increasing complexity of legislation. Establishing levels of taxation and the burden of taxation and social security contributions is, alas, much more dependent on factors that are outside the scope of tax law, irrespective of whether the latter is complicated or not. Rates of taxation are the outcome of political deliberations that embrace other elements besides merely fiscal considerations. Accordingly, the possibility of lowering tax rates lies outside the terms of reference of a committee set up to study the question of simplifying tax legislation. The stated requirement of budgetary neutrality has helped ensure the inclusion in the provisional statement by the government of the committee's proposal for a four-bracket structure of 40 percent, 55 percent, 65 percent, and 70 percent. The 40-percent rate consists of 10-percent income tax and 30-percent social security contributions and will apply to a broad initial tax band. The top rates, however, are largely provisional. They are the subject of a separate debate, which, it is hoped, will fairly soon produce tangible results. Public debate in the Netherlands on the subject is accelerating, so it is possible to speak about a cut of the highest tax rates to 60 percent without being called a dreamer. This result would be in keeping with the current international tendency to lower the rates. Furthermore, the Netherlands was a trendsetter a few years ago in lowering the corporate tax rate, and many countries have followed its example in recent years. That process can be expected to continue.

TAX BASE

The size of the tax base is also a consideration in tax reform. In many other countries tax reform has been accompanied by tax rate reductions that have in some cases been considerable and that have been financed by drastically limiting tax-deductible items in order to broaden the tax base. However, the tax base in the Netherlands is already fairly broad. The committee has examined, solely on the basis of mathematical calculations, the maximum tax reduction that could technically be achieved if almost all tax-deductible items, with the sole exception of tax relief on mortgage interest, were to be abolished. No attention was paid to the public acceptability of such a drastic plan. It was found that the proposed rates of 40 percent, 55 percent, 65 percent, and 70 percent could be lowered by a maximum of only two and one-half percentage points.

Other alternatives have been mentioned in professional journals. We are repeatedly led to conclude from these articles that a broadening of the tax base could offer only modest scope for tax reductions, or, in more drastic forms, only at the loss of public acceptance. The tax base is, moreover, an element looked at critically in the Netherlands from time to time, particularly whenever budgetary considerations necessitate choosing between increasing tax rates and broadening the tax base. A recent survey by the Ministry of Finance confirmed that the tax base in the Netherlands is fairly broad as it is, a conclusion that also applies to our corporate income tax. It is also worth noting that in the political debate on the committee's proposals, few hands were raised in favor of more far-reaching simplifications in the form of limiting other tax-deductible items apart from those suggested by the committee.

Tax reform in the Netherlands is a simultaneous process of achieving both major and minor reforms. The Netherlands is, for example, currently working on other major projects concerning adjustments in the tax base. These also have implications for the simplicity of the tax system. The Netherlands is revising provisions in both personal income tax and corporate income tax concerning retirement savings. The main aim is to express society's views on this subject and reduce the influence of legislation on private-sector decisions. A broadening of the tax base is not necessarily intended but could in practice be the result. The revenue raised in this way can be used for reducing tax rates.

CONCLUSION

It is realized in the Netherlands that the increasing burden of taxation and social security contributions and the growing complexity of tax legislation with emphasis on the income tax will gradually come to have an alienating effect on society. Another factor for consideration is that complexity and high rates will act as driving forces, as it were, on each other. The higher the rates, the greater the push to take account of particular circumstances, and so the spiral continues. At the same time it should also be admitted that the claims of the government as the source of expenditure with regard to income redistribution and fine tuning of the economy have not been fulfilled and are not now likely to be. Both these trends point directly to the need for simplification.

Any country faced with a similar task encounters its own particular problems. As far as the Netherlands is concerned, it must first be borne in mind that the relatively heavy burden of taxation and social security contributions is very much related to the size of the public sector. It is here that an important key to a substantial reduction in the Netherlands' high levels of taxation lies.

Second, it is relevant as far as the Netherlands is concerned that the tax base is already broad by comparison with many other countries. Even the most radical simplifications, such as a scrapping of tax-deductible items and tax relief, provide relatively little scope for lowering rates of taxation.

Third, seeking a firm social basis for simplifying the tax structure presents its own problems. The Netherlands has opted for what might be termed "the great debate." The sophisticated and subtle portrayal of all possible effects that this process engenders is a typical Dutch phenomenon. The consequences of the proposals regarding, for example, income distribution must be met with extreme caution.

Despite all the criticism leveled at the present income tax system, it has become clear that there is a great social need for a system of taxation that has built-in corrective mechanisms to enable the income and personal circumstances of individual taxpayers to be taken into account, albeit in a more general way than at present. Despite the fact that replacing income tax with levies of a less specific kind, such as a tax on consumption, may make the task of implementation for both government and business considerably easier, proposals for abolishing the income tax stand no chance.

The only way to make progress is to harness every effort and use the present tax system as a base for devising—in a step-by-step approach—a system that is simpler, more comprehensible, and, as a consequence, more acceptable to the public. We are confident that by the year 1990, the Netherlands will have made progress on all three elements of tax reform: integration, tax rates, and the tax base.

Comment by FLIP DE KAM

Nowadays the concept of tax reform is a highly successful American export article on the global market of ideas in public finance. In recent years tax reform has become a fashionable buzz word, notably among a select group of tax lawyers and tax economists. As everyone at this conference is aware, this trend may be explained because in practically all OECD countries the problem of high rates and growing complexity of taxes, especially the income tax, has finally attracted the attention of policymakers. Although citizens and private firms will mostly be interested to learn how changes in the tax legislation are going to influence their income and profits, this conference is a still more intellectually stimulating effort to come to grips with the theoretical and practical issues involved. My comments on the state of tax reform in the Netherlands will be in two parts. First, I will discuss tax rates. Second, I will concentrate on opportunities for broadening the tax base, which merits more attention. Of course, it would be interesting to speculate about the impact of U.S. tax reform on the Dutch economy. However, until now, no economic research on this matter has been done, at least as far as I am aware.

In the Netherlands, concerned academics, representatives of the Internal Revenue Service, and professional tax advisers have regularly voiced pleas for tax reform and tax simplification. Many proposals for improvement have been offered, though most of them were not ripe for immediate implementation by policymakers. It seems to me that recommendations to switch to an expenditure tax fall into this category.

In 1984–85 the ongoing process of complexification of the tax system culminated in the introduction of complicated legislation affecting the personal exemptions in the personal income tax. Time then proved ripe for a change. Because of the public outcry over the latest additions to an already overburdened tax system, Parliament demanded that a tax simplification committee be set up. The committee was appointed at the end of September 1985.

The committee produced a report within seven months of its first meeting (in May 1986). The report contains a proposal to combine the personal income taxes and the most important payroll taxes (contributions to the general social insurance programs) into one levy with an identical tax base, while ensuring that the identity and particular purpose of each part are maintained. Under the present system, social insurance contributions are deductible for income tax purposes. By absorbing the current deductibility into a lower rate of the combined levy, by far the largest deduction is eliminated (presently some 7 percent of GDP is involved).

The proposed rate scale has four brackets, instead of nine. On the basis of figures for 1985, 88 percent of all taxpayers have incomes in the proposed first bracket. Since the simplification committee had to develop its proposals within a frame of revenue neutrality, income in the first bracket is taxed at a stiff 40 percent. After the proposals are implemented (in 1990), the average production worker will pay (at the margin) 20 percent in contributions to employee social insurance programs, on top of the 40 percent in income levy. Thus total marginal rates will be about 60 percent. This is nothing new. At the moment, most taxpayers in the Netherlands contribute 55 percent to 65 percent at the margin. There is virtually no difference in tax rates between employees earning the statutory minimum wage, the average production worker, and employees earning twice the APW's wages: All face marginal rates in the 60-percent range.

The high rates of taxes and contributions are the result of high government spending and an extensive social security system. When the public sector siphons off approximately two-thirds of national income, as is now true in the Netherlands, taxes and contributions must be high. Simplification cannot directly contribute to lowering taxes (measured as a share of national income).

To attain lower tax rates—holding the budget deficit constant— three policy options are available: a reduction of public outlays; changing the tax mix, placing less emphasis on income taxes; and broadening the base of the income taxes.

Reducing public outlays would be difficult, mainly because between

1983 and 1986 public spending in the Netherlands (expressed as a percentage of net national income) has already been cut back by one and one-half percentage points, in spite of a strong growth in the number of benefit recipients under various programs.[1] Two-thirds of public outlays consists of transfer payments to families and private firms. Politically, it is nearly impossible to reduce public spending on transfers any more, at least at this moment.

Changing the tax mix has other drawbacks. The only alternative is a shift from income and payroll taxes to taxes on consumer spending. However, the rates of the value-added tax (general rate of 20 percent and a reduced rate of 6 percent for food and some other goods that satisfy basic needs) are already slightly above the average European level. In the light of efforts to harmonize VAT rates in Europe, there is no room to increase VAT rates in the Netherlands. Presently, excise taxes bring in about 2.5 percent of GDP. Even if all excise tax rates would rise by 50 percent, the extra revenue would only be sufficient to reduce the basic income tax rate (as proposed by the committee) by two points to 38 percent. The top rate could be lowered to just 68 percent. However, some would object to this policy option because a move toward taxing consumer spending would further increase the share of regressive taxes in the tax system. Between 1960 and 1985 the share of payroll taxes and taxes on consumption grew from 58 percent to 70 percent of total tax revenue.

Finally, broadening the base of the income taxes would be another way to attain lower tax rates. The current income tax system has many deductions of a widely differing nature, significance, and background. Most of these deductions are defended on the basis of the ability-to-pay principle (for example, the deduction of medical expenses). Other deductions permit deferral of taxes (for example, the deduction of contributions to private pension schemes); and still other deductions can be seen as an alternative to direct expenditures, in other words, an instrument to promote social or economic goals of government policy. The present refundable investment tax credit and the tax treatment of owner-occupied housing exemplify such tax expenditures.

The jungle of deductions and tax preferences already makes the

1. Organization for Economic Cooperation and Development, *OECD Economic Surveys, 1986/1987: Netherlands* (Paris: OECD, 1987), p. 80.

present tax system complicated and incomprehensible to the ordinary taxpayer. Moreover, taxpayers suspect that a tax system with fewer loopholes and tax preferential schemes would ensure more equitable treatment of a greater number of taxpayers. It has often been argued that income tax rates could be lowered considerably—after abolition or a drastic reduction of deductions and preferences. This is desirable not only on equity grounds, but also because it would simplify the income tax system. A less detailed tax structure is more readily acceptable at low rather than high rates.

Microeconomic simulations on a data set of a quarter-million tax returns for the year 1981, adjusted to reflect the conditions of the year 1985, have made it clear that even a drastic limitation of deductions plus the elimination of the investment tax credit would only permit a reduction of the rates that have been proposed by the simplification committee of at most six points in each bracket. A rate reduction of six points is a very "harsh" policy option indeed. All present deductions not related to an income source would be eliminated. Expenses of employees would be deductible only if they exceeded 4 percent of wages (the first 4 percent being considered part of normal household spending). Extra revenue from the corporation income tax after elimination of the investment tax credit and other tax subsidies to private firms would be used to lower rates of the personal income tax, increasing taxes of firms by over 1.5 percent of GDP. A slight increase of the imputed rent of owner-occupied housing is part of the "harsh" policy option. The deduction of interest, including mortgage interest, would be limited to the positive amount of net income from capital. Net capital income would include net imputed rent that is set at 1.2 percent of the market value of the property. Because of a lack of data, three items have not been included in the microsimulation carried out:

—A limitation of the deductibility of "mixed" expenses of firms and households, which combines elements of costs incurred in earning income and personal consumption. Recently I did some rough estimates of the potential effect on revenue of a limitation of deductibility of such mixed expenses to 75 percent of the amounts involved. This measure would probably produce extra tax revenues of about Dfl 0.3 billion, enabling a rate reduction of only one-seventh point at most.

—"Equity would be served by taxing realized capital gains with deemed realization in the event of death or similar circumstances." Many would add that such a measure might be considered, provided that net capital losses are fully deductible and other taxes on wealth reduced.[2] I have serious doubts whether extra revenue from the taxation of private capital gains would exceed a few billion guilders a year, enabling a further rate reduction by one point at most. Moreover, taxation of capital gains would not help to simplify the tax system, but, on the contrary, would complicate it.

—Finally, one might consider reducing the discrimination of conventional saving by eliminating the possibility for tax deferral from present private pension schemes to provide for old age. In 1986, untaxed investment income of public and private pension funds amounted to 5 percent of GDP. Moreover, contributions paid into pension funds exceeded pensions paid out of those funds by at least 1 percent of GDP. Adding this 6 percent of GDP to the personal income tax base would permit a reduction of all bracket rates by another five to six points.

By combining all policy measures mentioned, it would become possible to lower the basic rate of the income levy proposed by the committee to 28 percent. This basic rate would hardly be higher than comparable U.S. rates for two reasons:

—On average, 4 percent to 6 percent in state and local income taxes, which the Netherlands does not have, should be added to the 15 percent of the first U.S. federal income tax bracket.

—Seven percent in payroll taxes should be added to the, say, 20 percent in all U.S. income taxes. These payroll taxes finance the Old-Age, Survivors, Disability, and Hospital Insurance programs (OAS-DHI) in the United States. Comparable programs in the Netherlands are largely financed from contributions to the general social insurance programs, now incorporated in the new income levy proposed by the simplification committee.

However, to achieve a basic income tax rate of 28 percent in the Netherlands, policymakers would have to move toward a truly comprehensive tax base a lot further than the United States dared to go in 1986. Hardly any deduction of mortgage interest would still be allowed, the build-up of private pensions would be taxed, and so

2. Sijbren Cnossen, "Agenda for Income Tax Reform in the Netherlands," *Public Finance*, vol. 37, no. 2 (1982), p. 220.

on. Such drastic tax reforms might have dramatic consequences for the national economy and would certainly have a big impact on net disposable income of the large majority of all households.

The simplification committee knew that far-reaching policy changes would not be feasible. From the start the committee members were convinced that many deductions are so strongly believed to be socially justifiable or so directly related to earning personal income that abolition or even any substantial reduction in these deductions would stand little or no chance of political or social acceptance. In some cases reducing deductions would call for such complicated legislation (to counter the use of possible loopholes) that the committee ruled out such recommendations.

Later events have proved the prudence of this approach. Although first reactions to the committee report were on the whole remarkably positive, criticism from affected parties grew as they realized certain consequences of the proposals. Some rather modest committee suggestions for streamlining deductions have met with stiff opposition from pressure groups. It remains to be seen what the final outcome of the tax reform process in the Netherlands will be. But I am sure that progress will be made.

Though most public criticism focuses on the harshness of some of the committee recommendations, some observers must feel disappointed that both the report and the present government position on tax reform embody only a limited move toward a comprehensive income tax. For a number of years now, I have adhered to the view that the Netherlands should favor a far more comprehensive system of income taxation, which would be simple, clear, and economically efficient. However, all the evidence seems to prove that I cherish an impossible dream.

Sweden

Regardless of the method used to calculate the tax burden, Sweden heads the list. This is the case if taxes are calculated as a percentage of GDP, for which the 1985 figure is 50.5 percent. It is also true if the direct burden of tax on the individual is calculated in terms of the marginal rate or the average tax he is liable to pay. The most striking feature of taxes in Sweden, however, is the high level of individual income tax.

The structure of taxation in Sweden has changed character in the last couple of decades. Twenty years ago income tax was the dominant form of tax, representing almost 50 percent of the total taxes paid by a household. Today this figure has dropped to around 40 percent. More than two-thirds of this income tax consists of local tax and less than one-third of national income tax. During the same period, corporate taxation's share of total tax revenue has also dropped from 6 percent to just over 3 percent. The reduction in the percentage for direct income tax is mainly attributable to the continuous increase in social security charges, which now represent about 30 percent of the total revenue from taxes and such charges. Their share has risen by about eighteen percentage points. This increase is identical with an increase in employers' contributions, since employees have not had to pay these charges for many years. Employers' contributions now amount to over 37 percent of gross salaries.

The share of total tax revenue accounted for by indirect taxes has varied insignificantly during the last twenty years and represents today, as previously, about 30 percent of the total revenue from taxes and social security charges. Property taxes—the net wealth tax, inheritance and gift taxes, and others—have not varied much either and now represent about 1 percent of the total.

A TAX SYSTEM BASED ON LONGSTANDING PRINCIPLES

Sweden's income tax system is based on principles established almost sixty years ago with the passing of the Communal Tax Act in 1928. This act contains regulations concerning calculation of the taxable amount on which local taxes are charged, that is, taxes payable to municipalities and county councils. But this act is also generally referred to in the National Tax Act in connection with the method of calculating the taxable amount on which national tax is charged.

The basic principles underlying taxation of individuals are as follows. A taxpayer's income is divided into six categories subject to tax: income from agricultural property, income from other real property, income from business, income from employment, income from casual economic activities, and income from capital. In each category, income from different sources is calculated separately, and all expenses for the acquisition and maintenance of the gross receipts are in principle deductible. If a deficit arises when the net income from a source of income is calculated, this deficit may—with some exceptions—be used to set off net income from other sources. In addition, certain general deductions may be made from the aggregate net income of the different categories. The aggregate income from all sources after general deductions and deductions for loss incurred in a previous year constitutes the taxpayer's assessed income. From this amount, a so-called basic deduction is made in the case of private individuals, the result being their taxable income. In the case of companies, assessed income equals taxable income.

The provisions relating to tax have been amended many times since 1928, both in substance and in detail, but the Communal Tax Act is still the foundation of Sweden's tax system. No major review of the income tax system has been undertaken subsequent to its passage. Fundamental elements in this system are now obsolete and inappropriate to the present-day situation. While many attempts have been made to modernize the legislation in certain areas, these partial reforms have tended to render the system as a whole even more complex and impenetrable.

There is nowadays widespread criticism of the tax system in general and of income tax in particular. In some people's opinion taxes are so high that they discourage work, saving, and personal initiative. Others say that the system is unfair, since it is too easy for smart and unscrupulous people to evade taxes. Practically everyone agrees that the system is too complicated. Of course grumbling about taxes is nothing new, but there are good reasons for taking much of the criticism seriously. The Social Democrats, who regard a large public sector, primarily financed by taxes, as a prerequisite for social welfare, must constantly ask themselves whether the tax system is practical and just.

RECENT TAX REFORMS

During the last five years, after the change of government in 1982, the work of reforming the tax system has been more intense than at any time since 1928. The result has not only been a large number of reforms; the changes have in many cases touched on important matters of principle. A natural starting point for a discussion of the most significant of these reforms is the income tax reform carried out between 1983 and 1985. This reform was in all essentials based on ideas originally developed in Norway.

The reform introduced in Sweden was made possible by an agreement between the nonsocialist parties, which formed the government at the time, and the Social Democrat party, which was then in opposition. The main features of the agreement were reductions in the marginal tax rates and limitation of deductions.

Hitherto, deductions corresponding to the full marginal tax rate could be made for interest paid and other deficits, and in the early 1980s the highest marginal rate was 85 percent. As a result of the reform, the value of such deductions is limited to a maximum of 50 percent if it results in deficit in the revenue source. For example, for a deduction made for interest expenses amounting to Skr 10,000, the maximum reduction in tax in the case of a deficit is now Skr 5,000. The rules previously in force allowed a tax reduction amounting to a maximum of Skr 8,500 for a taxpayer in the highest marginal tax bracket.

The other component in the reform was a reduction of the marginal tax rates. A substantial adjustment was made in this respect, as a

TABLE 1. *Individual Income Tax Rates, 1988*

Annual income (kronor)	Total	National tax	Local tax[a]
10,000–80,000	35	5	30
80,001–150,000	50	20	30
150,001–200,000	64	34	30
200,001 and over	75	45	30

a. Average local tax.

result of which the marginal tax rates for those with average incomes were reduced by up to twenty percentage points.

There was another feature of the reform that was not very significant from a revenue point of view, but indicated a change in principle with regard to tax policy. The standard deduction of Skr 100, which had been introduced in 1956 and was taken by all wage earners, was raised first to Skr 1,000 and subsequently to Skr 3,000. This change was motivated by a desire to simplify the tax system. It is also an indication of the fact that we have now given up our ambition of achieving absolute fairness in taxation, which previously involved countless small deductions whose only practical result was to make the system complicated and anything but fair.

Another change designed to simplify the system was elimination, in 1986, of joint taxation of married couples' capital income. This means that there is no longer any joint taxation in the Swedish tax system except with respect to net wealth tax. Another change relating to income tax is that the number of tax brackets has been drastically reduced. There were fourteen in 1982; by 1988 there will be only four (table 1).

One further major reform was the introduction of a simplified income tax return beginning with the income year 1986. This radically simplifies the tax return procedure for the vast majority of the country's income earners. One of the factors that made this possible was the increase in the standard deduction, which means that almost 4 million income earners no longer need to fill out income tax returns at all. All they must do is sign a declaration that they have not earned any income apart from that reported to the tax authorities by employers in their statements of employees' earnings. The simplified income tax return symbolizes the effort to make Sweden's tax system simpler, both technically and in the sense that it is simpler for the taxpayer to understand. Many other reforms have also been motivated by the desire to simplify the system.

The next step after carrying out the tax reform in 1983–85 was to abolish indexation of the tax rates, which had been introduced in 1979. The pros and cons of indexing tax rates were among the most controversial issues in the political debate during the 1970s and 1980s. The fact that there was no formal indexation before 1979 did not prevent continuous adjustments from being made in the tax rates. These adjustments were, however, insufficient to keep pace with increases in prices and salaries.

TIME FOR A REVIEW

The reforms mentioned above are extensive, but can still be regarded as only partial reforms of the tax system. Sweden has now come to the next stage in reform, where the very principles of its present tax system are being questioned. It is right to say that the prospects are now better than ever before for a change of the system. There is now a willingness to review the tax system both by the political parties and by the various private organizations concerned with tax action. It is of course also a fact that the debate and reforms in progress in other countries have influenced the tax climate in Sweden.

In the fall of 1986 the union representing professional employees submitted a proposal for a new system. In January 1987 Minister of Finance Kjell-Olof Feldt put his name on a set of general proposals for a tax reform. Shortly afterward the Liberal party, one of the three nonsocialist parties represented in the Swedish Parliament, presented a tax reform proposal of its own. The Swedish Trade Union Confederation published a report recently in which it too offered proposals for changes in the tax system. The interesting thing about these proposals is that they all recommended a broader tax base, reduced tax rates, greater simplicity, and (to provide simpler and more uniform regulations) a reform of the taxation of income from capital gains and other income from capital. The proposals are by no means identical, but their essential features are remarkably similar.

HIGH TAX RATES

When progressive tax rates were introduced, they did not affect most income earners. Only large incomes were affected by high marginal rates. For most income earners the marginal rate was not appreciably higher than the average tax rate, and thus progressivity was not a burden.

With Sweden's expanding public sector and growing welfare ambitions, however, tax revenue had to be increased. As the pressure of taxation rose, progressive tax rates affected an increasing number of income earners. This was accompanied by a general increase in taxation, which was mainly due to a rise in local taxes, where the rates are fixed on a percentage basis regardless of the size of incomes. In 1960, local tax rates (payable to municipalities and county councils) averaged 15 percent, while today the average is more than 30 percent. This means that all income earners pay more than thirty kronor in local tax out of every one hundred kronor they earn above the basic exemption, more than twice the 1960 rate. It also means that higher local taxes have raised marginal tax rates by fifteen percentage points.

Soaring inflation, particularly in the 1970s, brought more and more taxpayers into income brackets in which they paid high progressive national income tax rates. These rates were only partially adjusted to the rapid rise in prices and incomes, and in some cases the national tax rates were even increased.

By the early 1980s the marginal tax rate exceeded 50 percent for almost half of all income earners, including a large majority of full-time employees. The 1983–85 tax reform altered this by appreciably reducing tax rates for the first time since World War II. As I mentioned earlier, this meant a reduction in marginal tax rates by up to twenty percentage points. With the additional adjustments decided on for 1987 and 1988, it is estimated that up to 90 percent of all income earners and 80 percent of all full-time employees will pay a marginal tax rate of not more than 50 percent. In the income year 1988 the maximum marginal tax rate will be 75 percent (assuming a local tax rate of 30 percent). The tax rates payable for the income year 1988 are shown in table 1.

An important point of departure in the debate is that progressive tax rates are an essential element in the Swedish tax system and promote an equitable distribution of wealth. The aim, however, should be to achieve the desired balance with tax rates that are as low as possible, since high tax rates entail a number of problems. They encourage tax evasion and tax planning. They also promote the growth of an informal, gray economy with a private exchange of services and do-it-yourself activities that are unproductive from the point of view of the national economy and probably inhibit development of the service sector.

Excessively progressive tax rates that are high even for ordinary wage earners complicate wage negotiations and make the task of keeping down price and salary increases more difficult. Rather high nominal increases in salaries have generally been required to achieve the intended rises after tax. This may have contributed to the difficulty experienced in bringing down the rate of inflation in Sweden to that of its main competitors.

An increase in income—from extra work, a change from part-time to full-time employment, or a move to a better-paid job—is not very rewarding. These drawbacks tend to be aggravated by other factors. Housing allowances, normally granted to low-income households, diminish with rising income; day nursery fees are often linked to income. As a result, a large number of taxpayers suffer considerably from the effects of high marginal tax rates. Cases have occurred in which these effects approach or even exceed 100 percent. In consequence, many people with a relatively low income and high tax margins are liable to end up in a "poverty trap" with little chance of working their way out.

The increasing internationalization of Sweden's economy is making it more susceptible to developments in the rest of the world. The necessity of bringing price and salary increases down to the levels of competitors is only one of the problems. Excessive differences in tax rates between Sweden and other countries also involve the risk of production, employment, and capital being transferred to countries where taxes are lower.

There is another aspect to be considered: the purpose of progressive tax rates is to reduce differences in income after tax by making those with high incomes pay more tax than those with low incomes. But progressive income tax entails a consequence that may not be so desirable: part-time work becomes more profitable than full-time work.

THE PROBLEM OF DEDUCTIONS

The Swedish tax system abounds in deductions. They can be divided into different categories. There is a basic deduction, which differs from all the others in that it constitutes an integral part of the tax scale. All taxpayers are allowed a basic deduction, which in 1988 will amount to Skr 10,000 in the assessment for both national and local taxes.

Another kind of deduction is that granted as a credit against tax. Single parents with children are allowed a tax credit amounting to Skr 1,800. The same applies to families in which only one parent is gainfully employed. Tax credits are also granted for trade union dues up to a maximum of Skr 480.

A third type of deduction is for specific categories of needy persons. For example, retired persons entirely dependent on a national basic pension are entitled to an extra deduction, which in effect makes them exempt from tax altogether. An extra deduction is also granted to cover expenses in connection with sickness, but only to people with relatively low incomes.

A fourth kind of deduction concerns expenses incurred in connection with earnings. All expenses related to income from employment are in principle deductible under the heading "income from employment" in tax returns. Expenses for travel to and from work are one example. All those with an income from employment of over Skr 30,000 are entitled to a standard deduction of Skr 3,000 without specification. If a person's itemized expenses exceed this amount, the actual amount is deductible. There are, of course, also a large number of deductible expenses and allocations related to business activities that will not be discussed here.

Two additional deductions that can be made by all taxpayers and are not related to expenses incurred in connection with earnings apply to payments for private pension insurance policies with a value of up to approximately Skr 50,000 and maintenance paid to children not living with the parent in question, the maximum being Skr 3,000.

The largest deductions relate to interest expenses. These are generally deductible, but, as already noted, the 1983–85 tax reform has limited their value to some extent.

The above deductions, as well as others not mentioned here, are, of course, justifiable in each particular case. There are, nonetheless, a number of problems connected with the generous opportunities for making deductions. One of these is that they entail a considerable loss of tax revenue—several tens of billions of kronor—to the national and local authorities. Another problem is that deductions relating to interest expenses, which are the major type of deduction, encourage people to incur debts and consume on credit. Few countries, in fact, have as generous regulations in this respect as Sweden. Another problem is that many deductions counteract an equitable distribution of wealth. The opportunities afforded by the tax system tend to be utilized mainly by people with high incomes, plenty of money, and access to tax experts. The effect of progressive tax rates is largely canceled out by deductions for interest expenses that in most cases give rise to deficits deductible from other income. There is a correlation between high tax rates and the generous scope of deductions. Many deductions have come into existence, or at least have been utilized on a large scale, in response to high tax rates. There has been no alternative to accepting extensive deductions as a means of moderating the unreasonable consequences of high tax rates in certain cases.

LACK OF NEUTRALITY

One of the most characteristic features of the Swedish tax system is the lack of neutrality and uniformity. Incomes from different sources are taxed differently. Even incomes from the same source may be treated differently depending on whether the taxpayer is a private individual, a corporation, a foundation, or an insurance company, and so on. Private individuals tend to be taxed more heavily than institutions.

Another feature is that work is taxed more heavily than capital, both in the case of private individuals and corporations. Capital invested or accumulated in a corporation is taxed at a low rate compared with labor. True enough, the tax rate on companies' taxable profits is fairly high, 52 percent at present, but the effective rate is usually less than half the nominal rate because of all the methods that can be used to reduce taxable profits by postponing taxation or reducing the tax base.

Many of the special regulations now in force were introduced to solve specific problems. The overall result has proved unsatisfactory; Sweden now has a complicated tax system with innumerable special regulations and exemptions. In consequence, it has become increasingly common for taxpayers to make deliberate use of the lack of uniformity for the purpose of reducing their total tax burden. This tax planning is practiced mainly by the wealthy, who possess the financial resources and expertise to use the tax system to their own advantage, and leads to a far from equitable distribution of wealth, as the following illustrations demonstrate.

A characteristic feature of the income tax system is the high tax payable on earned income and certain kinds of capital income (interest and stock dividends) and the low, and in some cases nonexistent, tax on other kinds of capital income. The tax on capital gains is generally rather low. Private individuals pay no tax on the income from certain favored forms of saving. Bank deposits (the commonest type of savings for many people with moderate incomes) are given unfavorable tax treatment, while private pension insurance premiums (mainly paid by high-income earners) have notable tax advantages. A common strategy is to transform earned or capital income, which is taxed at a high rate, into capital gains, on which the tax is low. One method, particularly common in the 1970s, was to purchase real estate with borrowed funds. Due to the high marginal tax rates and unlimited deductions, as much as 85 percent of the interest expenses could be passed on to other taxpayers. As property values rose, the assets could then be sold at a vast profit, which, because of the advantageous capital gains regulations, was liable to very little tax. Some of the very large fortunes that were amassed in Sweden in the past decade or so (including several in the billion-kronor class) were founded by this means.

The lack of uniformity is most marked with respect to taxation of capital gains and other income from capital. Taxation of nominal and real values, and in certain cases complete exemption from tax, are all mixed together in Sweden in an incomprehensible and sometimes apparently arbitrary manner. There is, for example, a purely nominal taxation of interest income and profits accruing from the sale of real estate when effected within four years of purchase. Profits accruing from the sale of real estate owned for a longer period are, however, adjusted for inflation. There are also a number of intermediate forms of taxation, for example, that are payable on the sale of stock. Finally, it should also be mentioned that profit accruing from the sale of personal property other than securities after five years of ownership is exempt from tax.

Borrowing is favored and saving is disadvantaged. Insufficient saving has been one of the Swedish economy's most serious problems since the mid-1970s. One symptom of this has been the chronic external deficit. Insufficient domestic saving has made it necessary to finance part of Sweden's investment with foreign borrowing. The situation has improved in recent years, but the lasting external surplus that is needed to start paying off foreign debt has not yet been achieved. In addition, increased saving is needed to finance the increase in investment that is necessary to generate future economic growth, thus providing a prospect of full employment and a higher standard of living.

Increased saving should, to a great extent, be achieved in the public sector, particularly in the national budget, because this is the major source of the deficits. A substantial improvement in public finances has, in fact, been achieved since 1982. But an increase in private saving is also desirable both from the point of view of the national economy and because it is good for households to have a nest egg.

The private saving ratio (the percentage of available income saved) dropped in the early 1980s from 3–4 percent to around zero. In the last few years the savings ratio has actually been negative; instead of saving, private individuals have, as a group, borrowed. This may seem surprising in view of the marked improvement in the climate for saving in recent years. Marginal tax rates have been reduced, and the tax value of deficit deductions has been restricted. As a result of reduced inflation, Sweden now has a high real rate of interest. Recently, moreover, the downward trend in real incomes has been reversed, thereby providing more money for private saving. Several measures have, in addition, been taken to encourage saving, such as exempting certain types of saving, with a ceiling of Skr 800 per month, from tax on the interest, and doubling the amount deductible from interest on other savings to Skr 1,600.

There may be several reasons why private saving, far from increasing, has continued to diminish. The increase in real incomes has not yet made up for the lean years following the mid-1970s, and households may consider it more important to satisfy their deferred needs than to save. Perhaps people simply need a few years to adjust to the improved conditions for saving. Another reason may be that, on the whole, the tax system still gives more favorable treatment to borrowing than to saving. With few exemptions, income from savings is taxed in full at the nominal value, with no allowance made for capital depreciation due to inflation. It has, therefore, been more profitable to finance the purchase of capital goods by borrowing instead of with savings.

Similarly, a combination of advantageous tax deductions and high inflation has generated large capital gains for many people who have taken loans to buy a house or tenant-owned apartment. Although the 1983–85 tax reform has restricted the tax benefit of deductible interest, most people still only pay about half of their interest expenses themselves.

The popularity of accounts that, as a result of the measures taken to encourage saving, provide tax-free interest is therefore understandable. However, these savings accounts have not necessarily increased the total volume of savings. Nothing prevents people from transferring other savings to these favored accounts in order to secure the concomitant tax benefits without any resulting increase in saving as a whole. It is even profitable to borrow money (and deduct the interest in the usual way) in order to invest in the favored savings accounts. This is just another example of so-called tax arbitraging, that is, the state (in reality other taxpayers) pays profits to people whose only effort consists in transferring funds from one account to another.

COMPLICATED REGULATIONS

The Swedish tax system is a reflection of a society that has become highly complex. There have certainly been good reasons for most of the special regulations that have been made to encourage some activities and discourage others, for example, to achieve a fair distribution of wealth, to close loopholes in the tax laws, and so on.

For a long time Sweden disregarded the drawbacks of adding new, complicated tax regulations to the existing system, which thus became increasingly incomprehensible. Only in recent years has serious attention been paid to the disadvantages of an excessively complicated tax system and significant efforts made to simplify it. The simplified income tax return is a good example of this.

There are many reasons for simplifying the tax system still further. People have a democratic right to demand a system that is reasonably simple and easy to understand. Otherwise many of them will have little chance of having a say in matters that have an important effect on their lives.

A complicated tax system leads to unnecessary bureaucracy and costs to society. A large administrative apparatus has had to be developed to apply the present tax regulations and enforce them. Even so, many errors are made because these regulations are difficult to apply and interpret, which in turn means additional work for tax authorities and taxpayers alike.

A complicated tax system leads to injustice. Only high-income earners can afford to hire experts and lawyers to help them derive the maximum profit from tax deductions and loopholes in the law. Complicated regulations are also subject to different interpretations, as a result of which taxpayers are not given uniform treatment. Despite the size of administration, its resources are not sufficient for effective tax control. Control is especially inadequate in the case of corporations and people whose incomes and wealth present a complex picture, while ordinary wage earners are checked in detail.

A complicated tax system is not likely to command public confidence. People suspect that the system is neither fair nor effective. Such suspicions may or may not be justified, but in any case they cause lack of confidence and risk low tax morale.

THE INCOME TAX COMMISSION

The Swedish government recently appointed a parliamentary commission to review the entire income tax system as it applies to private individuals. The commission is to submit its report by the end of 1988. According to its directives it is to make proposals designed to achieve the following:

—Lower and less progressive tax rates
—A broader tax base
—Uniform and fairer taxation of capital gains and other income from capital that stimulates increased saving and less debt incurrence

—A tax system that is as simple and comprehensible as possible
—A tax system that should last for a long time

Lower Tax Rates

The commission is to draft a new scale for a national income tax with lower tax rates. The tax scales in use so far have contained rather a large number of tax rates for different income brackets. Even small increases in income have, therefore, placed taxpayers in higher brackets. As mentioned earlier, the number of income tax brackets will have been reduced from fourteen in 1982 to four by 1988. The objective of a future tax scale should also be a small number of brackets, the result being a simple system without rapid escalation of the effects of marginal tax rates. A reduction of the highest total marginal tax rate from the present 75 percent to 60 percent has been advocated in the debate on this question. It has also been argued that the highest rate should apply only to the really high income group, which is not the case at present.

Broadening the Tax Base

Deductions become less important if tax rates are reduced, since they will no longer be so profitable. Limiting deductions and thus broadening the tax base will help finance at least part of the cost of lower tax rates. The regulations should be simplified as far as possible, and consideration should be given to the possibility of limiting deductions, the aim being to retain as few as possible. But there must, of course, be a balance between limiting deductions, on the one hand, and lowering tax rates, on the other, to ensure that the effect on taxpayers is not unreasonable.

The standard deduction allowed to all those with income from employment is at present 10 percent of income, with a maximum of Skr 3,000. Increasing this deduction from Skr 1,000 has simplified tax assessments considerably, since neither taxpayers nor the tax authorities now have to consider minor expenses. As the cost of travel to and from work and other expenses related to earnings rise, a growing number of wage earners will tend to have expenses in excess of the standard deduction. To retain the advantages of simplicity, it is reasonable to increase the standard deduction to keep pace with the increase in these expenses. This would, however, lead to a loss of tax revenue and be in conflict with the goal of broadening the tax base. A solution to this problem that is worth trying is to reduce the basic deduction substantially, or even abolish it, while raising the maximum standard deduction considerably. The proposal presented by the minister of finance in the spring of 1987 discussed an increase in the standard deduction for all wage earners to Skr 10,000.

Taxation of Income from Capital Gains and Yields

Amending the regulations applying to taxation of income from capital is an important element in an income tax reform. The purpose is to simplify the tax system, encourage a more efficient use of capital, reduce opportunities for planning, and, at the same time, make the system fairer.

The regulations concerning taxation of capital gains and other income from capital should be as uniform as possible in the future system. It is particularly important that the new regulations ensure neutral treatment of gains arising from the sale of houses and tenant-owned apartments. In addition, the difference in the taxation of capital gains and other income from capital and of income from work should be minimized. The new regulations should be more favorable to savings and less favorable to debt. Lastly, the changes should result in an increase of the revenue from taxes on capital gains and other income from capital.

In the present system, the imputed income from a one- or two-family dwelling comes under the heading "income from other real property." Profits arising from the sale of stock, real estate, and so on, come under "income from casual economic activities," while income consisting of interest and stock dividends is taxed as "income from capital." A possible model for uniform taxation of capital gains and other income from capital would be to treat all of these as one type of income. Interest expenses payable for loans on houses, including holiday houses, would thus be deducted from income from capital gains and other investment income. Capital gains and losses would likewise come under income from capital gains and investment income. In this solution all types of capital income and capital gains not connected with business activities would be taxed in the same way, that is, as income from capital.

Another central question relating to taxation of income from capital is the extent to which nominal or real values are to be taxed, in other words, whether the tax system is to take inflation into account. With a few exceptions, the present system does not do so. In an economy subject to inflation, however, part of the income from capital constitutes compensation for capital depreciation. If this part is taxed, as is the case today, taxation tends to discourage saving. The opposite holds for debt incurrence and deductions for interest expenses. Thus deductions can be made under the present system for the part of the interest that corresponds to depreciation of debts due to inflation.

These problems would be solved, to all intents and purposes, by taxation of real values, that is, the real income over and above inflation. Real income from capital could be taxed to its full value according to uniform principles. There are, however, several difficulties connected with full taxation of real values, for example, assessment of the real profit or income and the question of how to deal with negative real interest. There is a risk that the regulations in these respects would be very complex, difficult to apply, and incomprehensible to the individual taxpayer.

Another solution would be to tax only part of the income from capital and grant deductions for interest expenses to the same extent. This is a more standardized method of allowing for the consequences of inflation.

Regardless of the main principle decided on with respect to taxation of income from capital, it may still be necessary to find special solutions to certain problems. One such problem is taxation of income from capital gains on stock, for which a standardized routine should be considered.

A consistent system with uniform regulations governing taxation of income from capital would offer great advantages; it would, for example, encourage saving and counteract debt incurrence and tax planning. However, a prerequisite for a reform of the taxation of income from capital is that the increase in tax resulting from the limitation of deductions must be compensated for by lower tax rates or some other means.

A reform on these lines would tend to be especially hard on those who have rather large loans on their houses or tenant-owned apartments. It is not feasible to exclude the interest on such loans completely from the limitation of deductions. It would be wrong as a matter of principle to favor a certain type of debt in this way. It would, moreover, upset the system of uniform taxation of income from capital and complicate the relevant regulations. It would also cause considerable problems from the point of view of tax control, since loans that are ostensibly granted for the purchase of real estate can be used to finance private consumption of a quite different nature. To ensure that the effects of such a reform on the distribution of wealth are acceptable, measures may have to be taken in the field of housing and family policies.

Simpler Regulations

The fourth important element in a new tax system is simpler regulations. This is important not just because it simplifies administration; the most important aspect is an equitable distribution of wealth. A system, like that currently in force, under which those with the expertise, or the money to hire such expertise, can evade high taxes by getting round the various rules, is not acceptable. Simplifying the tax system is, therefore, not a mere question of technicalities. The tax system must be designed in a logical and consistent manner. It is important, especially in a country with high taxes, to have a system that taxpayers can accept as a means of financing the public sector. Simpler regulations are to be preferred, even if they do entail a certain amount of standardized routines.

CORPORATE TAXATION

Corporate taxation in Sweden is payable on net profits and is by and large based on nominal values. The tax rate on companies' taxable profits is fairly high, 52 percent at present, but the tax base is relatively narrow owing to the generous opportunities for allocating funds to various reserves. As a result, the effective rate of taxation, that is, the percentage of tax paid in relation to profits before allocations, is usually between 15 percent and 25 percent.

A traditional view holds that a combination of high nominal tax rates and a narrow tax base has certain advantages, but also creates problems. The system allows companies with large profits to finance continued expansion with deferred taxation. Moreover, various studies have shown that profitable companies with high growth rates pay less tax under this system.

During the first twenty to thirty years after the war, when a satisfactory and stable market structure prevailed, there was reason to stress the need of consolidating existing companies. The crisis in industry that occurred in the 1970s, and increasing uncertainty as to which industries and companies had best potential, created a new situation that showed up the shortcomings of the tax system in force. A system with a narrow tax base tends to trap profits in existing companies. As a result, mediocre projects may be realized by companies that are traditionally profitable, while more profitable projects never materialize because they emanate from newly established companies or ones that are not so profitable. A system with a narrow tax base can therefore be an obstacle to an optimal resource allocation.

This problem is aggravated by the difficulty of effectively taxing income from capital accumulated by a company's owners. Because of the low tax rate on companies' net profits and the fact that tax rates applying to interests and capital gains are lower than those applying to income from dividends, owners prefer to appropriate a company's profits in the form of capital gains rather than dividends. In Sweden this problem is, however, somewhat less serious owing to the special tax relief allowed for dividends at the corporate level, which enables corporations to deduct dividends from new capital issues.

Apart from the problem of efficiency in a system with a narrow tax base, like the present one, there are several other problems. First, this system leads to certain undesirable destabilizing effects, since the tax load is higher in recessions than in boom years. Second, there is a lack of equality in the taxation of income from work as against income from capital, the former being subject to higher rates. The existence of interest-free tax deferral in the narrow tax base system contributes to the variation in the tax load.

Steps have been taken in Sweden in the last few years to broaden the base for corporate taxation. Thus in 1984 restrictions were introduced on allocating funds to inventory reserves, at the same time as the nominal tax rate was somewhat reduced. In 1985 changes were made in the system of investment funds that had been in force for more than fifty years. Under this system, corporations can, in years with high profits, make deductible allocations to a corporation fund, while depositing a certain percentage of these assets in an interest-free account in the Bank of Sweden. The assets thus allocated can, following a decision by the authorities, be used for investment, during a recession for example. The changes made in 1985 in this system involved a reduction of the subsidies, the share of the fund to be deposited in the Bank of Sweden being raised from 50 percent to 75 percent. A further rise in this figure, to 100 percent, has now been announced.

Taxation of individual wage earners has not been the only subject under review. Since 1985 a government commission has been at work on a general review of corporate taxation. This work is to be completed by 1988. The commission is at present considering a proposal for a system with a substantially broader tax base combined with reduced tax rates. However, changing a system based on nominal values involves certain problems, such as the risk of greater susceptibility to inflation. The present opportunities for building up reserves provides some protection against inflation.

A broader tax base and lower tax rates are in line with developments elsewhere, and the Swedish economy is greatly dependent on other countries. It is therefore important that not only corporate rates but also the structure of the tax base not differ too much from those in other countries.

Discussion of corporate taxation is focused on taxation of incorporated companies, which is natural since they have a dominant role in industry for production, exports, employment, and so on. The government commission, however, is also concerned with taxation of the business income of individuals.

There are various requirements concerning tax regulations for the business income of individuals. It is generally accepted that the same rules should apply to taxation of this business income as apply to corporations. At the same time, it is considered desirable that self-employed persons should not have advantages not open to ordinary wage earners.

For this reason, it has been proposed that the finances of self-employed persons should be divided into two parts, private and business. The business part would be subject to a low rate of taxation, but when such a person withdrew funds for private consumption he or she would be liable for income tax in full. It has also been proposed that partnerships should be a separate tax category. The commission's goal is to consider, in a unified context, the future taxation of corporations, partnerships, and the business income of individuals, and to make relevant proposals.

INDIRECT TAXES

The indirect taxes levied by the state consist of a general sales tax—value-added tax—and special taxes on goods and services. The revenue from these taxes is substantial, representing almost 30 percent of all revenue from taxes and other charges.

The value-added tax (VAT) corresponds essentially to that in other Western European countries. It was introduced in 1969 and replaced a tax that was charged at the retail stage and had more or less the same scope as the present VAT. There were several reasons for replacing the former tax, one of which was the desire to avoid cumulative effects on investments in industry.

The present VAT is payable at a uniform rate of 19.0 percent of prices including tax, which is equivalent to 23.46 percent of the price of goods or services excluding tax. There is no variation in the tax rate, but in certain cases the tax is payable on a reduced basis. For example, the price of building contracts on which the tax is paid is reduced to 60 percent, and to 20 percent for land development in certain cases. There is no VAT on some goods and services, the most important area being energy, where excise duties are levied instead, for example, on electric power, oil, gas, carbon fuels, and other fuels.

An issue that has often been discussed is the VAT on foodstuffs. Most of the studies on this subject indicate that reducing the tax on foodstuffs involves technical complications. Nor would this have a great effect on the distribution of resources. Further, abolishing or reducing the tax on foodstuffs would lead to a greater administrative workload for both those liable to pay the tax and the tax authorities, and this in its turn would result in higher costs, control problems, and a probable loss of tax revenue. Increasing tax subsidies for food is an ineffective way of redistributing resources, since the support would not necessarily benefit those for whom it is intended. The government has decided instead to give direct support to the groups most in need of it, for example, by increasing children's allowances, which is a more effective instrument of redistribution policy.

The tax base for the VAT consists of more or less all commodities. The service sector is not subject to this tax to the same extent, and the relevant legislation specifies the services that are subject to taxation. Value-added tax covers about 60 percent of all private and public consumption.

Excise duties on goods and services, in addition to those on energy, are levied on the following: tobacco, alcoholic liquors, sound recordings and video cassettes, video tape recorders, charter tours, and advertising. There are also taxes on lotteries, horse racing and other forms of gambling, as well as taxation of road traffic in the form of excise duty on automobiles and motor vehicle taxes.

The intention now is to undertake a comprehensive review of indirect taxes. The government has appointed, in addition to the two commissions already mentioned, a government commission for this purpose. Its chief directives are to study how to broaden the tax base for value-added tax and make an assessment of the possibility of restricting or altering other indirect taxes. The goal with respect to the VAT is that it should be generally applicable and a neutral factor in competition between goods and services. The special regulations making the tax payable on a reduced basis in certain cases should be abolished, if possible. An evaluation is to be made of the consequences of making energy subject to the VAT. The directives also include special consideration of the the VAT systems in the European Community and other Nordic countries. The commission is expected to complete its work by the end of 1988.

NET WEALTH TAX

The regulations governing the existing Swedish net wealth tax are contained in a law dating from 1947. Taxation occurs once a year and is calculated on the basis of taxpayers' assets at the end of the year preceding the tax assessment. Those liable to tax are generally individuals resident in Sweden. Swedish corporations are not liable to this tax, since the stockholders are liable to tax on their holdings of stock in corporations.

Certain assets are exempt from tax, for example, pension insurance funds, other pension rights, personal property, and art and book collections. The reason in the latter case is the difficulty of control.

Assets liable to tax are usually taxed at their market value. In the case of real estate, the assessed value applies. Special tax relief is granted in valuing assets invested in a business enterprise or a farm, which are generally taxed at 30 percent of the estimated net value.

Private individuals pay tax on property valued at more than Skr 400,000. The tax rate rises with the value of their property: the minimum rate is 1.5 percent and the maximum, for property valued at over Skr 1.8 million, is 3.0 percent. Married couples and their children are taxed jointly. Taxation is limited by a special rule stipulating that the sum total of income tax and net wealth tax shall not exceed 75 percent of a person's taxable income.

INHERITANCE TAX AND GIFT TAX

Inheritance tax in Sweden is calculated on the share of an estate left to each heir and is based on the data in the estate inventory. Assets are valued in basically the same way as for net wealth tax, that is, they are generally taxed at a conservative estimate of their market value. The reduced valuation of business and farm assets also applies in the case of inheritance tax.

If a deceased person was married, the estate is first divided so as to give the surviving spouse half of their joint property free of tax. Before calculation of the tax, standard deductions are made from each share of the estate. For a surviving spouse this deduction will, after January 1, 1988, amount to Skr 200,000. The deduction for children of the deceased is Skr 50,000. The tax rates vary depending on the relationship between the deceased and the heirs. They are lower in the case of close relatives—spouse and children—than other heirs. The tax is progressive. For close relatives the highest rate, payable on the value of their share exceeding Skr 8 million, is 60 percent. The highest rate for other heirs is 65 percent and is payable on the value of shares over Skr 2 million.

In addition to the inheritance tax there is a general gift tax that is similar in essentials. The regulations concerning valuation and tax rates are thus the same, but the basic deduction is limited to Skr 2,000. The tax is based on special gift declarations that the recipients are obliged to submit.

ORGANIZATION, CONTROL, AND SANCTIONS

Administration of Sweden's taxes is a government responsibility exercised by the Ministry of Finance. Tax administration is supervised by the National Tax Board, whose board of directors includes laymen in order to provide the possibility of control and influence for nonspecialists. The National Tax Board exercises supervision in many different ways. In some cases its role is equivalent to that of legislator in that it issues mandatory regulations even in matters subject to legislation. Its main task, however, is to give advice and make recommendations in cases where it is necessary to ensure uniform application of the law. These are mainly addressed to subordinate authorities, in particular the twenty-four county tax boards responsible to the board for tax administration in counties.

There are 120 tax offices at the local level. The regional and local authorities perform most of the actual work of taxation, but the National Tax Board is the taxation authority in charge of the majority of excise duties, such as the duties on energy and tobacco. Decisions relating to the assessment of income tax and net wealth tax are made by assessment boards, which act independently of the authorities and whose members are elected. In the future, however, these decisions too will be made by the tax authorities. The number of tax officials is at present about 12,000.

The tax system is primarily based on the information provided by taxpayers and third parties. Returns must be filed every year with respect to income tax and net wealth tax. About 7.0 million tax returns are filed each year, out of a total population of about 8.5 million. Third parties are also obliged to submit information. Employers, those who make pension payments, and others must notify the authorities of salaries and pensions paid. The same obligation was introduced a year ago for stock dividends and for banks and financial institutions, for interest payments. In addition, the tax authorities can in special cases request information from third parties, for example, from entrepreneurs for payments to and from other entrepreneurs.

The tax authorities are authorized to carry out certain checks on the accuracy of the information submitted. For instance, a tax charge office may audit an employer's accounts to check whether the information relating to salaries paid to employees is correct and complete. The authority to carry out such audits is, however, primarily the prerogative of the regional tax boards, and the main object of the checks is the information given by companies about their economic circumstances.

Legal proceedings can be instituted to punish those who furnish incorrect information, but this normally occurs only in cases of serious offenses against tax regulations. In the last few years, about 1,500 persons a year have been convicted of tax offenses. The penalty in these cases is usually payment of a fine. The most frequent penalty incurred for supplying incorrect information on income tax returns, however, is the imposition by the tax authorities of additional tax in the form of an administrative fee. This is based on the tax that would have been evaded had the authorities accepted the incorrect information. This additional tax amounts to 20 percent or 40 percent of the sum involved, depending on the circumstances. No extra tax is charged if there are mitigating circumstances, for example, if the taxpayer is inexperienced or if the amount in question is small. A decision concerning additional tax, like any other decision relating to tax assessment, can be appealed to a court of law. Additional tax is charged in about 40,000 cases every year.

SUMMARY

Sweden is currently engaged in intense activity in the field of tax policy, and the entire tax system is under review. This may result in the near future in a radical reform of the system, which will in that case be based on principles of lower tax rates, a broader tax base, great symmetry, and simplicity.

The tax reforms shortly to be proposed must be financed in a responsible manner. Therefore, Sweden cannot anticipate an appreciably lower tax burden in the immediate future. Obviously, it is not possible to reduce taxes without simultaneously undertaking major reductions in public expenditure, which would cause a risk of serious adverse effects on redistribution policies.

By some time in the 1990s, Sweden is likely to have greater flexibility, provided that it has succeeded in eliminating the budget deficit and balance has been restored to the national economy as a whole. It should then be possible to discuss the desirability of increasing expenditures in order to finance various social reforms or whether it would be preferable to reduce taxes instead. It would, however, be pointless to embark on such a discussion at present.

Comment by LEIF MUTÉN

The most remarkable feature of the Swedish tax system is the extremely high ratio of taxes to GDP. The 50.5 percent mentioned in Claes Ljungh's paper is at the top of the list of countries in the OECD statistics for 1985. The ratio probably rose even further in 1987, possibly as high as 55 percent.

Ljungh has rightly made the point that this tax ratio is being criticized as too high. In an international context, I don't think anybody would disagree. But it is somewhat disturbing to find that so little is said about government efforts to bring about a reduction. Even after the tax reform now under discussion, signs are clear that Sweden will remain at, or close to, the top of the OECD list. Reform, of course, involves difficult political decisions. In the context of a technical discussion, suffice it to say that maintaining this kind of a tax ratio poses a challenge to reformers.

Contrary to what might have been expected, Sweden, while topping the tax ratio list, does not claim a similar high position in tax evasion and fraud. The late professor Gunnar Myrdal exclaimed in despair a few years ago that the tax system had made a "people of cheaters" out of the once law-abiding Swedes. All available studies so far, however, seem to show that the underground economy, tax evasion, and fraud, while certainly important problems, are still well within the limits of what is typical in countries with much lower tax pressure than that of Sweden.[1] While it would be naive to assume that tax

1. U. Laurin, *På heder och samvete: skattefuskets utbredning* (Stockholm: Norstedts, 1986), presents an interesting study as well as an account of results found by others.

evasion is unrelated to the tax ratio, it is simplistic to see the tax ratio as the only, or even the main, element influencing the rate of tax evasion.

Perhaps the apparently low rate of evasion in Sweden is explained by traditional respect for the law. Furthermore, Swedish law provides for rigorous control of taxpayers. Another explanation is the remarkably widespread acceptance of the way public monies are spent. Frugality rather than conspicuous consumption is the order of the day for the royal family as well as for political leaders. The main elements of the welfare state are widely accepted. Although Swedes may not necessarily agree on how the services are organized, they generally agree that government should care for the needs of the sick, the old, children, and the unemployed. Even an expenditure category such as foreign aid is hardly an issue in Sweden. In fact the percentage of GDP spent on foreign aid is almost four times greater than that of the United States and, to a much larger extent than is true of the United States, goes through international organizations. And defense appropriations, while contested, can hardly fuel any hot debate about their tax implications, given that the party most against taxes is also most in favor of higher defense expenditure.

A high level of taxation presupposes a high degree of fairness in the system. Fairness, of course, lies in the eyes of the beholder. The Swedish taxpayer is confronted not only with his own tax return form but with more information on his fellow citizen's tax situation than is usually available in other countries. Tax reform efforts in recent years have gone far in establishing rules against zero-assessment of well-to-do taxpayers. Those assessments do not sit well with the taxpaying public.

On the other hand, in the eternal conflict between simplicity and equity, the trend is toward greater simplicity at the expense of equity. I might be wrong, but my impression from assessment work back in the 1950s, as well as from casual contacts with Swedish taxpayers in later years, is that the man in the street in Sweden is rather fond of his deductions and thinks they suggest a system geared toward just and equitable treatment of all. My misgiving is that by going too far in the direction of standard deductions, tax-free amounts, and rough rules for the evaluation of fringe benefits, the tax legislator may well teach taxpayers the wrong lesson: that small amounts really do not matter that much. If they don't, then how can Sweden make taxpayers report them as income? Yet as the tax administration strives to satisfy one taxpayer's claim for justice, another taxpayer sees the administration as delving into ridiculous detail, or, even worse, snooping into areas that should be respected as private.

But progress is inexorable. We must assume that it is progress when the trouble of filling out the yearly tax return is taken away from the great number of taxpayers, even if it is at the price of some equity being sacrificed to simplification. Sweden is particularly well suited for a fully automatic individual tax system; the taxpayer identity number that follows every Swede from the cradle to the grave is available virtually everywhere. (The law-abiding Swedes accept without noticeable complaint that personal checks are embossed with the ID number, even though the number starts with six digits revealing the birthday of the holder.) The population is completely and currently registered. Hence nonfiling is a minor problem.

The present review of the whole tax system has started on a promising note. The shock wave from the United States has hit Sweden forcefully. The general approach taken in the 1986 U.S. tax reform has gained broad acceptance in principle, though with a much more prudent approach to slashing the tax rates.[2] It is extraordinary to find in Ljungh's paper such references to broad agreement among the minister's proposals, the Liberal party program, and the trade union proposals. Ljungh could have achieved an even stronger effect by including the reform program presented by the academic trade union as well as the program for business tax reform submitted this year by the Federation of Swedish Industry. He could then have indicated not only that the commissions now preparing the tax reform envisaged for 1989 are multipartisan—that is par for the course—but that important technical studies have been commissioned from leading spokesmen of party and industrial groupings outside the government circles.

In his discussion about deductions, Ljungh should perhaps have

2. For an illustration of the need for lower rates see, Deloitte Haskins and Sells, *Taxation of International Executives* (Boston: Kluwer Law and Taxation, 1985). In a comparison among twenty-one host countries of an employer's cost of keeping an expatriate with $30,000 net income, housing, car, and two children in a local international school, the cost usually did not go much higher than $100,000, except for Sweden, where the cost was $237,400.

mentioned that interest deductions are a problem in Sweden, even though Sweden, in contrast to most countries around the world, imposes income tax on the imputed value of the taxpayer's residence. However, in the opinion of most experts, the evaluation of that imputed income is on the low side, at least for less expensive homes. An interest deduction is also available for consumption credits that have nothing to do with the cost of the taxpayer's residence.

In connection with the opportunities for tax arbitrage (that is, giving income from capital a form that defers tax or avoids it altogether), the interest deductions have been intensely discussed. Part of this examination refers to indexation, but even under the assumption that the system is based on nominal values, arguments can be advanced for a more restrictive attitude than exists now. Some experts argue in favor of a more comprehensive tax on all income from capital, including capital gains, and possibly dealing with some or all cases of tax deferral. Other experts argue that since, at least for individuals, net income from capital on balance is negative, with interest deductions exceeding taxable gross income, excluding all capital income items from the tax base, positive as well as negative, would be a rational approach.

But that approach is probably not acceptable. Tax arbitrage can take more than one form, and the prospect of wealthy taxpayers relabeling their corporate salaries to represent loan interest, to cite just one example, is not appealing.

It is certainly true that the relatively favorable treatment of capital gains has been an incentive to invest in property with growth prospects. Such investments are made with the intention of offsetting the fully deductible interest expense by a capital gain, the tax on which is deferred until realization and mitigated by favorable treatment of such gains. (Incidentally, these provisions are not as liberal as Ljungh says: The gains on personal property that are tax exempt after five years of ownership do not include gains on securities nor those on condominiums.) Yet the general level of taxation makes it questionable whether the system can take such a drastic change as to equalize capital gains with ordinary income. On this question, Sweden might learn from the United States, where the capital gains tax rates will be the same as the rates on ordinary income. The top U.S. capital gains rate—28 percent in 1987 and 33 percent beginning in 1988—represents less than half of the present Swedish top rate.

This may indicate that a sweeping change such as the abolition of separate treatment for capital gains may work in a low-rate setting but may create serious problems in a system with high rates.

Ljungh's paper states quite properly that the household saving ratio in Sweden is low. Whether an improvement can be achieved by a higher tax on capital gains and abolishing other features aimed at promoting saving is a big question. Perhaps Ljungh should have included some reflections on the special once-and-for-all levy on pension insurance funds, aimed at soaking up their excessive interest accumulations during the high-interest years around 1980. Or he might have mentioned the special corporation tax deduction now allowed over a limited period of time to build up the "wage-earner funds." This is a half-hearted appropriation of corporate funds to establish an institutionalized participation in corporate ownership on behalf of wage earners. It can be argued that both provisions, by changing the rules under which investors took out their pension insurance or invested in corporate stock, had a disincentive effect. Needless to say, the extremely high yield of the pension funds and the remarkable development of the Stockholm stock exchange may well be attributed to special incentives, though not of the fiscal kind. But in the face of recent stock market developments and the reductions in interest rates, it could be argued that savers in Sweden have received mixed signals.

This issue takes on particular significance because the social security system in Sweden faces a difficult situation. From the early 1960s, the system, although basically a redistribution system rather than a funded system, built up larger reserves, thus compensating for the relatively low household saving ratio. At present, the overcompensation to the older generation, in combination with the maturity of the system, makes it difficult to achieve any accumulation at all in the system. If accumulation is ensured by increasing the social security tax, the dangerously high wedge between net wage income and employers' cost will become even greater. If the loss of savings must be made up elsewhere, the household saving ratio becomes even more important than before.

Some recent proposals presented to the Swedish public have emulated the U.S. reform because some people foresee a shifting of the tax burden from individuals to corporations. The paper by the Federation of Swedish Industry does not support the idea of greater taxation on corporations, however. Instead, the paper suggests a drastic curtailment of the whole panoply of special investment funds, stock valuation rules, and other gimmicks in favor of a much lower corporate tax rate (to be reduced from 52 percent to 25 percent). Some Swedes say that by offering the abolition of all the incentives, the federation has invited the government to broaden the corporate tax base, but without paying the price in the form of a lower tax rate. Others feel, however, that the recommendation for lower corporate tax rates is realistic. At this stage, it is difficult to predict the outcome. However, I must confess that I feel a bit awkward since I was an enthusiastic supporter of the Swedish system at the 1963 conference on foreign tax policies and economic growth, sponsored by the National Bureau of Economic Research and the Brookings Institution. The system that I and other Swedish experts were bragging about is now on the verge of being scrapped. Is this just another swing of the pendulum? Will a new generation of tax policymakers rediscover all the old gimmicks and reestablish a system with high rates and full of such loopholes as investment reserves, accelerated depreciation, stock valuation reliefs, and the like?[3]

At any rate, it is interesting that the Swedish authorities are apprehensive about the influence of tax rules on the choice of legal form for businesses. The present U.S. trend toward partnerships has not gone unnoticed. And while certainly not new, the idea of a uniform business income tax, with private owners held liable on their withdrawals of funds from business just as they would be liable to income tax on dividends, has much to speak for it, although the technical implications are most complicated.[4]

I shall not say much about indirect taxes. The VAT functions reasonably well, and Nordic cooperation does not indicate that any revolutionary steps are needed; the destination country will impose

3. See Leif Mutén and Karl-Olof Faxén, "Sweden," in National Bureau of Economic Research, *Foreign Tax Policies and Economic Growth* (New York: NBER, 1966), p. 341. For a recent positive evaluation, see Sven Steinmo, "So What's Wrong with Tax Expenditures? A Reevaluation Based on Swedish Experience," *Public Budgeting and Finance*, vol. 6 (Summer 1986), pp. 27–44.

4. The idea—a tax called Betriebsteuer—was developed by Conrad Boettcher in 1949. It was discussed in a parliamentary committee and dismissed as impractical. It was, however, cited as an inspiration for later measures to integrate the corporate tax with the tax on shareholders.

the final tax, as is now the case. As for taxes on gambling, it is interesting that Ljungh calls them indirect taxes. Historically, they have been imposed in lieu of income taxes on winnings. A low tax of 20 percent to 30 percent levied at the source is much less of a discouragement to official gambling than the full income tax. I take it that the people running state lotteries in the United States would envy their Swedish colleagues.

The net wealth tax does not raise much revenue. The exemption of such items as antiques, art, and stamps is necessary for administrative reasons, but it is a most unfortunate disincentive to productive investment. Valuation is difficult, and the need for a ceiling at 75 percent of income reveals the negative effect of the tax.

The excellent quality of Ljungh's paper, the fine tradition of Swedish government commissions, especially in the tax field, and the open mind with which the minister of finance and his staff have approached reform promise that the commission reports, when they are available by the end of 1988, will make interesting reading. Having said that, I fear that adapting the Swedish system to current international trends, however necessary to maintain international competitiveness, prevent brain drain, and keep tax compliance at a reasonable level, will pose a formidable task for reformers, if the tax ratio must remain unchanged. Luckily, the Swedes have been good at making compromises. That talent will be in considerable demand next year.

IAN C. R. BYATT

United Kingdom

Tax policy is an element in the approach to economic policy adopted by government. Hence it is not surprising that the whole direction of tax policy in the United Kingdom in the 1980s has changed significantly, compared with the dominant approach of the 1960s and 1970s. In the 1960s and 1970s, tax policy was concerned with conjunctural policy (demand management), with achieving a "better" distribution of income, and with devising incentives to correct market failures and to intervene selectively to increase the growth of productive potential. In the last category, the United Kingdom had a selective employment tax to encourage employment in manufacturing rather than in services and a whole series of experiments with incentives designed to raise the level of investment. During the 1970s these investment incentives were changed from investment grants to allowances against tax—but they remained devices to encourage investment in physical capital, especially in plant and machinery.

The changes in the economic environment that took place during the 1970s—and the progressive recognition of these changes—have led to a different approach to economic policy, which has been reflected in taxation policy. The problems of the 1970s, including the increase in public expenditure against a background of slow growth and poor economic performance, led to a rise in the tax burden and concern about the damage this was doing to the performance of markets, particularly with the adverse effects on take-home pay and work incentives. The burden was exacerbated by the interaction between higher tax rates and other economic policies, for example, the effect that pay policy had in squeezing pretax differentials in earnings.

I am grateful for help from numerous colleagues in both the Treasury and the Inland Revenue. I am particularly grateful to Geoffrey Smith, Robert Weeden, Michael Johns, Ian Scotter, and Mark Courtney.

The reemergence of concern for market efficiency goes wider than tax reform. This is not the occasion for an exposition of general economic policy. But tax reform is one instrument of microeconomic policy. And, in this context, the main message is the need to strengthen market mechanisms and to allow markets to work more freely.

At a wider level of social as well as economic policy, there has been a strong desire by the government to leave people with "more of their own money." While I shall talk particularly about economic issues, one should not underestimate the wider social objectives behind the changes that have been made.

CHANGES SINCE 1979

First, let me run quickly through the main changes made in the last eight years, looking first at the abolitions, reductions, and simplifications of taxes that have taken place and then at measures to improve the workings of specific markets:

—Some taxes, for example, the investment income surcharge, the national insurance surcharge, and the development land tax, have been abolished. Capital transfer tax has been reformed and renamed inheritance tax following the abolition of the charge to tax on lifetime gifts.

—Some tax rates have been greatly reduced. The basic rate of income tax was reduced from 33 percent to 30 percent in 1979 with the long-term aim of a reduction to 25 percent. The rate has been subsequently reduced to 27 percent. The maximum income tax rate on earned income was reduced from 83 percent to 60 percent in 1979. Income tax thresholds have been raised in successive budgets and are now 22 percent higher in real terms than in 1979. Since 1982 capital gains have been indexed (modified in 1985) before being charged to capital gains tax (CGT); since 1985 the threshold for CGT has also been indexed. Capital transfer tax, now inheritance tax, has been made less onerous; the threshold has been raised by 360 percent since 1979, the top rate reduced from 75 percent to 60 percent, and the number of rate bands reduced from fourteen to four. Stamp duty on transactions in shares has been reduced from 2.0 percent to 0.5 percent.

—Some taxes have been restructured, sometimes substantially.

Within personal tax, a substantial switch from income tax to value-added tax (VAT) occurred in 1979; the VAT rose from 8 percent and 12 percent to 15 percent, and there were modest extensions of the VAT base in 1984 and 1985. Business taxation was reformed in 1984. Capital allowances were restructured, and the rate of mainstream corporation tax reduced from 52 percent to 35 percent over a period of three years. Contributions to the national insurance fund were restructured in 1985 by reducing employers' and employees' contribution rates for lower-paid workers and abolishing the ceiling (known as the upper earnings limit) on employers' contributions. Taxes on oil production have been adjusted to take account of the substantial changes in the oil market since 1979.

—Some elements in the tax system have been simplified. Relief and deduction at source have made taxation easier for individuals. The arrangements whereby companies make returns for corporation tax will be simplified and streamlined in the 1990s. The United Kingdom has taken measures to reduce the burden of the VAT on small businesses.

—Schemes to encourage noninstitutional savings and enterprise have been introduced—the business expansion scheme, share options, personal equity plans, and the tax arrangements for occupational (employer-run final salary) pensions have been extended to personal (that is, portable, money purchase) pensions. Income tax relief on life assurance premiums was withdrawn in 1984.

—Changes have been made to improve the operation of financial markets. The tax treatment of deposit interest paid by banks and building societies has been aligned. The tax treatment of U.K. corporate bonds has been broadly aligned with that of government securities.

—A scheme for tax relief for profit-related pay is being introduced to encourage the flexibility of pay and the identification of workers with the performance of the firm who employs them. It should improve the operation of the labor market and help to deal with what is perhaps the most serious problem in the running of the British economy.

Complementary measures in social security legislation have changed the arrangements for the withdrawal of means-tested benefits. In particular, beginning in 1988, a combined rate of tax and benefit withdrawal of over 100 percent will no longer exist.

The government recently published a report with suggestions for reforming the taxation of husband and wife.[1] It is planning to introduce a community charge that will replace domestic rates (the local domestic property tax) and reform nondomestic rates (on business property) by applying a uniform national rate.[2] But these changes have still to be implemented.

The structural changes have taken place over a period when taxes have been changed for macroeconomic reasons. In the early 1980s aggregate taxation, as a percentage of gross domestic product (GDP), rose rather than fell. Although the government wanted to reduce taxation, it gave first priority to reducing the fiscal deficit. More recently, as public expenditure has fallen as a percentage of GDP, reducing taxation and the fiscal deficit have become possible.

CRITERIA

In this talk, I want to look at these changes analytically. What threads have run through these measures? What criteria have guided action?

The changes have several objectives—simplification, reduction of administrative and compliance costs, distributional consequences, and other aims. I propose to concentrate on the issue of economic efficiency.

The general objective has been to enable markets to work better by reducing distortions caused by the tax system. This aim contrasts with the approach of the 1960s and 1970s, which was to use tax (and other) interventions to correct what was perceived as a market failure. One should not exaggerate matters. Market failures have not disappeared. But the adverse consequences of intervention have also become apparent. The onus of proof has shifted sharply; markets have to be clearly demonstrated rather than presumed inefficient, and the many disadvantages of intervention have to be considered.

This is closely parallel to the philosophy of the level playing field or, perhaps I should say, a more level playing field—a concern to remove the bumps and fill in the hollows in what has become over

1. Cmnd. 9756, *The Reform of Personal Taxation* (London: Her Majesty's Stationery Office [HMSO], 1986).

2. British Department of the Environment, *Paying for Local Government: The Community Charge* (London: Department of the Environment, 1986).

the passage of time some pretty rough land, ploughed in a number of different directions. Absolute flatness is scarcely attainable; but departures from it should be carefully justified.

In considering tax reform, the United Kingdom has been much concerned with the "high ground" of ideal tax systems. Following the Meade report on the British tax system, a lively academic debate has occurred in the United Kingdom on the relative merits of an expenditure rather than an income base for the taxation of individuals and companies.[3] While this debate has illuminated issues in several areas, for example, company tax and the taxation of savings, it has not made a practical contribution to reform. The British tax system is a hybrid of income and expenditure tax bases, and Britain has found it more useful to direct attention to reducing the major distortions within a hybrid system. This has involved concentration on equalizing the tax treatment of activities that are close substitutes for each other.

I propose to evaluate the measures taken against five headings:
—Work incentives (more generally, incentives to effort)
—Business capital formation
—Employment and the labor market
—Stimulus to enterprise
—Financial markets

WORK INCENTIVES

Table 1 shows the changes in marginal tax rates for different income bands between 1978–79 and 1987–88. Have these reductions in marginal rates affected the supply of labor—or effort? As everyone knows, there is no easy answer.

Economic analysis has been primarily directed to the effect of taxation on hours of work in existing jobs and its short-term effect on participation in the labor force. There has been a certain amount of empirical work in this area in the United Kingdom in recent years. This work shows results that are consistent with U.S. work. Large

3. *The Structure and Reform of Direct Taxation: Report of a Committee Chaired by J. E. Meade* (London: Allen and Unwin for the Institute for Fiscal Studies, 1978).

TABLE 1. *Marginal Tax Rates, 1978–79 and 1987–88*

Marginal income tax rates	Annual income (pounds)[a]	
	1978–79[b]	*1987–88*
0	0–3,200	0–3,800
25	3,201–4,800	. . .
27	. . .	3,801–21,700
33	4,801–19,900	. . .
40	19,901–22,000	21,701–24,200
45	22,001–24,100	24,200–29,200
50	24,101–26,200	29,200–37,100
55	26,201–29,400	37,100–45,000
60	29,401–32,600	50,000 and over
65	32,601–36,800	
70	36,801–42,100	
75	42,101–53,600	
83	53,611 and over	

a. For a married man.
b. Tax bands indexed to 1987–88 levels.

effects for men (and single women) are not found, although the short-run supply elasticity seems significantly greater for married women.[4]

But the short-term consequences for labor supply are only part of the story and indeed play a relatively minor part in the consideration of most governments. Large substitution effects, even if offset by large income effects, imply significant interference in the working of markets. And the government is more concerned with the longer-term consequences of high marginal tax rates on people's willingness to be enterprising, take personal risks, undertake training, and be prepared for work that is demanding and stressful. High marginal tax rates also encourage avoidance—an industry of its own—and evasion. In an increasingly international labor market, especially for highly qualified people, marginal tax rates can influence the decision

4. Richard Blundell and Ian Walker, "A Life-Cycle Consistent Empirical Model of Family Labour Supply Using Cross-Section Data," *Review of Economic Studies*, vol. 53 (August 1986), pp. 539–58.

to stay in or return to the United Kingdom. In this context, it is relevant to report that net emigration of managerial and professional talent has now become net immigration.[5]

In the longer term, the cumulative effects of high tax rates on these factors can be pervasive. In the current state of knowledge, these more Schumpeterian aspects of taxation may be matters more for judgment than for technical analysis, but that does not make them any less important. They are important elements in the policies designed to revitalize the enterprise economy.

Interestingly, in Britain, as in the United States, reductions in top rates of income tax have been accompanied by an increase in the share of income tax paid by top-rate taxpayers. For example, in 1978–79, 24 percent of income tax was paid by the top 5 percent of taxpayers; by 1986–87, the figure had risen to 28 percent. The tax changes have been associated with significant changes in the distribution of factor income—profits have risen faster than earnings—and in the distribution of earnings, higher salaries have risen faster than those of workers generally. One reason why there are more high incomes is that it has become more worthwhile to pay, earn, and declare such incomes, and to set up business or otherwise work in the United Kingdom.

The highest marginal tax rates—if the marginal rate of withdrawal of means-tested benefits is included—are found in the bottom part of the income distribution. Here we find the poverty trap and the unemployment trap. But although the issue is acute for those affected, the total numbers involved are small; on an entitlement basis, only 1 percent to 2 percent of families face combined marginal tax and benefit withdrawal rates of above 70 percent, and only 2 percent to 4 percent have replacement ratios (net income out of work in relation to net income in work) above 80 percent.

In this complex area, action is caught between the conflicting objectives of reducing poverty and avoiding disincentives to work, and policy has sought to achieve a balance between objectives rather than concentrate on reducing disincentives for work. But the following steps have been taken to improve incentives:

—Raising tax allowances in real terms (British income tax starts at

5. Kent Matthews and Patrick Minford, "Mrs Thatcher's Economic Policies, 1979–87," *Economic Policy*, no. 5 (October 1987), pp. 57–92.

27 percent) has significantly reduced marginal tax rates for some of those in the poverty and unemployment traps.

—The reform of social security announced in 1985—and coming into operation in 1988—will reduce maximum marginal rates.[6] Because benefit will be related to income after payment of tax and national insurance contributions rather than before it, marginal tax rates of above 100 percent will disappear. These two changes interact; future increases in tax thresholds will float out people from the top of the traps by raising their posttax incomes rather than reducing significantly the marginal tax rates of those deep in the poverty trap.

—Some employees' national insurance contributions have been reduced by the introduction of lower contribution rates for low-paid workers.

BUSINESS CAPITAL FORMATION

The main interest here is the taxation of fixed investment. The pre-1984 system of business taxation—essentially a high rate of corporation tax combined with high initial allowances for some, but not all, investment—led to the following:

—Subsidization, through the tax regime, of investment in plant and machinery and industrial buildings, stimulating the quantity of investment at the expense of its quality. Investment with low pretax rates of return was made profitable by the tax system, and investment in some sectors, for example, manufacturing, was encouraged at the expense of other sectors, for example, services.

—Subsidization of investment (combined with the taxation of labor) biased economic activity toward capital intensity and against employment at a time when unemployment was high.

—Very different tax treatment of different kinds of assets, financed in different ways. Investment in plant and machinery was subsidized, while investment in commercial building was taxed. Debt interest was fully allowable against tax, while dividends were subject to the imputation system and retentions taxed at the high corporate tax rate.

6. British Department of Health and Social Security, *Reform of Social Security*, vol. 1 (London: HMSO, 1985).

To show the extent of the differences that the arrangements for taxation made to the return to investment after tax, compared with the return before tax, it is possible to calculate a whole set of "tax wedges" (some analysts work in terms of effective tax rates) for specimen projects. It is also possible to show the consequences of tax reform on the size and distribution of these wedges.[7] Actual projects will be some combination of specimens.

The 1984 reform retained the overall structure of business taxation (the imputation system, with interest deductibility) but, in four stages, over a period of three years accomplished the following:

—Reduced the rate of mainstream corporation tax from 52 percent to 35 percent.

—Abolished the 100-percent first-year allowances for plant and machinery and replaced them with 25-percent per annum declining balance depreciation allowances.

—Abolished the 75-percent initial allowances for industrial buildings and replaced them with 4-percent per annum straight line depreciation allowances.

The consequences of reform for the tax wedges for specimen projects are shown in table 2. To construct such figures it is necessary to assume rates of return and rates of inflation. These figures assume a 10-percent nominal return posttax on capital and a 5-percent rate of inflation. Other assumptions are possible, and since the calculations were done, the nominal rate of return on capital has risen, and the inflation rate has fallen. But changes in assumptions would not destroy the main message shown in table 2, that is, the high dispersion of tax wedges before reform and the much lower dispersion afterward.

For example, table 2 shows that, under the regime in place before 1984, in order to give suppliers of finance a 5.0-percent real (that is, adjusted for inflation) return—after company tax, but before personal tax—on debt-financed investment in plant and machinery, it was only necessary to earn −0.2 percent before tax; that is, negative pretax returns were "made economic" by the tax system. By contrast it was necessary to earn 7.7 percent before tax on equity-financed commercial buildings in order to achieve a 5.0-percent return after

7. *Fourth Report from the Treasury and Civil Service Committee: The 1984 Budget*, House of Commons Paper 341, sess. 1983–84 (London: HMSO, 1984), app. 10.

TABLE 2. *Pretax Returns Needed to Earn Five-Percent Real Return,*
Net of Company Tax, Pre-1984 and Postreform

Investment category	Debt finance	Equity finance	Retained profit finance
Pre-1984 (5-percent inflation)			
Plant and machinery	−0.2	2.0	5.0
Industrial buildings	−0.1	2.2	5.5
Commercial buildings	3.2	7.7	13.9
Postreform (5-percent inflation)			
Plant and machinery	2.5	3.1	6.7
Industrial buildings	2.7	3.4	7.7
Commercial buildings	4.1	4.8	9.4
Postreform (zero inflation, 25-percent personal tax rate)			
Plant and machinery	3.9	4.5	6.0
Industrial buildings	4.3	5.0	6.8
Commercial buildings	4.7	7.5	9.4

tax. After the 1984 reforms, these figures became 2.5 percent and 4.8
percent, respectively. The wedge on debt-financed plant and machinery projects was raised by 2.7 percent and that on equity-financed
commercial building projects was reduced by 2.9 percent. Table 2
also shows what the wedges would be if there were no inflation and
if the basic rate of income tax were 25 percent.

Analysis by specimen projects is less than fully satisfactory. All
actual projects will be some combination of these rates of return. But
there are problems with any attempt to construct weights. There are
the usual information and index number problems. The latter is acute
when substantial changes in incentives—and therefore potentially in
behavior—are involved. The advantage of showing specimens is that
they can illustrate the detailed changes in incentives facing decisionmakers in many different situations.

Inventories

The 1984 reform also changed the taxation of inventory gains. In
1974, during the course of the profit crisis that followed the events
linked with the fivefold increase in oil prices in 1973, a system of

stock relief was introduced. Before 1981 the relief was given on the increase in the value of a business's stocks, subject to a profits restriction. After 1981 the system was reformed to limit relief to inflationary gains, even though tax relief was allowable on the interest costs of holding stocks. This system was abolished in 1984. In fact U.K. stock and output ratios rose over the period 1974–80 but have declined continuously since that date, and the evidence suggests that the 1981 rather than the 1984 reform had more impact on stock holding behavior.[8]

Other Assets

Under the post-1984 system, spending on intangible assets such as research and development (R&D) and training, which typically is counted as current rather than capital spending (and thus "expensed"), remains favored relative to other assets. The 100-percent first-year allowance for capital spending on scientific research assets remains in place. However, as a recent (1987) Inland Revenue-Treasury paper, *Fiscal Incentives for R&D Spending*, has indicated, the tax treatment of R&D in the United Kingdom is broadly in line with most of the other major industrial countries.[9]

Interaction with Economic Developments

Not only did the pre-1984 system of business taxation bias the choice of asset and method of finance, but it also produced some odd consequences because of the way it had interacted with changes in rates of profit. Profits fell dramatically in Britain during the 1970s. Many companies had become "tax exhausted," that is, their tax reliefs and allowances were more than sufficient to exhaust any liability for mainstream corporation tax. This interaction further increased the dispersion of tax incentives—and disincentives—to investment.

8. C. Kelly and D. Owen, *Factor Prices in the Treasury Model*, Government Economic Service Working Paper 83 (London, 1985).
9. British Inland Revenue-HM Treasury, *Fiscal Incentives for R & D Spending: An International Survey* (London: Inland Revenue, 1987).

The Quality of Investment

Commentators responded favorably to the 1984 reforms. There was a general welcome for the increased neutrality in business taxation. There has also been a big increase in profitability, and companies are beginning to feel the benefit of the reduced rate of corporation tax.

There seems to be a growing realization that in British conditions, the quality and composition of investment may be a more important concern than the quantity of investment. What is striking about the performance of the British economy is not that the amount of capital per worker has been insufficient, but that poor use has been made of the capital Britain has. This problem is shown, for example, by the relatively low returns to fixed capital in Britain, the relatively low level of output achieved per additional unit of capital (Britain had a high ratio of net investment to changes in output), and the low levels of output per unit of the capital stock.

In Britain, and in Europe generally, evidence indicates that investment has been too much concerned with capital deepening rather than capital widening. This problem also involves the taxation of labor, to which I will turn in a minute. But wider economic concerns, such as the real wage controversy, are also at issue. Real wages have been a problem in Britain—and in Europe generally.[10] These affairs take me away from my terms of reference, but, in this wider context, one must ask whether tax policy is going with the grain of policy. In this context, there is a good case for drawing back on subsidies designed to increase the volume of investment.

Oil Taxation

Rather different considerations apply to the taxation of profits from North Sea oil. Oil is a national resource, which, in the most profitable fields, generates a considerable amount of economic rent. Oil can be taxed at high rates without affecting economic activity unduly. Britain's objective has been to maximize tax revenue from the profitable fields while leaving incentives for new, more marginal

10. H. M. Treasury, *The Relationship between Employment and Wages* (London: H. M. Treasury, 1985).

investments. And the government has had to react to the rapid increases in oil prices in 1979–80 and ensure that the system was still appropriate after the reduction in 1986.

The changes have taken three main forms. First, measures were taken to accelerate and increase revenue in 1979–80. The smaller, less profitable fields were protected by limiting the acceleration to those fields producing more than 20,000 barrels a day. A few fields over this limit proved rather unprofitable after the oil prices fell again, and some of the accelerated tax was paid back last year to reflect this situation. Second, measures were taken to curb reliefs that were encouraging wasteful investment. Third, measures have been taken to encourage new activity where the economic rent was much lower. In 1983 reliefs were introduced for exploration and appraisal and for new fields. There is a delicate balance to be struck here, and the situation must be kept under review. But so far the United Kingdom has managed to raise considerable tax revenue while keeping up the pace of new exploration and development and, as far as we can tell, avoiding the worst distortions to investment.

EMPLOYMENT AND THE LABOR MARKET

The relative price of capital and labor involves consideration of taxes on labor as well as on capital. I propose to avoid the issue of the final incidence of taxes and concentrate on employers' contributions to the national insurance fund and the surcharge on these contributions, which was introduced in 1977. The latter was widely regarded as a "tax on jobs." Mainly as a result of this tax, which rose to 3.5 percent, taxes on labor, as a share of payroll costs, rose from 13.0 percent in 1970 to 17.5 percent in 1980.

National Insurance Contributions

The surcharge on national insurance contributions has been progressively reduced and was finally abolished in 1984. This reduction in the cost of employing labor, combined with a reduction in the subsidies to investment, altered, in a way favorable to employment, the relative posttax cost of capital and labor. This measure went some way to correct the bias against employment that arose during the 1970s.

This process was taken a step further in 1985, when employers' national insurance contributions were restructured. Lower rates were introduced for low-paid workers—and employees—and the upper earnings limit on employers' contributions was abolished. This increased the incentive to employ lower-paid workers and, as there seemed little shortage of demand for higher-paid workers, was expected to increase employment overall.

Profit-Related Pay

A further tax measure, designed to improve the functioning of the labor market and so reduce unemployment, is the introduction of profit-related pay in the 1987 Finance Act. Income tax relief will be available for participants in profit-related pay (PRP) schemes registered with the Inland Revenue. One-half of PRP will be free of income tax up to the point when PRP is equal to £3,000 a year or 20 percent of pay, whichever is lower. The prospective PRP pool (that is, the total of PRP to be distributed among employees) at the time of registration must equal at least 5 percent of pay.

The government expects two advantages to flow from such arrangements:

—The work force would have a more direct personal interest in the profits earned by the firm or unit of the firm where it works.

—There would be more flexibility in pay in the face of changing market conditions.

The debate on the scheme, following the government's consultation document, owed something to the work of Martin Weitzman.[11] We were persuaded that more widespread linking of pay to profits would benefit aggregate employment stability and growth—protecting jobs that might be at risk and getting the jobless back into work more quickly. But we were not convinced that profit-related pay was a panacea and would work quickly to bring the dramatic benefits suggested by Weitzman. In the longer term, we saw potential benefits,

11. Cmnd. 9835, *Profit-Related Pay: A Consultative Document* (London: HMSO, 1986).

on a large scale, in altered attitudes and more flexibility in the labor market.

The treatment of employee share schemes has been made more generous. Gains on disposal in approved schemes are treated as capital gains rather than income. This was done to encourage the spread of schemes for executives and other employees that link rewards directly to company performance. In total there are now 1,300 approved schemes, and about 1.5 million employees have benefited.

STIMULUS TO ENTERPRISE

There is widespread concern that Britain is deficient in business enterprise. There has been particular concern that in the economic environment in the 1960s and 1970s, small businesses were squeezed out. By contrast the present government intends to encourage them. Tax measures taken to remedy this situation are only part of a wider policy for improving the climate for small businesses. There are other nontax initiatives such as the loan guarantee scheme. But compared with other countries that have also wanted to encourage small business, the United Kingdom seems to have placed more emphasis on tax measures.

The main tax measures are the following:

—The reduction in income tax, which has lightened the tax burden on the self-employed. Benefits in kind have become less attractive. The small company tax rate has been reduced from 40 percent in 1979 to 27 percent today. The abolition of the investment income surcharge, combined with the reduction of income tax, has reduced the top rates of tax on investment income from 98 percent in 1979 to 60 percent today. Reform of capital gains will have encouraged risk taking, while at the same time the revenue yield has risen.

—The business expansion scheme (BES). This plan was introduced in 1983 as a successor to the business start-up scheme. Initially it was an experiment but was extended indefinitely in the 1986 budget. The BES provides for income tax relief on amounts up to £40,000 a year for new investment by individuals not closely connected with the firms concerned, which must be unquoted U.K. trading companies. The shares must be held for at least five years but are exempt from capital gains tax on first sale. The investment has to be in new, genuinely additional, and full-risk ordinary capital. Certain activities such as dealing in land, shares or commodities, leasing, banking, insurance, and farming are excluded. In 1986 low-risk asset-backed activities, such as wine and antiques, were excluded. The BES was evaluated in 1985 by a firm of management consultants. Their report showed that 70 percent of the finance raised would not otherwise have been raised as equity and that half of the companies involved raised sums of less than £50,000 each. The latest figures show that more than £150 million is being raised each year through the BES.

FINANCIAL MARKETS

The last few years have been a period of great change in British financial markets. Government activity has focused on deregulation, but there have also been significant tax changes.

During the last decade, British saving became increasingly insti-tutionalized. The year 1986 was the first year in which the net flow of personal saving into shares was positive—before that there had consistently been net disposals of shares by individuals, while over 30 percent of saving went into life assurance and pension fund contributions. As a result, the share of life assurance and pension fund assets in personal wealth, including housing, grew from 13.0 percent in 1975 to 24.0 percent in 1985, while the share of equities in wealth declined from 8.5 percent in 1975 to 5.5 percent in 1985 before recovering to 7.0 percent last year. One objective of government policy has been to encourage noninstitutional saving, partly with the economic objective of increasing risk taking and individual enterprise and partly with the social objective of promoting wider share own-ership.

Measures have been introduced to improve the neutrality of the tax system among different financial institutions, instruments, and channels:

—The tax treatment of deposit interest paid by banks and by building societies has been broadly aligned.

—Special income tax relief on life assurance premiums has been abolished for new contracts.

—The corporation tax measures of 1984 reduced the extent to which tax distorted companies' choice between debt and equity.

—A scheme for tax relief on direct investment in equities has been introduced. This plan brings the treatment of such saving closer to the treatment (in terms of tax wedges) of saving in pensions and housing. This has been done by introducing personal equity plans (PEPs), which permit individuals to invest up to £2,400 a year in quoted shares without incurring tax liability on either capital gains or reinvested dividends if the investment is held for at least one complete year.

—The level of tax relief for certain forms of saving, such as pension saving and home ownership, has been reduced as a result of reductions in income tax rates and, where employers' contributions are concerned, reductions in rates or corporation tax.

Transactions have been eased (locking-in reduced) by a reduction of stamp duty from 2.0 percent to 0.5 percent. And personal investment in securities has been encouraged by the reform of capital gains tax and by the abolition, in 1984, of the income tax surcharge on investment income.

What have the effects of these changes been? Isolating cause and effect is always difficult when other changes are going on, but the volume of share transactions has increased sharply as stamp duty and other share dealing costs have come down.[12] In addition companies have made greater use of the new issues market since 1984, largely because of the buoyant U.K. stock market but also possibly for tax reasons. The composition of insurance companies' business has changed, but it continues to grow. Other policies, such as the introduction of PEPs, will have a longer-term effect, and so perhaps it is unwise to look for a major shift in behavior in the short term.

CONCLUSION

The tax system in Britain has been reformed significantly in recent years with consequences that are likely to be very far reaching. The following major changes have occurred:

12. P. D. Jackson and A. T. O'Donnell, "The Effects of Stamp Duty on Equity Transactions and Prices in the U.K. Stock Exchange," Bank of England Discussion Paper 25 (London: Bank of England, 1985).

—In 1979 there was a major reduction in the top rates of income tax, a 3-percent reduction in the basic rate of tax linked with a switch of tax away from direct taxation and toward indirect taxation as a result of the increase in the VAT rate.

—In 1984 there was a major change in business taxation, reducing the rate of tax by seventeen percentage points from 52 percent to 35 percent and replacing tax investment incentives by annual depreciation allowances.

Measures have also been designed to do the following:

—Lower the tax cost of employing labor, especially lower-paid labor.

—Encourage personal saving and direct personal investment, especially where risks are high.

—Encourage closer involvement between the employee and his or her firm, in particular to relate remuneration more closely to profitability.

The guiding principles behind these changes have been the following:

—Increase the scope for the individual to use his or her money according to personal choice.

—Remove tax-induced distortions in decisionmaking and thereby make individual decisions depend more on underlying economic conditions and less on the characteristics of the tax system.

—Encourage enterprise, particularly individual enterprise among the employed and the self-employed, in job and work decisions.

All these changes are designed to allow markets and market processes to work more effectively and efficiently.

Comment by JOHN HILLS

In Ian Byatt's otherwise comprehensive survey of current U.K. tax policy, two interesting omissions occur. First, the paper is almost wholly concerned with efficiency with little or no mention of its usual partner in tax analysis, equity. Byatt is, however, presenting an official view of policy and that balance in his paper accurately reflects the British government's priorities.

Second, he makes only the most cursory reference to one of the more interesting developments—one could hardly call it an innovation—in U.K. tax policy: the reintroduction of a poll tax (under the alias of a "community charge") to finance local government instead of property taxes ("rates"). Apart from brief periods during the English Civil War, this charge has not been seen in England since it caused the Peasants' Revolt. It was, however, imposed in many British colonies, and its reintroduction will, appropriately enough, start in what some see as one of England's few remaining colonies, Scotland. If nothing else, the move should win the government awards from the organizations concerned with the preservation of endangered species.

THE LEVEL PLAYING FIELD

One concern of this conference is how tax policy is formulated. It is interesting therefore to read that the "lively academic debate . . . in the United Kingdom on the relative merits of an expenditure rather than an income base. . . . has not made a practical contribution to reform." In fact, the center of that debate has been precisely the issue of equality of treatment of different activities financed in different ways, which is described by Byatt as a "level playing field."[1] If nothing else, the academic debate does seem to have influenced how policy is described.

But has policy on personal taxation really produced the leveling effect claimed, and argued for, in the academic debate? Perhaps the most important development affecting taxes—the fall in the inflation rate—has had nothing to do with tax policy. In many ways, inflation leads to the worst distortions in the tax system. The problems with

1. See, in particular, *The Structure and Reform of Direct Taxation: Report of a Committee Chaired by J. E. Meade* (London: Allen and Unwin for the Institute for Fiscal Studies, 1978); and J. A. King and M. A. King, *The British Tax System* (Oxford University Press, 1978).

discrimination between debt and equity in company taxation, between interest income and capital gains, with allowing deductibility of homeowners' mortgage interest payments, and so on become much worse at high inflation rates. The fall in the inflation rate from the two-digit levels experienced in the 1970s and early 1980s to 4 percent to 5 percent now has greatly helped to reduce tax distortions. To pursue the analogy, the playing field has been moved to a site with less of an inflationary slope.

Major reductions in tax discrimination have also been achieved through eliminating the highest tax rates on individuals. The theoretical top marginal tax rate of 98 percent on interest income can only have been paid by those individuals with so much money that they could not bother to ask their accountant how to convert it into capital gains taxed (with a useful delay) at 30 percent. The current maximum of 60 percent offers far less of a reward to the outer reaches of the tax avoidance industry. However, at the other end of the income scale, the problem of disqualification from welfare benefits has become more severe. The poor and elderly with small amounts of savings have more limited options for avoiding tax discrimination. The shift in the composition of taxation away from income tax with its many deduction provisions and toward social security tax (national insurance contributions) and expenditure taxation (value-added tax) also affects the lower-income population.

Finally, as Byatt argues, a few measures have removed bumps in the playing field. The most notable example is the removal of the tax subsidy of 15 percent for life insurance payments on new policies (although the tax remains for policies taken out before the 1984 budget).

However, the big mountains remain, at least as far as the taxation of saving is concerned. The major tax privileges associated with pension funds and owner-occupied housing remain intact. The chancellor ducked the possibility in the 1985 budget of phasing out tax-free lump sums paid by pension schemes on retirement. The replacement of local property taxes with a poll tax removes the only offset to the tax advantages of owner occupation, further increasing its privileged position. Given the political pressure to favor owner-occupation, it has, however, been a major achievement for the Treasury to have kept the maximum amount of a mortgage eligible for interest deductibility down to £30,000, a significant reduction in real terms since 1979. Nonetheless, the cost of the tax expenditure on mortgage interest tax relief has risen from 6.7 percent of income tax revenue in 1978–79 to 11.7 percent in 1986–87.

Other policies, rather than leveling the field, throw a few more boulders onto it. The business expansion scheme is an example. An income taxpayer at the top rate can sacrifice just £40 of after-tax income to purchase assets worth £100, which can be sold in five years: a subsidy equivalent to an addition of 20 percent of initial capital value a year to their return. The Inland Revenue's figures show that, almost exclusively, only the richest taxpayers have used this scheme. Other devices that have narrowed the tax base include the opening up of employee-share options as a way for top executives to receive almost tax-free pay, the new tax-free "personal equity plans," and the new "profit-related pay" arrangements, which could constitute up to 10 percent of someone's wages tax free. Capital gains tax has been restricted to real gains, with indexation of the base for calculating gains after 1982–83. Despite this condition, the rate remains at 30 percent rather than being integrated into the normal income tax base, and a generous exemption remains. One could own assets worth £130,000 (more than ten times average earnings) without paying any tax on capital gains if they yielded real gains at a rate of 5 percent a year.

Thus it would not be accurate to describe the changes in the United Kingdom's personal taxation as base broadening: many of those taxpayers benefiting from lower rates have also been offered some additional forms of exempt income.

CORPORATION TAX

By contrast, the 1984 reform of company income tax exemplifies how tax reform can, in fact, be popular, please (almost) everyone, and involve both base broadening and rate reduction. Businessmen and women are pleased because the rate of tax has been cut from 52 percent to 35 percent. They are also pleased by the prospect that—if inflation remains below about 8 percent—long-run tax liabilities will be lower than under the old system.[2] The Treasury is happy because

2. John King and Charles Wookey, *Inflation: The Achilles' Heel of Corporation Tax*, Institute for Fiscal Studies Report 26 (London: IFS, 1987), p. 8.

revenues are higher in the short term than they would have been under the old system.[3] This is due to the bulge in taxable incomes until the new depreciation allowances (replacing the old 100-percent allowance) build up in value. Accountants are happy because the system is based on old-fashioned, historic cost accounting rather than including weird adjustments for the effects of inflation. Commentators are happy because, as Byatt's paper shows, the dispersion in the tax wedges imposed on different kinds of investment and sources of finance has been narrowed. The only people who are not happy are economists who are pessimistic about inflation and who are worried about the disincentives imposed by the new system on new investment.

The new system has recently been described as "wide open to the effects of inflation."[4] Because it is based on historic cost accounting principles, the tax base diverges from real profits if the inflation level is significant. The effective level of taxation on real profits rises in general, and distortions such as the discrimination between debt and equity worsen. Having said that, the pre-1984 system was also vulnerable to inflation, with the effective rate of tax on real profits falling as inflation rose. The critics argue mainly that the chance for reform of the system into one that would be impervious to inflation has been lost and that a reemergence of inflation will prompt unsatisfactory ad hoc adjustments as happened in the past.

Critics also say the new system increases the cost of capital for most firms making investments while reducing long-run revenues from the tax.[5] This combination occurs because the tax charged on "pure profits" has been reduced—the reverse of the outcome argued for by economists.

WORK INCENTIVES

Whether the overall effect of changes in tax policy since 1979 has been to improve work incentives by cutting marginal tax rates for all

3. Michael Devereux, "On the Growth of Corporation Tax Revenues," *Fiscal Studies*, vol. 8 (May 1987), pp. 77–85.

4. King and Wookey, *Inflation*, p. 8.

5. Jeremy Edwards, "The 1984 Corporation Tax Reform," *Fiscal Studies*, vol. 5 (May 1984), pp. 30–44.

but the rich is more dubious. The main marginal rate of income tax has been cut from 33 percent to 27 percent, but this cut has been accompanied by increases in the main rate of national insurance contributions (social security tax) from 6.5 percent to 9.0 percent and in value-added tax from 8.0 percent to 15.0 percent. Overall, for all but the small minority paying income tax above the basic rate, the "wedge" between gross labor costs to employers and net spending power of employees has increased since 1979.[6]

As Byatt's paper indicates, the research in this area suggests that the labor supply of married women is most sensitive to tax treatment. It is therefore rather surprising to find the government considering a change in the tax treatment of husband and wife toward "transferable allowances" (described in the recent Green Paper on personal taxation). This move would have a significant threshold effect, making participation in the labor force less attractive to married women and reducing work incentives.

EQUITY

The distributional effects of changes in tax policy since 1979 are also important. First, the ratio of taxes to GDP rose steeply between 1978–79 and 1981–82 (from 38.4 percent of GDP at factor cost to 46.2 percent); since then it has declined very slowly (to about 45.0 percent in 1987–88). The distributional effects of changes in policy have to be judged against this general background of an increase in the overall tax burden. Income tax has been cut, but most other taxes have been increased. Table 1 shows how the burden of direct taxes (income tax and national insurance contributions less the child benefit that has replaced the former child tax allowance) has changed for different income groups since 1978–79. The gains shown are calculated by comparing the tax burden on a sample of families under the actual 1987–88 tax system and that of 1978–79 (uprated by the increase in national income, so that all other things being equal, the tax burden as a percentage of income would have been constant). The results are derived from TAXMOD, the model of the U.K. tax and benefit

6. Andrew Dilnot and others, "The 1987 Budget in Perspective," *Fiscal Studies*, vol. 8 (May 1987), pp. 48–57.

TABLE 1. *Effect of Changes in Direct Taxation between 1978–79 and 1987–88*[a]

Decile group[b]	Average gain (pounds each week)
Bottom	No change
Second	−0.20
Third	−0.40
Fourth	−0.80
Fifth	−1.10
Sixth	−0.70
Seventh	0.50
Eighth	1.90
Ninth	3.40
Top	32.40

Source: Author's calculations using TAXMOD model of U.K. tax and social security system, developed by A. B. Atkinson and H. Sutherland, London School of Economics.

a. Income tax and social security contributions (national insurance contributions), allowing for child tax allowances and child benefit. For 1978–79, widths of tax brackets, allowances, and so on are adjusted to 1987–88 levels by growth in gross domestic product (market prices) to eliminate effects of fiscal drag.

b. Families by level of equivalent income (that is, adjusted for family size).

system developed by A. B. Atkinson and H. Sutherland at the London School of Economics.

The bottom 80 percent of the population has experienced virtually no change: direct tax reductions and increases have canceled one another out. Only the top 20 percent of the population, in particular the top 5 percent to 10 percent, have emerged as significant gainers. Meanwhile everyone has had to pay higher indirect taxes. According to the Treasury's figures (information supplied to House of Commons Library), the total tax burden on a two-child family on average earnings increased by two and one-half percentage points between 1978–79 and 1987–88. The direct tax cuts have offset the indirect tax increases only for those earning well above twice the average earnings.

At the same time the rates of welfare benefits have struggled to maintain their real values despite the rise in overall real national income. The poorest part of the population has been cut adrift from the overall improvement in living standards. In addition, the distribution of pretax incomes has become steadily more unequal. In 1979 the top one-fifth of the population received 45 percent of original income; according to 1982 and 1987 data from the Central Statistical Office, by 1985 the share of the top one-fifth had risen to 49 percent.[7] At the same time the share of the bottom two-fifths fell by one-third as unemployment rose. The tax and benefit system cushioned this rise in inequality to some extent, but even after allowing for all taxes and benefits, the share of the top one-fifth still rose from 36 percent to 38 percent.

The reduction in the progressivity of the tax system—even before the threatened poll tax—has been part of an overall increase in inequality in Britain. Although undoubtedly some improvement has occurred in the efficiency of the British tax system, the cost in equity has been high.

7. *Economic Trends*, no. 350 (December 1982), p. 102, and no. 397 (November 1986), p. 96.

LAWRENCE B. GIBBS

United States

Thanks to the sophistication of today's technology and the extended reach of telecommunications, people can communicate with one another instantaneously around the world. In October 1987 stocks plummeted on Wall Street, and overnight—in an altogether new way—the interrelatedness of world financial markets was recognized. In 1986 the United States fundamentally reformed its tax laws, and in 1987 the worldwide ripple effects of those changes have become apparent.

As members of the global community, our countries are inextricably tied together. When anything economically important happens to any one of our countries, it affects the rest of us in good times and in bad times. So any time we have the opportunity to take a broader look at our economic and tax policy issues—not just in a parochial way but in worldwide terms—we should relish it.

During the long months of 1986, when U.S. legislators were deliberating the fate of tax reform, many doubted that consensus would ever be reached. Yet it was—and the rest is history. The new U.S. tax law is fundamentally different from the previous tax laws with which I have been working during the last twenty-five years.

Recognizing how untraditional the new law is, the Internal Revenue Service (IRS) has tackled its implementation in what I believe are untraditional ways. For more than a year, the IRS has been doing everything it can to make sure that its employees and taxpayers in general are ready for tax reform.

Although I could easily devote my whole discussion to tax reform and the readiness efforts, I think it will be more useful to offer some reflections about life beyond tax reform implementation—some reflections about what tax administration in the twenty-first century may be like.

A RETURN-FREE TAX SYSTEM

Several years ago, when the U.S. Department of the Treasury began soliciting ideas for tax reform proposals, the IRS suggested the possibility of a return-free tax system. Between the time the department announced its first tax reform proposal in November 1984 and the time Congress put the final touches on the Tax Reform Act of 1986, there were many legislative changes, but the return-free concept remained alive. The act, as finally passed, required the IRS to report to Congress on the pros and cons of such a system. In October 1987 it did just that.

A return-free system works like this. On the basis of the information reports it receives from employers, banks, and financial and other institutions, the IRS would use its computers to prepare returns for taxpayers. By the agency's calculation, millions of taxpayers with relatively simple and straightforward tax situations would be eligible to participate. Basically, the concept is simple. The tough part comes when one tries to mesh the return-free concept with available technology.

The report that the agency provided to Congress outlined certain criteria that would have to be met before a return-free system would be practical. First, for a return-free system to be feasible, the information that the IRS receives from employers, banks, and others relating to taxpayers' income and deductions would have to be accurate—only a small error rate could be tolerated. Second, the IRS would have to receive the information as soon as possible after the year end and be able within a short time to process the information and prepare each taxpayer's return. Third, the IRS would have to give the taxpayer the opportunity to review the return and either confirm that it was correct and complete or provide the necessary information or changes so that the return could be accurately finalized.

Thus far the IRS has not been successful in its attempts to match up the design and price of a return-free system with the features I just mentioned. That is not to say that over the long term, technology improvements in the tax processing system will not enable the IRS to do so. But at the moment the cost of generating accurate and timely returns for a return-free system is prohibitive. The agency did announce plans to conduct a market research study to gauge taxpayer interest and potential participation in a return-free type of program. The results of such a study should be available in 1989.

The IRS will also be closely watching the experience of other countries—including Sweden and Japan—with their return-free systems. Their experience and recent editorials in the United States already suggest that if a return-free system is to be compatible with voluntary compliance objectives, the agency must find a way to avoid the perception that IRS-generated returns are no longer taxpayer returns. That is, tax administrators must find a way to communicate effectively to taxpayers that, even though the IRS may gather the tax information and prepare the return, the taxpayer still has the obligation to assure the agency that the return information is correct and complete.

INNOVATIVE APPLICATIONS OF TECHNOLOGY

But as the IRS works today to design a more effective tax system for tomorrow—more effective for tax administrators and their customers—I do not want to leave the impression that it is putting all its eggs in the future basket. Yes, it is looking ahead to information systems designs for the twenty-first century, but in the meantime it is also working on current problems.

The IRS is testing the electronic filing of tax returns and the use of optical laser disks for storage of tax return information. Recently it also created an artificial intelligence laboratory to develop expert systems applications for tax administration.

Electronic filing is perhaps the best hope for substantially reducing the cost and burden of collecting tax information. It essentially automates the taxpayer and IRS steps for filing and processing a tax return.

The agency first tested electronic filing in 1986. Every year since then has been a major turning point for the process. There were three filing sites in 1986 and seven medium-sized metropolitan area sites in 1987. In 1988 the electronic filing option will be available in ten entire states and in major parts of four other states. By 1990 the system is expected to be nationwide. In 1986, 25,000 individual returns were electronically filed; in 1987, about 80,000. In 1988 the program has the potential of reaching 40 percent of the taxpayer population.

On the individual side, the IRS pilot system will accept computer-prepared individual tax forms. For the first time this year, the agency also opened the project to business returns. Experience has shown that first-year participants rated the program "highly favorable" for business, electronic and magnetic media filing of business returns is technically and economically feasible, and there is a market for this type of service. Unlike the electronic filing of individual returns, the electronic filing of business returns has no geographical restrictions.

Electronic filing emphasizes the fact that no value is added by processing paper. If the IRS can eliminate the paper and thereby divert resources from the present manual processing of paper returns, it can focus more on true value-added services, such as taxpayer assistance, tax examinations, and collection of delinquent accounts.

Another technology at work to help reduce the massive amount of paper involved in tax return processing is the optical laser disk, which holds thousands of pages of information and requires little space. Present technology could permit storage of sixteen cubic feet of documents on a disk the size of a long-playing record. In 1986 the IRS began testing equipment to store and retrieve tax return information using laser technology.

Another technology threshold already crossed involves artificial intelligence: the study of how to make computers act like humans—reasoning through a problem, learning from experience. Major areas of artificial intelligence research today include robotics, image processing, speech recognition, and expert systems.

It is the latter, expert systems, that appears to be the best bet for tax administration. But the IRS is not satisfied with consulting the experts. It is creating some of its own. Since January 1985 the agency has been offering to some of its employees advanced training with an artificial intelligence firm or two years of academic training at one of three institutions, the University of Pennsylvania, the Massachusetts Institute of Technology, or Carnegie-Mellon University.

Let me mention just a few of the expert systems projects the IRS is working on. It is now developing expert systems to do the following:

—Identify specific tax issues with good audit potential;

—Set up parameters for determining when to abate certain taxpayer penalties;

—Automate the scheduling and management of mainframe computers at the service centers where those millions of tax returns are processed; and

—Provide backup assistance in terms of technical information to IRS telephone assistors, thus freeing more technical people who now provide the backup assistance.

MANAGEMENT IN THE NINETIES

Advances in technology hold tremendous promise for the Internal Revenue Service and for its customers, the taxpayers. But the greater the IRS's exposure to and experience with new technologies, the more convinced it is that success will depend on the ability to manage these changing technologies.

The IRS is the first to admit it does not have all the management answers. Three years ago, however, the agency took a big step closer to finding many of them when it joined nine corporate sponsors of a research consortium known as Management in the Nineties. Sponsors cover all kinds of business interests. But they have one thing in common—a desire to help their organizations cope with the demands and opportunities inherent in the emerging large-scale information technology with which each of them is increasingly confronted.

The IRS is working with companies such as American Express, Digital Equipment, Eastman Kodak, General Motors, and International Computers, Ltd., and its research is being coordinated by the Massachusetts Institute of Technology. It has the benefit of the perspectives of some of the leaders in private industry, who are helping the agency examine its directions in technology. And, at the same time, it is exploring areas of common interest for the public and private sectors. For example, in April 1987 the IRS hosted a workshop on artificial intelligence and expert systems.

CONCLUSION

Many know the words of Chief Justice Oliver Wendell Holmes that are etched on the front of the main IRS building in Washington: "Taxes are what we pay for civilized society."

Humorist Will Rogers said it more simply: "It's a great country, but you can't live in it for nothing."

Before tax reform, too many individuals and businesses tried to do exactly that. Tax reform has made a difference. It did not make the U.S. system perfect. But it did make it better—by a long shot. The important question now is, where do we go from here?

If there is one point to remember, it is this: wherever the IRS is headed, it intends to keep open the international channels of communication. It has learned an important lesson from its Management in the Nineties experience—there is strength in numbers.

Tax administrators around the world have their work cut out for them. They must

—Contribute in a unique way to finding short-range and long-range solutions to our countries' serious economic challenges;

—Respond to a variety of tax reform changes;

—Manage the evolving technology of taxation; and

—Make certain that those who owe tax pay it, that those who need tax assistance receive it, and that those who encounter problems are offered prompt, accurate, consistent, and courteous solutions.

Economically speaking, these are uncertain times for most nations of the world. That fact makes tax officials—the policymakers and collectors of their nations' revenues—important players. The administrators at the Internal Revenue Service look forward to doing what they can in the months and years ahead to work with others to find lasting solutions to the difficult problems we collectively face.

C. EUGENE STEUERLE

United States

The assigned subject of my talk—the international implications of U.S. reform—is so broad and comprehensive that I cannot possibly do it justice. I am reminded of the time that Winston Churchill was introduced to an audience by a moderator who made reference to Sir Winston's legendary consumption of alcohol. "If all the whiskey drunk by Sir Winston were to be put in this room," the moderator stated, "it would fill the room up to here," and he drew an imaginary line halfway up the walls. When Sir Winston stepped to the podium, he looked at the imaginary line, glanced at the ceiling, then sighed and said, "Ah, so much to do, and so little time in which to do it."

TAX REFORM: AN INTERNATIONAL PHENOMENON

Tax reform is truly an international phenomenon. Countries learn much from one another these days and at a much faster rate. When we see things we like, we quickly imitate them. This imitation is as true of public-sector endeavors as it is of private-sector innovations, and it is reciprocal. Reform is international because our economies and businesses have become international in scope. At the same time, many countries have recently undergone similar economic experiences. Inflation, for instance, has had an important effect on each of our tax accounting systems and on the distribution of tax burdens among taxpayers.

THE BASIS FOR TAX REFORM

At its core, tax reform is an attack on hidden and inefficient government. It is also a call for simple honesty in the tax code.

Through the elimination of many special exclusions, deductions, credits, and deferrals, lower rates are made possible for everyone. It is extraordinarily difficult to apply simplistic political labels to the reformers. I think those who favor tax reform basically distrust hidden agendas in government, even when they might otherwise agree with the thrust of the agendas. They do not like tax code provisions that pretend to do something, but do not—incentives that do not provide incentive, high rates that do not apply, or an income tax base unrelated to income. Reformers reject the economic notion that people see through a multiplicity of tax "veils" in some costless manner because it is costly to obtain information.

Tax reform also represents a fundamental belief that growth, increased well-being, and wealth formation depend on individuals' development of their skills and knowledge, the opportunity to test their ideas in the marketplace, and the free use of their own capabilities. Those capabilities can be and have been as constrained by discriminatory tax rules as by other legalistic rules and regulations that tend to deter innovation.

THE NAYSAYERS

Of course, there are the naysayers. In the United States tax reform was presented as a reform for the long run. Opponents immediately decried that in the short term the economy would fall apart, that it is simply impossible to develop policy for the long run. But look at the real situation. The U.S. tax reform process started at the beginning of 1984, and the economy has done all right since then. The United States is now enjoying its longest peacetime expansion ever; the unemployment rate dropped about one percentage point between 1986 and 1987, and investment spending is expected to be higher in 1987 than in 1986. Moreover, all this took place not only while tax reform was being put into place but while the deficit was being reduced from fiscal 1986 to fiscal 1987 by more than $70 billion, or almost 2 percent of gross national product (GNP). These observations do not prove that tax reform had a short-term beneficial effect on the economy, but, make no mistake about it, those who decried the inevitable short-term devastating effect of major tax reform on the economy have been proved wrong.

At present, of course, each of our governments is devoting renewed attention to the financial markets and to our macroeconomic budgetary and monetary policies. Though tax reform aims at long-term growth through structural reform, in no way does it supersede or mitigate the need for sound policies in these other areas. I remain optimistic both about the U.S. budget outlook and about the response of the U.S. monetary authorities to recent market disturbances. Clearly, success at one type of reform should not and will not deter this country from other important policy efforts.

A second set of U.S. naysayers claimed that tax reform would hurt international competitiveness. But after enactment of the U.S. reform, many foreign governments were besieged with the same argument, only this time it was their economies, not the U.S. economy, that supposedly were put at a competitive disadvantage by the U.S. tax reform. Obviously, both arguments cannot be right at the same time.

The bottom line of all our economic analysis is that the best way to be competitive internationally is to be competitive domestically. Yet there are some in every country who do not like to hear this argument. They mistakenly believe that "beggar-thy-neighbor" tax and trade policies are somehow going to spark so much domestic growth that the net international harm will be suffered only abroad.

A third group of naysayers ventured that high, not low, tax rates were the answer. While purporting to favor less government, these people implicitly, and sometimes explicitly, argued that the government should impose high tax rates and then grant tax credits or deductions for favored activities. This approach—which is tied to the notion that a government can regularly impose so-called windfall taxes on existing wealth—abandons the hope of building a tax system for the future. Long-run objectives are rejected, and one is left to stand on the shaky ground that the government can confiscate old wealth in ways that will not affect the future behavior of individuals.

This high-tax-rate approach also places unrealistic reliance on the ability of government policymakers to apply tax credits and preferences in the right places at the right time. Finally, it ignores or discounts the noncompetitive effect of the selective credits and subsidies as well as the distortions created by the high tax rates that support those preferences.

LESSONS FROM TAX REFORM

Two sets of lessons can be gleaned from the U.S. tax reform effort that I believe have future application both here and abroad. The first are political or institutional in nature; the second, economic.

Political and Institutional Lessons

The United States was blessed, I think, with the necessary institutional structure through which reform could be achieved. Talented staffs of public servants were in place in both the Treasury and Congress to develop, design, and implement tax reform. These staffs are cohesive and committed to the task of developing an efficient and equitable tax code. They maintain a strong tradition and a high standard of honor that are passed from one generation of workers to the next.

In addition, as elaborate and complicated as the U.S. decisionmaking process turned out to be, it was simplified by the placement of both cost and benefit analysis within the same department of the executive branch and the same committee of each house of Congress. On the direct expenditure side of the budget, trade-offs of costs and benefits are difficult to achieve. In most cases, it is not possible for one department of the government or one committee of Congress to propose that an expenditure item be cut back to reduce tax rates or to pay for another expenditure not under the jurisdiction of that department or committee.

Even in tax reform, however, I must add one caveat about the government's ability to make the trade-offs that would be possible in an ideal world. One of the more revealing moments in the reform process came when a debate arose about whether the original Treasury study could make use of the traditional tax policy argument that a tax preference should be rejected if it could be better designed as a direct expenditure. Unfortunately, I had to veto the use of that argument. The only trade-offs the tax reform committees could offer were in our area of jurisdiction: the tax code. They could propose to redesign or eliminate a preference within the tax code, they could exchange one tax preference for another, and they could trade off preferences for lower tax rates. They could not propose to substitute a direct expenditure for a tax preference. Fortunately, because so many tax subsidies were inefficient and worth eliminating, this restriction was less severe than it first appeared. Nevertheless, there clearly were areas where reform could not be accomplished by either the Treasury or the tax-writing committees because neither had the jurisdiction to propose expenditure policies to replace some popular tax preferences.

Working on reform also taught another lesson: that comprehensiveness can be an important tool for reform. Rightly or wrongly, in the early stages of tax reform, I decided to push forward as comprehensive a list of proposals as I could get on the table. My reasons were several.

First, under what I call the "hopper theory of reform," the more good things that get into the hopper, the more good and the fewer bad things come out. And a comprehensive agenda usually serves better than a scramble of special interest legislation that might take its place.

Second, many of the problems of modern democratic governments today stem from the unwillingness of policymakers to deal with thousands of issues that, individually, can be considered minor. For over a decade I had heard the argument that tax reformers should deal only with the multibillion dollar programs. My view, however, came to be just the opposite: the totality, duplication, and incomprehensibility of all programs on both the tax and expenditure sides of the budget are responsible for much of the inefficiency of government today.

Third, comprehensiveness helps convince the public that action is being sought in the public interest, not simply to attack a particular constituency that may be as worthy of support as any other.

Economic Lessons

The economic lessons are no less important. First, governments should not develop fiscal and monetary systems that encourage wasteful use of resources. In particular, taxpayers should not be able to make an after-tax profit by investing in assets that produce a

negative return for the economy. Such a situation readily occurs in
any economy that has high tax rates, generous subsidies for particular
investments, and inflation. Indeed, as I have argued elsewhere, the
stagflation of the past can be explained in part by this induced
movement of saving (and work effort) toward less productive and
often unproductive uses.

A corollary of the first lesson is that fiscal and monetary policy
must over time keep interest rates positive and real in after-tax terms
for most borrowers. In the United States the reattainment of positive
after-tax interest rates was accomplished recently both through a
reduction in tax rates and through a lowering of the inflation rate.

I realize that this lesson and its corollary are not fully accepted by
everyone. Some believe few social costs are associated with very high
rates of subsidy or negative after-tax interest rates. I would argue,
on the contrary, that the lesson is more important now than ever
before. Both the sophistication of financial markets and the capabilities
of the accounting and legal professional have grown exponentially.
Individuals and firms can now arbitrage easily in the tax and financial
markets. Given the correct set of incentives, they can quickly turn
positive saving into unproductive investment. The rapid growth of
the tax shelter market in the United States is only one of the more
obvious cases in point.

Tax reform has also taught us, or retaught us, that domestic
protectionism does not promote international competition. Often the
results are just the opposite of the desired outcome. Perhaps Warren
G. Harding was not so confused when he said that "the United States
should adopt a protective tariff of such a character as will help the
struggling industries of Europe to get on their feet."[1] Protectionism,
of course, comes not only from tariffs and quotas at the border; it
also derives from tax and regulatory processes that prevent competition from developing internally.

Again, this is not an issue for the United States alone. How do
nations compete in this world? Treasury Secretary James A. Baker III
was exactly on target when he stated that "because the integration
of the world economy is so extensive, we need an 'integrated'
competitiveness policy. Basically, this means removing barriers to

1. Cited in Paul F. Boller, Jr., *Presidential Anecdotes* (Penguin, 1982), p. 231.

growth in our entire society—in the public and private sectors, and abroad.''[2]

Is the battle against protectionism over, even in the tax arena? Hardly. Tax reform has may parallels with tariff reform of past decades. The case against direct and obvious barriers to competition—high tariff and tax rates that apply only to a portion of consumption or investment goods, or only to a portion of productive human and capital assets—is strong and difficult to reject directly. Many, therefore, push for special-interest legislation and for protection against competition through the use of hidden, backdoor, and indirect barriers. Thus protectionism will still be fostered through rules, regulations, and quotas, as well as through tax accounting systems that are designed to mismeasure. The protectionist agenda is often one of hidden government. The battle in this arena is much more difficult because the costs to the economy are much less obvious than in the case of the tariffs or credits that are more clearly identifiable as favoring particular firms or individuals.

Another major economic lesson, and one with application in many democratic countries, is that new businesses and households—the producers, innovators, and competitors of tomorrow—are underrepresented in the democratic process. In the United States, for instance, postwar investment incentives were available only as tax reductions and were available almost immediately, either at the time of investment or soon after. These two features implied that the greatest amount of tax saving per dollar of investment would be received by firms with significant outside income; only they could take immediate advantage of the preferences. For a given marginal investment, new firms with little outside income had to face higher tax rates than most established firms. We need to be constantly watchful of this tendency to favor existing wealth over new wealth and today's voters over tomorrow's voters.

A related economic as well as political lesson is that it is not harmful to try to design policies for posterity. Indeed, it is actually a good thing to do. To be shortsighted used to be thought of as an accusation; in some of modern public finance, it has become a claim of attribution.

2. Remarks before a conference sponsored by the Institute of International Economics, Washington, D.C., September 14, 1987.

Many were fond of misusing Keynes's remark that in the long run we are all dead.

I have already stated my philosophical as well as economic objections to those who would design a permanent policy only by significantly discounting or ignoring long-run costs, inefficiencies, and distortions. History should have taught us by now that our greatest statesmen and stateswomen had a vision that went beyond the present. Nonetheless, I recognize that designing for posterity or at least for the longer run requires both some degree of optimism about the future and some degree of humility about our own knowledge and abilities. Perhaps Piet Hien suggested the proper mix: "We must expect posterity to view with some asperity the marvels and the wonders we're passing on to it; but it should change its attitude to one of heartfelt gratitude when thinking of the blunders we didn't quite commit."[3]

A GLANCE AT THE FUTURE

The U.S. tax reform, I believe, shows the kinds of processes that the United States and many other industrial nations are going to have to use to deal with the reform of health, labor, welfare, housing, and other areas of economic and social policy. In many ways, our governments are involved in carrying out policies that were developed decades ago to deal with the problems of those times. We could debate whether those policies themselves were correct at the time—indeed, much political debate centers on the past—but that is not the right focus. What is crucial is that many of those policies do not provide the greatest social benefits at the least social cost.

Why? For one reason, we have the benefit of both experience and hindsight. We see some distortions and inequities in many of those past policies; we recognize better the constraints on government activity. We have come to realize that a government monopoly can be as inefficient and unfair as any private monopoly. For another reason, some of those past policies have already achieved their success. The problems they addressed, if not eliminated, have been reduced substantially. They no longer represent the problems to which we need to devote so many marginal resources and efforts.

3. Piet Hien with Jens Arup, *Grooks* (Doubleday, 1969), p. 26.

At the same time, the needs of our societies have changed and will continue to change as new demands and new problems arise. Governments have to evolve in much the same way as households: according to changes in need, opportunity, and knowledge.

Whether one agrees with it or not, tax reform was a policy directed at the future. It looked at many past policies and reformed them— not because they were aimed at bad objectives, but because they achieved their objectives at too great a cost. The people were paying a dollar to get back ninety, seventy-five, or fifty cents in benefits. The benefits were not inconsequential; they were just not worth the cost.

As our economies have matured, our options have changed. In a time of expanding government, revenues were often generated through bracket creep and scheduled increases in social insurance and other tax rates. On the expenditure side, there was little indexing of many expenditure programs for inflation or real growth.

Much of that budgetary slack is now gone. Those who want to increase particular expenditures and those who want to reduce taxes, liberals and conservatives, have all learned how to design their programs so that they are effectively indexed over time. As a result, much less apparent slack exists. At the same time, there has been increasing recognition of the limits of government. We have come to better understand resource limitations, constraints on human ability, and some of the costs of administration.

Tax reform cannot be understood outside that environment. Few tax or expenditure changes can now be made in isolation. Every action creates an inevitable reaction; every gain carries with it a more identifiable loss. New initiatives and directions can now be achieved only by cutting back old initiatives. One need not be pessimistic about this development or maturation of our economics. No former tax reform effort in the United States operated under the set of constraints prevailing in the 1980s, but then none succeeded as well either.

It's a new world, and those who would be most successful in operating in it will be those who recognize both its possibilities and its limitations. Those who would move to the future might note some of the institutional and economic lessons from U.S. tax reform: the vital role played by talented and committed staff, with a well-developed tradition; the need to limit jurisdictional squabbles and find mechanisms to allow broader trade-offs and more unified decisionmaking; the importance of comprehensiveness, especially in a period when trade-offs are more important than ever before; the requirement that policies encourage the productive use of scarce saving and labor resources and not rely on discouragement of domestic or international competition; and, finally, the recognition that good policy can be designed for the long run and with posterity in mind.

SIJBREN CNOSSEN

Overview

Since World War II there have been four waves of tax reform in industrial countries: (1) the widespread introduction of social security taxes to finance income-maintenance programs for the aged, the sick, the unemployed, and other less privileged groups; (2) the adoption by most countries of the value-added tax (VAT) as the main form of consumption tax; (3) the introduction of the imputation system or some other form of corporate-income-tax integration to relieve the double tax on dividends; and (4) reductions of the highest marginal income tax rates and the corporation tax rates, in conjunction with some selective base-broadening measures that are mainly confined to the elimination of various investment tax incentives. I consider the introduction of social security schemes and the adoption of the VAT major waves of tax reform. In comparison, dividend relief measures and base-broadening or rate-flattening operations are, generally speaking, minor tax reforms, although they have assumed large proportions in some countries.

In my view, social security reform and payroll taxation, greatly aided by the pervasive introduction of tax withholding schemes for labor income, have been the most significant developments in the structure of taxation in the industrial world. In the European Community (EC), social security contributions on a weighted average basis now account for 14 percent of gross domestic product (GDP), which make them the most important source of tax revenue.[1] Social security from cradle to grave has a profound effect on the attitudes and institutions of our societies, with long-term benefits and costs that have not yet been fully understood and appreciated. The system appears to be headed for a significant overhaul as populations age rapidly in the next thirty years.

1. See Sijbren Cnossen, "Tax Structure Developments," in Cnossen, ed., *Tax Coordination in the European Community* (Boston: Kluwer Law and Taxation, 1986), p. 24.

The second major wave of tax reform is the adoption by seventeen out of twenty-four OECD member countries of the consumption-type, destination-based, value-added tax, collected through the tax credit or invoice method. The value-added tax has become a permanent feature of the tax mix in most countries, and according to one astute observer, Charles E. McLure, Jr., even the United States is only one president away from the VAT. In my opinion, the VAT will win the fight from the retail sales tax, which is troubled by end-use exemptions and which has greater difficulties in reaching services.[2] The continuing discussions on the VAT will center on its coordination in common markets and federal countries, on the most appropriate rate structure, and on means to include financial and insurance services in the base. As regards the last issue, the paper on Canadian tax reform proposes the use of the subtraction method to tax those services, though at the cost of introducing a questionable cumulative element of tax in the system because business use of financial services is not relieved of tax.

The third, smaller wave of tax reform is the relief of double taxation of corporate source income: (1) at the shareholder level through the imputation system in seven out of twelve EC member states and four non-EC countries and (2) at the corporate level through a dividend-deduction or split-rate system in seven OECD member countries.[3] All these integration systems, it will be remembered, can be made identical in the degree of double tax relief if one assumes that integration does not affect the payout rate. Australia is the latest convert to the imputation system, and New Zealand has announced that it will also introduce that system in 1989. This leaves five OECD member countries (Luxembourg, the Netherlands, Spain, Switzerland, and the United States) still clinging to the classical system that taxes distributed profits twice: at the corporate level and in the hands

2. See Sijbren Cnossen, "VAT and RST: A Comparison," *Canadian Tax Journal*, vol. 35 (May-June 1987), pp. 559–615.

3. Although a member of the Organization for Economic Cooperation and Development, Iceland is not included in the analysis. See Sijbren Cnossen, "Alternative Forms of Corporation Tax," *Australian Tax Forum*, vol. 1 (September 1984), pp. 253–79, reprinted as "Corporation Taxes in OECD Member Countries," *Bulletin for International Fiscal Documentation*, vol. 38 (November 1984), pp. 483–96.

of the shareholders. In my view, dividend relief, in one form or another, is also here to stay.

The last wave of tax reform, not a thundering wave in my opinion, is the move to level the playing field of the income taxes through base broadening and rate flattening, the subject of this conference. To assess the effect of this reform movement, I believe the various measures should be judged primarily in light of the normative income concept developed by Schanz, Haig, and Simons (S-H-S) and elucidated by Goode, Musgrave, and our host, Pechman.[4] The normative implications of the S-H-S concept of income for income tax design are broadly the following: (1) income in-kind should be taxed at its full market value, and it is important, if often difficult, to distinguish clearly between taxable consumption and deductible costs in earning income; (2) claims to future income, such as pensions and annuities, should be included in income, that is, deductions for premiums should not be allowed and interest accruing on accumulated premiums should be taxed; (3) the net imputed rental income of owner-occupied houses should be taxed after allowance has been made for mortgage interest, repair and maintenance costs, depreciation charges, and so on; (4) all capital income and gains, realized as well as accrued, should be taxed as ordinary income after the base of capital gains has been adjusted for inflation; (5) gifts, bequests, and lottery winnings should be taxed; (6) the corporation tax with respect to undistributed as well as distributed profits should be fully integrated with the income tax of the shareholder; and (7) foreign income should be taxed in full, but a credit against tax should be given for foreign income or corporation taxes. My discussion does not cover the last three criteria, but I admit that much more attention needs to be given to the international implications of various income tax reforms.

As regards labor income, Australia has enacted a separate fringe benefits tax on employers at the corporation tax rate of 49 percent, although de minimus provisions and concessional valuation rules

---

4. For the classic treatment on the income tax, see Richard Goode, *The Individual Income Tax*, rev. ed. (Brookings, 1976). For an up-to-date analysis of the U.S. income tax in light of the accretion concept of income, see Joseph A. Pechman, *Federal Tax Policy*, fifth ed. (Brookings, 1987), chap. 4. For a useful review of the role and implications of the accretion concept, see John G. Head, "The Carter Legacy: An International Perspective," *Australian Tax Forum*, vol. 4, no. 2 (1987), pp. 143–59.

soften the application of the tax. Other countries have not addressed the tax-favored treatment of fringe benefits as squarely as Australia, but Denmark, Germany, and Sweden have dealt with the related issue of deductible costs in earning income by curbing allowances for professional and personal expenses. No doubt, the deductibility of "mixed" expenses, involving elements of personal consumption, for, say, commuting, entertainment, travel, lodging, and moving, will continue to be debated. If compensating wage movements are ignored, a generous attitude toward fringe benefits or deductible mixed expenses will encourage people to seek jobs that provide remunerations with a high proportion of nontaxable benefits, or induce employers to pay a large part of wages in such forms of income. As a result, labor resources will be misallocated. It should be noted that the 1986 U.S. tax reform scarcely made an attempt to tax fringe benefits more fully. Notably, the tax advantages of so-called cafeteria plans were left intact.

Perhaps the most glaring deviation from the accretion concept of income with respect to labor income is the continued deductibility of savings for retirement in almost all the countries under review here. To be sure, pension premiums are not deductible in France, and life insurance premiums are not allowed against income in Sweden. On the other hand, the Netherlands and Australia have no ceiling on pension contributions and life insurance premiums, respectively.[5] Apparently, Canada intends to impose a ceiling on the deductibility of retirement contributions. Of course, the favorable treatment of retirement saving discriminates against other forms of saving and promotes the concentration of wealth in risk-averse institutions. Assuming that future benefits are fully taxed and the interest on accumulated premiums is exempt, retirement savers enjoy a tax benefit that can be compared to a tax-free loan from the government. Admittedly, this would not be true if contributions for retirement were quasi-compulsory, that is, similar to a tax that cannot be avoided.

In all countries, favorable treatment is also extended to income from owner-occupied housing. Such treatment results in a tax saving that lowers the price of housing consumption or, what is the same

5. For the information, see Organization for Economic Cooperation and Development, Committee on Fiscal Affairs, *Personal Income Tax Systems under Changing Economic Conditions* (Paris: OECD, 1986), p. 31.

thing, increases the net return on the investment. Consequently, more capital will be invested in housing (and other durable consumer goods) than in industrial or financial assets. Some countries partially tax imputed rental income. Some other countries (Australia, France, Italy, and the United Kingdom) impose a ceiling on deductions for mortgage interest, while Germany restricts the deduction to the size of associated income. Exemption or partial taxation of imputed rental income raises troublesome questions of second-best taxation. For instance, the restrictive treatment of interest payments other than those for home mortgages (essentially limiting their deductibility to related investment income), as well as the taxation as ordinary income of all capital gains except those on housing, may have accentuated the discrimination in favor of owner-occupied housing under the 1986 U.S. Tax Reform Act.[6] In such a situation, second-best policies might call for a surcharge on economic-life depreciation as a compensating incentive for investment in manufacturing.

Similar second-best problems are encountered in the field of capital gains taxation. Australia has introduced a comprehensive capital gains tax, and the United States has removed the 60-percent exemption for long-term capital gains. Unlike Australia, the United States has not introduced base indexation measures, perhaps because the U.S. income tax rate is much lower than Australia's. Canada continues to tax half of capital gains, whereas most European countries do not tax capital gains that do not arise in the course of a trade or business. The U.S. capital gains tax as well as the Australian grandfathering scheme have accentuated lock-in effects arising from the apparent impracticability of taxing accrued gains. In Canada this result is partially countered by including capital gains unrealized at death as income in the final year's tax return. In short, the appropriate treatment of capital gains, as Andrews has observed, remains the Achilles heel of the accretion concept. In attempting to move closer to the accretion concept, I note that administrative problems loom much larger in the capital gains area than in the fields of owner-occupied property and retirement saving, where full taxation is a contentious political issue.

6. See Charles E. McLure, Jr., and George R. Zodrow, "Treasury I and the Tax Reform Act of 1986: The Economics and Politics of Tax Reform," *Journal of Economic Perspectives*, vol. 1 (Summer 1987), pp. 46–47.

Selective base-broadening measures in several countries have been accompanied by reductions in high marginal income tax rates and corporate tax rates. According to a recent study by Tanzi covering many countries, the average of the highest personal income tax rates have fallen by eleven percentage points since 1985.[7] This move was accompanied by a sharp reduction in the number of brackets, which on average fell from eleven to four. In addition, the corporate tax rate was on average reduced by five percentage points, although effective rates increased, possibly with detrimental effects on economic growth. Generally, these measures should reduce the distortions of the income taxes in dollar amounts and diminish, but not eliminate, the return on intertemporal and intersectoral tax arbitrage. While U.S. income tax rates have come down substantially, average income tax rates in most other countries remain very high because of much greater revenue requirements.

The Australian operation involving a fringe benefits tax, a comprehensive capital gains tax, and a full imputation system should probably be described as a major tax reform. In most other countries, however, base broadening and rate flattening seems best described as "repair" rather than "reform" of the income taxes. As two expert observers and close participants in the U.S. reform state: "Instead of fundamental reform, the 1986 Act is better characterized as using the revenues from elimination of most tax shelters, the investment tax credit, sales tax deductibility, and other politically vulnerable provisions to reduce tax rates dramatically."[8] This result may not be as undesirable as some observers think, because the tax systems of democratic countries have a quasi-constitutional character; in other words, a high degree of stability is desirable.

Surveying the field, I believe that if the normative implications of the accretion concept of income are taken seriously, much more vigorous efforts are needed to fully tax in-kind fringe benefits, to tax claims on retirement income as they accrue, to tax imputed rental

7. See Vito Tanzi, "The Response of Other Industrial Countries to the U.S. Tax Reform Act," *National Tax Journal*, vol. 40 (September 1987), pp. 344– 48.

8. McLure and Zodrow, "Treasury I," p. 39. For a more optimistic assessment, see Joseph A. Pechman, "Tax Reform: Theory and Practice," *Journal of Economic Perspectives*, vol. 1 (Summer 1987), pp. 11–28.

income, to fully tax realized capital gains, to move toward an accrual tax on other capital gains, and to fully integrate the corporate tax with the personal income tax. Doing so, however, invites enormous and possibly insuperable valuation, imputation, and inflation adjustment problems. But failure to do so leaves the income tax stranded in a labyrinth of second-best approaches that are informationally demanding and an administrative nightmare.

Second-best issues are further complicated and clouded by doubts about the incidence pattern of the income taxes. Whether income tax reform is regressive, proportional, or progressive depends very much on the assumption about the incidence of the corporation tax. Does it fall on shareholders or on all owners of capital, or is it borne by consumers or by labor? Particularly the latter possibility, that the corporation tax is borne by labor (because they have less capital to work with), has been considered likely for small, open economies in Europe. That implies a cautionary approach to raising taxes on corporations, noncorporate business income, and other capital income.

This efficiency point has its counterpart on the equity side of the argument, when, as Feldstein has pointed out, horizontal inequities of not fully taxing capital income would be largely self-eliminating through tax capitalization. In other words, tax corrections on the accretion principle would generate windfall gains and losses in violation of horizontal equity norms. Moreover, as Musgrave reminds us, "when determining an equitable distribution of the tax burden, the latter should be defined so as to include deadweight loss, not only tax dollars paid; when measuring efficiency cost, allowance should be made for the social valuation of the tax burden and not (as is typically done) for dollar amounts only."[9] Again, problems of definition and measurement loom large. Major analytical puzzles remain, and even when the theory is clear, statistics are hopelessly inadequate.

In practice, then, the modern income tax, despite sometimes heroic efforts at reform, remains awkwardly suspended between the accretion and the consumption concept. There are two alternatives. Either governments move toward a lifetime income tax under which income

9. Richard A. Musgrave, "Short of Euphoria," *Journal of Economic Perspectives*, vol. 1 (Summer 1987), p. 67.

is defined as the sum of consumption and gifts and bequests by the taxpayer to others, or they examine the possibility of an indirect income tax, that is, a value-added tax of the income type. The move nearly everywhere to flatten rate schedules has brought the latter possibility within reach. My preference is for the lifetime income tax for which Henry Aaron and Harvey Galper have made such an eloquent plea at Brookings.[10]

A final word on the role of the income tax, which I have always considered a fundamental democratic institution and an essential counterweight to the income distribution arising from an economic order that relies heavily on market forces. In this light, rate flattening in the United States should probably be deplored, since it legitimizes the previous shortcomings of the income tax. In most European countries, however, it has long been realized that poverty issues must largely be addressed through the welfare system. As a result of these countries' pervasive social security systems, the income distribution has become much less unequal than, say, forty years ago. Their rate-flattening moves, therefore, may signal a demise of the income tax as the cornerstone of the tax system. Politically, and in my view unfortunately, this demise is accentuated by measures to remove large numbers of taxpayers from the tax rolls and to extend the reach of withholding systems.

10. Henry J. Aaron and Havey Galper, *Assessing Tax Reform* (Brookings, 1985).

Overview

A version of tax reform that has gained wide recognition combines base broadening with reduction of nominal rates. All the countries considered in this National Issues Forum have accepted the rate-reduction prescription. They have cut individual income tax rates, especially the top rates, or are considering official proposals to do so. Several have also cut corporation income tax rates. But not all countries have broadened the bases of the income taxes. Australia, the Federal Republic of Germany, and Japan have deliberately reduced their tax revenues, and others have done so to a lesser extent by reducing nominal tax rates without broadening the bases. The United States and Denmark have emphasized revenue neutrality, and both have achieved it by raising corporate taxes to replace some loss of individual income tax revenue. The United Kingdom has increased total revenue by raising value-added tax rates.

INDIVIDUAL INCOME TAXES

The extent of reduction of individual income tax rates differs greatly among countries, and there are striking differences in beginning and top rates. The United States has the lowest top rate in this group of countries, though such comparisons are of limited significance owing to differences in the definition of taxable income and in the income level at which the top rate applies and also in other features of the tax system. A reduction in the share of revenue obtained from the individual income tax is an acknowledged objective in the United Kingdom, Australia, and Canada and somewhat less explicitly in Germany.

What explains the general desire to cut individual income tax rates? I suggest three factors: politics, inflation, and concern about incentives.

First, political developments led to conservative governments in several countries (and a Labor government in Australia that appears rather conservative from the other side of the world). Those governments brought with them a diminished support for income redistribution, an emphasis on markets, and a desire for deregulation.

Second, inflation in the 1970s and early 1980s aroused hostility to the income tax because of bracket creep. The rapid growth in revenue from the individual income tax, and in its share of total revenue, alarmed those who wished to restrict the role of the state.

Third, many felt concern about the adverse effect on economic incentives of high marginal tax rates. This concern is hard to separate from the political developments; conservatives are always worried about the incentive effects of taxation. However, economists have come to share the concern much more than in the past. Although it would be too simple, and cynical, to conclude that economists followed the election returns, surely they were not immune to the influences that determined the election results.

Economic research has produced some credible, quantitative evidence that participation in the labor force and hours worked are sensitive to marginal tax rates. Studies in the United States and the United Kingdom have found that second earners in families will indeed work more when net rates of pay are high than when they are low because of income taxes or other factors. Primary earners, in contrast, display little sensitivity to marginal rates of take-home pay. Although it is hard to reconcile this evidence with the great increase in participation in the labor force by married women, the extent of their participation ensures that the reactions of second earners are important. I find little indication in the papers and discussions presented here that empirical research on labor markets influenced governments' decisions on income tax rates, or that income tax laws have been designed to discriminate between primary and secondary earners.

The empirical evidence, though better than it was a generation ago, does little to resolve uncertainties about the influence of taxation on occupational choice, investment in education, acceptance of responsibility, and retirement decisions. Those aspects may be the most significant.

The evidence on the effects of taxation on saving is less convincing than that on labor force participation and hours of work. Probably the size of the budget deficit (or surplus) has a greater effect on national saving than any feasible alteration of the tax structure and tax rates.

A feature of most of the reforms is a reduction in the number of rate brackets of the individual income tax. This is commonly, but erroneously, represented as a simplification. Actually, the number of brackets is inconsequential when taxpayers fill out their returns— they have only to consult tables prepared by the tax department. But a decrease in the number of brackets may have economic advantages, provided the first bracket is wide. The large number of persons falling in a wide first bracket are not exposed to a possible increase in marginal tax rate when their earnings rise because of overtime work or transfer to a better-paying job. The significance of this point is problematical, in my opinion, because surveys have shown that few people are accurately and acutely aware of their marginal tax rate. Beyond the first bracket the span of rates is more significant than the number of brackets.

The U.S. Tax Reform Act of 1986 includes an odd set of rates. Eager to achieve a low top rate and a drastic reduction in the number of brackets (fifteen at the time), Congress adopted what is usually described as a two-bracket schedule with rates of 15 percent and 28 percent. But to satisfy revenue and distributional objectives, the benefits of the 15-percent bracket and of personal exemptions will be phased out by applying an additional tax of 5 percent over a certain range of income. The result is a third bracket of 33 percent, which is applicable, for example, to married couples with two dependent children and income between about $85,000 and $198,000 (assumes standard deduction used; no allowance for inflation adjustment). Although predictions on such matters are hazardous, I venture the forecast that this anomaly will be eliminated before long, particularly since many of those affected fall in what American politicians think of as the middle-income group, that is to say, themselves and leading citizens in many constituencies. Less confidently, I expect the rate schedule will be vulnerable to the criticism that it is unfair to apply the same marginal rate to taxable incomes of, say, $30,000 and $3,000,000.

CORPORATE AND OTHER BUSINESS INCOME TAXES

The actual and proposed reforms of income taxes on corporations and other enterprises are not easily summarized. The post-1979 legislation in the United Kingdom, the 1986 act in the United States, and the proposals still under consideration in Canada go furthest in combining base broadening with rate reduction. It should be recalled, however, that a large part of the 1986 change in the United States was a reversal of the 1981 liberalization of depreciation allowances. In Germany a reduction in the corporate tax rate was accompanied by a cutback in both special depreciation allowances and regional incentives. But I am unclear about the relative magnitude of their effect on revenues. In the other countries, apparently little has been done about the corporate tax base, though interest in the subject in Sweden is reported.

The case of Denmark is surprising, involving an immediate ten-percentage point increase in the corporate tax rate, to be followed in 1990 by elimination of the double taxation of dividends. Progress toward integration of corporate and individual taxes in two other countries was a by-product rather than a primary objective. In Australia it resulted from a late political compromise rather than from an initial government proposal. In France the degree of integration has been increased as the incidental consequence of a reduction of the corporate tax rate (the *avoir fiscal* being set at half the amount of the cash dividend).

In the United Kingdom and the United States, the combination of cutting back investment incentives and reducing the corporate tax rate has been vigorously supported as an improvement in economic efficiency. This argument is largely a matter of faith—belief in the inherent efficiency of market allocations and lack of faith in the rationality of government intervention. It has not been accepted by business interests that benefited from the discontinued investment incentives or by a few well-credentialed economists. The position of those economists seems to me to have more merit than has been generally acknowledged. They argue that a large part of the revenue loss caused by a tax rate cut benefits owners of old capital and that more stimulus to investment and growth can be obtained by focusing incentives on new investment, through an investment tax credit, an initial allowance, or accelerated depreciation. Of course, this argument is itself subject to depreciation—or obsolescence—but so are many other arguments.

Canada is a striking example of a country whose government refuses to accept the market as a guide to which investments are socially most desirable. It supports the continuation of corporate tax rate differentials across industries and of an investment tax credit for regional development and research and development.

PERSISTENCE OF INCOME TAXATION

It is noteworthy that none of the governments embarking on tax reform accepted the idea of substituting a personal expenditure tax for the individual income tax or a cash-flow business tax for the corporation income tax, as urged by many academic writers. Some will regard this as a regrettable failure. In my view, it is rather a triumph of common sense and political wisdom. But I do not expect the issue to disappear soon.

Despite the rejection of the expenditure tax, governments showed no clear tendency to eliminate preferences for saving in the income tax. The United Kingdom did abolish (for new contracts) a long-standing special relief for life insurance premiums, but it added new provisions for personal equity plans and a business expansion scheme. Japan somewhat curtailed its generous saving preferences, and the United States restricted individual retirement accounts. Among the countries being discussed, deductions for employee contributions to private pension plans are common. The last-mentioned deductions are not necessarily regarded as an incentive for saving. They may be thought of, rather, as a way of bringing taxable income into line with currently disposable income.

Except in the United Kingdom, I have noticed no tendency to expand the preferential treatment of saving in the income tax. I hope that my observation is correct, because I think that an incremental approach to an expenditure tax, by gradual enlargement of preferences for saving, as proposed by some economists, would entail many inequities and arbitrary classifications of savings without ensuring an increase in net saving.

UNRESOLVED ISSUES

In concluding, I wish to mention a few unresolved issues in the income tax field that merit further consideration. The first is the appropriate scope and form of inflation adjustments. During the period of rapid inflation in the 1970s, several countries introduced indexing of bracket limits, personal exemptions, and some other items. In many cases, however, these provisions were overridden because of revenue needs. On the more fundamental matter of the definition of income, no progress was made. Accelerated depreciation and the preferential treatment of capital gains were often rationalized as rough-and-ready inflation adjustments, though they were unsatisfactory for that purpose. Now that inflation has abated, there is little interest in perfecting inflation adjustments in the tax system. Although I am ambivalent on the policy issues, I agree with the critics who urge consideration of the subject. One cannot be sure that inflation will remain quiescent.

My ambivalence on the policy issues springs at bottom from a feeling that it is incongruous to try to devise rational adjustments to minimize the influence on income taxation of an essentially arbitrary and irrational method of capturing control of resources. More specifically, I doubt whether comprehensive adjustments are feasible, and I wonder whether partial adjustments bring a net improvement. It would be easy enough to adjust inventory costs, depreciation allowances, and capital gains for inflation. But a satisfactory adjustment of interest income and expense is hard to visualize. In my judgment, the proposal in U.S. Treasury I was not satisfactory, for reasons that I cannot elaborate here. Despite complications and inconsistencies, I think the United States will be unable to maintain the taxation of capital gains at regular rates without adjustment of the basis for inflation if the price level continues to rise even at moderate rates.

Second, the treatment of capital gains and losses is, in my opinion, a major weakness in most of the tax systems under discussion. The omission of capital gains from the tax base or their preferential taxation results in inequities, administrative complications, and economic distortions. However, I detect little inclination in most countries to deal with the issues.

Third, the general omission from the taxable income of employees of the value of fringe benefits also produces inequities and inefficiencies. As with capital gains, it is hard to be optimistic about the subject. Perhaps the Australian solution of imposing a special tax on employers for noncash fringe benefits, or the alternative of simply denying employers deductions for the cost of the benefits, will be the most expedient solution. Discussion at the conference, however, raised questions about the difficulty of correctly defining fringe benefits and the social acceptability of discouraging employer contributions to health insurance and retirement schemes, two important fringe benefits.

Finally, I think that international competition and coordination in taxation merit more systematic attention than they appear to have received in the recent reforms. Worries about the influence of taxation on migration and international capital movements are mentioned in some of the papers, but it is not clear that the worries prompted any reaction except to reinforce the arguments for rate reduction. Surely, a case exists for strengthening efforts through the Organization for Economic Cooperation and Development and other forums to limit destructive tax competition among countries.

Overview

In commenting on the tax reform labyrinth, it is almost impossible to avoid repetition. I will do my best.

It is better to avoid defining what constitutes a "tax reform" as distinct from minor adjustment operations, since different sets of people have different criteria and motives for evaluating the distinction. For example, politicians may wish to take a high-profile approach and call a patchwork operation a major tax reform or a low-profile approach and call a major tax reform a minor adjustment; tax practitioners may focus on the number of "tax winners" and "tax losers" and the practical consequences for their work; academics may judge reform by whether there are major structural changes to the tax system. These differences came out clearly in the conference discussion. Here I use the concept of tax reform in its widest sense to cover all changes recently undertaken or that may shortly take place in the eleven countries under review.

FOUR QUESTIONS ABOUT TAX REFORM

Tax reform raises four basic questions: Why do it? When should it be done? In what direction should it go? How should it be implemented?

Why Do It?

The papers of the eleven countries give similar answers at more than one level of generality. The broad objectives of tax reform are simplicity, economic efficiency, and the improvement of horizontal (no longer vertical) equity, along with that ever-conflicting pair: the promotion of economic and social goals and the achievement of tax neutrality, the latter now predominating except in certain sensitive areas. Other replies relate to more specific goals such as improving the labor supply, encouraging private saving, and reducing the attractions of the underground economy. Most specifically, governments go straight to the methods they think will achieve some of these objectives and announce their intention, for example, to cut rates of personal and corporate income tax, to broaden the base of those taxes, and to move from income and payroll to consumption taxation.

When Should It Be Done?

There are both long-term and short-term considerations. In the long term the consensus is that in good economic times (for example, the 1960s and early 1970s), it is not worth undertaking tax reform because the potential winners will not react and the potential losers will be resentful. Nevertheless, there may be other reasons for undertaking a particular tax reform, and the move to a value-added tax (VAT) by seven of the eleven countries during that period was probably more far-reaching than anything they did subsequently by way of tax reform. Again, during the 1970s, when inflation was continuous and growth was gradually lessening, little major tax reform occurred, though certain issues were addressed. In particular, most governments felt compelled to offset, at least partially, fiscal drag from the income tax, whether by discretionary measures or indexation. Also, in a number of countries (Denmark, the Netherlands, Sweden, and the United Kingdom), the growth of two-earner families led to a change from joint taxation to separate taxation, or at least the option for such. Since that change led to a tax gain for higher-earner couples, many governments gave aid to parents outside the tax system or replaced tax deductions by tax credits. During the 1980s, when lower levels of growth, employment, and inflation have prevailed, as well as the feeling that tax systems are unfair, inefficient, and unnecessarily complicated, governments have been persuaded that tax reform may be a vote winner rather than a vote loser, a view reinforced by the U.S. experience. It now stands high on the political agenda of almost all OECD countries.

Short-term considerations refer to the election cycle. The United States began reform early in the cycle; Australia was probably frustrated from getting its broad-based sales tax (even if achieving much else) by beginning too late in what is an exceptionally short (three-year) parliamentary term; Canada began late in the election cycle on its VAT proposals, which will be for the next government to implement or not to implement; and France, Italy, the Netherlands, Sweden, and the United Kingdom now appear to be deferring changes. These are political choices.

In What Direction Should It Go?

Though in theory all countries are dedicated to rate cutting and flattening and base broadening, in practice much depends on where a country starts from in terms of tax levels, tax structure, tax system, and so on, and from where it has recently been moving.[1] For example, base broadening and rate reducing seem to have limited possibilities in Italy and the Netherlands because with a revenue-neutral constraint base broadening will probably not attract sufficient revenue to lower rates significantly. Or again, the Swedish paper clearly shows how the need to attract saving is probably frustrated by the favorable tax treatment given in that country for borrowing in relation to saving. The same situation applies to several other countries under consideration, though not to Japan, where private saving is very high and tax incentives to save are to be reduced on revenue and equity grounds.

How Should It Be Implemented?

There are many ways to get tax reform through the legislature; the constitutional and institutional characteristics of a country as well as its perceptions and habits will evidently play a part. Such elements as high profile or low profile, universal consultation or selective consultation, and degree of prior consultation vary from country to country. The more ambitious the reform, the higher the profile that may have to be taken and the greater the risk that it will not work. Canada is now in this situation, and Australia and the United States were in it recently. Both the Australian and U.S. administrations got some but not all they wanted, and at certain moments, especially in the United States, it looked as though reform were totally doomed

1. Tables 2 and 3 give some relevant quantitative information and table 1 some descriptive information.

for many years to come. This tends to be forgotten in the euphoria of the narrow escape. Political negotiations loomed equally large in the Danish reform and Swedish proposals. Implementation is now generally accepted as a multifaceted and often inconvenient constraint that cannot be ignored. To put it less pedantically, tax reform projects are a gamble that may or may not see fruition.

POLICY ISSUES

A checklist of major tax policy issues that are currently of concern in some or all of the eleven countries would include the following:

Personal income tax and social security contributions

—Integration of the personal income tax and social security

—Rate reduction and flattening of the income tax

—Base broadening of the income tax

—Tax neutrality between sources of income and forms of company organization (the Danish reform)

—Social aspects of the income tax (thresholds, starting rates, deductions versus credits, negative income taxes, relative income tax treatment of one- and two-earner couples, married and unmarried couples and single persons, and parents and nonparents)

Corporate income tax

—Rate reduction and flattening[2] and base broadening

—The choice between systems such as separate and imputation

—Coping with inflation

General consumption tax

—Choice of general consumption tax

—Rate and base structure

Changing the tax mix

—From households to enterprises

—From income and payroll to consumption tax

The revenue-neutral assumption

In commenting briefly on some of these issues, I try to avoid repeating territory already covered by Richard Goode and Sijbren

2. In fact three separate changes are proposed to tax schedules: lowering of top rates, reduction of difference between top and bottom rate, and fewer brackets.

Cnossen. I rest mostly with the equity issues (both horizontal and vertical). The general consensus that vertical equity is more suitably addressed through reductions in primary incomes or the transfer payment system than the tax system does not prevent several current tax policy choices from being influenced by considerations of vertical equity. Though by definition equity issues entail value judgments, they seem to me more clearly defined than issues relating to economic efficiency and simplicity, which are systematically ambiguous and change over time.

As regards economic efficiency, there is clearly a trend toward rate flattening and base broadening, toward neutrality rather than interventionism, but perhaps the reasoning behind it is somewhat overstated and unconvincing. For example, as already mentioned by Richard Goode, the evidence from the second-generation studies that lower rates improve hours worked by primary earners seems to be confined to the United Kingdom and the United States and neglects, among other things, high unemployment levels in those countries in certain regions and among certain age groups and ethnic minorities. Also there is little evidence that tax incentives increase the overall volume of savings, even if they influence their allocation. Though a move toward a preference for tax neutrality as against interventionism has occurred, it has been limited. Governments seem rather to have moved to more narrowly targeted fiscal interventionism to reflect political realities (aid to homeownership) and current economic preoccupations, such as subsidizing small traders and important productive investment.

As for simplicity, tax reforms, with their necessarily complicated transition procedures, probably limit the possibilities. As several speakers observed, taxpayers' perceptions apart, the reduction in the number of rate brackets will not contribute much to simplicity, though other administrative measures, such as the possibility of a return-free tax system, clearly would do so.

On another issue, many have suggested that full imputation is the ideal system, the method chosen recently by Australia, Italy, and Germany and contemplated by Denmark, New Zealand, and U.S. Treasury plan I. I do not agree, and the several different systems (see table 1, column 5) adapted by other countries suggest that others share my view. I find the conventional terminology (economic double taxation) irrational in this context, since dividend income is being

TABLE 1. *Some Comparative Aspects of the Tax Systems in Eleven OECD Countries*

Country	Personal income tax unit (1)	Relief for parents within tax system[a] (2)	Relief for interest payments on home mortgage for principal abode (3)	Relief for interest payments on home mortgage for second abode (4)	Corporate tax system (5)
Australia	Individual	None	Tax credit partially deductible subject to ceiling	None	Full imputation[b]
Canada	Individual	Refundable tax credit plus allowance	None	None	Credit against income tax for domestic investment
Denmark	Individual	None	Tax allowance for 50 percent of interest[c]	Same as column 3	Partial imputation[d]
France	Family	Family quotient	Tax credit fully deductible up to ceiling	None	Partial imputation
Germany	Joint-income splitting	Tax allowance[e]	Tax allowance fully deductible	None	Full imputation plus split rate
Italy	Individual	Tax credit inversely related to income	Tax allowance fully deductible to ceiling	Same as column 3	Full imputation

				Split rate plus partial imputation[f]
Japan	Individual	Tax allowance	Tax credit partially deductible to ceiling	None	
Netherlands	Individual	None	Tax allowance fully deductible	Same as column 3	Separate
Sweden	Individual	None	Tax allowance fully deductible	Same as column 3	Primary dividend
United Kingdom	Optional	None	Tax allowance fully deductible to ceiling	None	Partial imputation
United States	Joint-income splitting	Tax allowance plus refundable tax credit	Tax allowance fully deductible	Same as column 3	Separate system[g]

Sources: Organization for Economic Cooperation and Development, Committee on Fiscal Affairs, *Personal Income Tax Systems under Changing Economic Conditions* (Paris: OECD 1986); and OECD, *Taxation in Developed Countries: An International Symposium* (Paris: OECD 1987).

a. All countries allow tax transfers. This column does not refer to the single-parent case.

b. Replacing in 1987 a separate system.

c. Before tax reform, fully deductible.

d. Future full imputation contemplated.

e. To be increased.

f. Proposals for modification under consideration.

g. Treasury proposal supported full imputation.

subjected to two *different* taxes, just as consumption tax is levied on purchases from income that has already been subject to income tax. The real issue is the relative treatment of distributed and undistributed profits, which may legitimately vary between countries and within countries over time according to governments' main economic objectives. The arguments in favor of the separate system are that it gives companies a built-in protection against the overdistribution of company profits through shareholder pressure (which perhaps is why such a system is preferred in countries such as the Netherlands and the United States where many head offices of multinational enterprises are situated) and that it causes the fewest complications for double-taxation agreements. The counterargument, that separate systems accentuate the tax bias toward investment in bonds rather than equities, cannot be denied, though no clear evidence exists on whether financing through the market provides better-quality investment than self-financing by firms, the other main issue in this particular debate.

Next, I refer briefly to two proposed changes in the tax mix. The first removes burdens from the household sector and moves them to the business sector (as has been done in the United States and Denmark and is proposed in Canada). It is difficult to believe that this tendency will be general, since the United States, unlike most of the other ten countries, has considerably reduced the relative taxation of business income to household income, as shown in the following table. (The figures are percentages of total tax receipts.)[3]

	Corporate		Personal	
	1965	1985	1965	1985
United States	16	7	30	36
Unweighted average of Europe	7	7	25	29

The second proposed change in the tax mix refers to announcements by several governments of intentions to move from income and payroll taxation toward consumption taxes. Table 2 shows that changes in tax structures were relatively small between 1975 and 1985, the most frequent change being a move from income tax to

3. Organization for Economic Cooperation and Development, *Revenue Statistics of OECD Member Countries, 1965–1986* (Paris: OECD, 1987), tables 11, 13.

TABLE 2. *Tax Revenues as a Percent of Gross Domestic Product and Distribution of Tax Revenues, by Source, Eleven OECD Countries, 1975 and 1985*

Country	Tax revenues as percent of GDP	Distribution of tax revenues (percent of total)		
		Income taxes[a]	Social security contributions	Consumption taxes
1975				
Australia	28	55	0	29
Canada	32	47	10	32
Denmark	41	59	1	34
France	37	18	41	33
Germany	36	35	33	27
Italy	25	21	46	29
Japan	21	45	29	17
Netherlands	44	35	38	24
Sweden	44	50	19	24
United Kingdom	35	44	17	25
United States	29	44	25	18
1985				
Australia	30	54	0	32
Canada	33	44	13	31
Denmark	49	57	4	34
France	46	17	44	29
Germany	38	35	36	26
Italy	35	37	35	25
Japan	28	46	30	14
Netherlands	45	26	44	26
Sweden	50	42	25	26
United Kingdom	38	39	17	32
United States	29	43	29	18

Source: OECD, *Revenue Statistics of OECD Member Countries, 1965–1986* (Paris: OECD, 1987).

a. Includes individual and corporation income.

social security contributions. A move toward greater reliance on consumption taxes is not yet evident, but a twenty-year or more trend away from consumption taxes has been halted.

A REVIEW OF ELEVEN OECD COUNTRIES

The papers show that in almost all the countries tax reforms must operate under the revenue-neutral constraint because of the difficulty of reducing government expenditure under present high unemployment, demographic trends, and current budget deficits. Only Germany and the United Kingdom envisage tax reform accompanied by net tax cuts. Few, if any, of the eleven envisage future increases in the ratios of total tax receipts to gross domestic product (GDP), but most see little prospect for much reduction. The first column of table 2 shows recent developments in the ratios of total tax receipts to GDP: they have increased greatly in Denmark, France, Italy, Japan, and Sweden but have scarcely changed in Australia, Canada, Germany, the Netherlands, and the United States. The United Kingdom occupies an intermediate position.

A most important issue, addressed only in the papers from France and the Netherlands, and not on the tax reform agenda in many countries, is the relation between the income tax and social security contributions (table 3). To avoid the old interminable debate, let us assume social security contributions are a tax, though of a special kind.[4] They do not exist, or hardly exist, in Australia, Denmark, and Sweden (at the employee level), are extremely important in France and the Netherlands and until recently in Italy, with Canada, Germany, Japan, the United Kingdom, and the United States occupying middle ground. Employees' contributions are evidently regressive, there being usually little or no threshold, flat rates, no account taken of the family circumstances of the contributor, and for the most part subject to ceilings. Employers' contributions are more ambivalent, but the conventional wisdom is that, though they may be a short-term burden on employers (which discourages them from

4. Comparisons between income tax rates are meaningless if one does not take into account social security contributions paid by employees. This is technically difficult to do on the basis of rate comparisons, but see table 3 regarding the amounts of each paid by an average production worker.

TABLE 3. *Income Tax and Social Security Contributions Paid by an Average Single Worker as a Percentage of Gross Earnings, Eleven OECD Countries, 1986*

Country	Income tax	Social security contributions	Total
Australia	22	1	23
Canada	20	4	24
Denmark	40	6	47
France	7	16	23
Germany	18	17	35
Italy	17	9	26
Japan	9	7	16
Netherlands	11	26	38
Sweden	36	0	36
United Kingdom	22	9	31
United States	20	7	27

Source: OECD, *The Tax/Benefit Position of Production Workers, 1983–1986* (Paris: OECD, 1987). Total figures for the Netherlands and Sweden are rounded.

substituting labor for capital), they are ultimately reflected in lower wages and so become in effect a proportional income tax up to a ceiling and regressive once the ceiling is passed.

The distinctive nature of France's income-payroll tax system follows logically from its great reliance on social security contributions. Having such an important regressive tax means that the income tax should be very progressive, and, as noted in the French paper, its revenues come substantially from the wealthy. That in turn has other consequences peculiar to France: nearly half the French people do not pay income tax, and rich parents relative to poor parents and to rich nonparents get a more substantial reduction in their tax bill than in other industrialized countries.

These comments lead to a more general problem: though vertical equity has been thrown out of the tax policy door, it is lurking in some areas of tax reform—the idea being not to soak the relatively few rich, but to protect the many poor. For example, what should be the threshold and starting rates of an income tax? There are two distinct philosophies among the countries surveyed: France, Japan, and the United States take the view that the poor should not pay income tax, and so a large percentage of the populations do not pay it; Denmark and Sweden believe all or nearly all citizens should contribute to the income tax, even if they get more back in transfer payments than they pay in taxes. Canada has pioneered a way of providing transfers through the tax system by refundable tax credits,[5] under which benefits in excess of tax due are paid directly to the (potential) taxpayer. This method could extend, if used systematically, to a complete integration of the tax and social welfare system by way of a negative income tax, ignored for many years but apparently now under consideration in New Zealand and by certain people in the United Kingdom.

Vertical equity is also a live issue in the consumption tax area. Countries having recently introduced the VAT (New Zealand) or contemplating its introduction (Canada) are aware not only of the many advantages of a one-rate VAT but also of political resistance to taxing hitherto tax-free goods such as food and medicines. Proponents of a one-rate VAT argue that nowadays consumption patterns vary little among the population, so that a one-rate VAT should not be regressive. However, even if a one-rate VAT is perceived as regressive, the means for remedying this exists: increase social welfare benefits to the needy (Scandinavian style) or provide nonwastable tax credits (Canadian style).

Finally, vertical equity considerations arise in the base-broadening and tax-expenditure-reduction field. Tax expenditures have been attacked not only from the point of view of economic efficiency but also on distributional grounds, since they largely benefit the rich. The replacement of tax allowances (whose value is a function of the marginal rate of tax) by flat tax credits unrelated to income has been a feature of several countries (Australia, Canada, Italy, and Japan), regarding, for example, tax subsidies to parents and homeowners (see table 1).

One final word on base broadening of the personal income tax: I am inclined to agree with the view expressed during the conference that the scope for base broadening in most of the ten other countries

---

5. Since nothing is refunded in most cases, the OECD prefers the term "nonwastable tax credits."

is less than that existing in the United States, even after the U.S. tax reform. It is true that some of the countries could get more revenue from base broadening than the United States by increasing capital gains taxes and by making work-related expenses and social security contributions nondeductible. On the other hand, outside the United States, local income and property taxes are not deductible, and deductibility for mortgage interest on two homes is far greater in the United States than in most of the other ten countries (see table 1, column 4). I suspect too that in other important areas such as fringe benefits, interest payments on loans other than for home mortgages, insurance premiums and private pensions, and health contributions, postreform United States remains more generous than most of the other countries under review. It is also a fact that in recent years there has been a broadening of the tax base by eliminating or reducing deductions and extending the taxation of fringe benefits in many of the eleven countries.[6]

CONCLUDING COMMENT

To conclude, a word on my OECD connection. First, all opinions expressed here are my own and in no way commit the OECD or its member governments to agreement with any of them. It is especially important to emphasize this because several issues under discussion remain controversial. Second, especially in the Australian contribution, the question was raised about the desirability of coordinating certain international aspects of tax reform. That is a priority of the OECD Committee on Fiscal Affairs, which provides a forum for discussion among senior tax officials on how to minimize conflicts arising from different tax levels, rate structures, and systems. Third, as Joseph Pechman has kindly said, the OECD's comparative studies on the tax policies and current tax practices of member countries do provide a unique source of information. During 1988 the OECD hopes to publish comprehensive surveys of wealth and capital gains taxes and of consumption taxes, with special emphasis on value-added taxation.

6. For details, see OECD, Committee on Fiscal Affairs, *Personal Income Tax Systems under Changing Economic Conditions* (Paris: OECD, 1986); and OECD, *The Taxation of Fringe Benefits* (Paris: OECD, forthcoming).

Conference Participants

with their affiliations at the time of the conference

Participants from the United States

Michael Abrutyn
Cole and Corette

Donald C. Alexander
Cadwalader, Wickersham and Taft

Anthony G. Alexandron
Omnicom Group Inc.

Martin J. Bailey
Department of State

Cheryl D. Block
George Washington University

Mortimer Caplin
Caplin and Drysdale

Sheldon S. Cohen
Morgan Lewis and Bockius

Robert T. Cole
Cole and Corette

Ann Davidson
Internal Revenue Service

Edward N. Delaney
Delaney and Young, Chartered

Larry L. Dildine
Price Waterhouse

Carl A. DiLisio
Monsanto Co.

David K. Edmonds
Eaton Corp.

Marcia Field
Department of the Treasury

C. David Finch
Institute for International Economics

Arnold Jay Fries
Merrill Lynch

Thomas B. Gallagher
E.F. Hutton

Harvey Galper
Peat Marwick Main and Co.

Lawrence B. Gibbs
Internal Revenue Service

Al J. Golato
H & R Block, Inc.

Hernan Gonzalez
Deloitte Haskins and Sells

Richard Goode
Brookings Institution

Jane G. Gravelle
Congressional Research Service

Joseph H. Guttentag
Arnold and Porter

George Guttman
Research Institute of America

Daniel I. Halperin
Georgetown University

Dennis K. Hoover
American Telephone and Telegraph

Nirjhar Jain
*Port Authority of New York
and New Jersey*

Suzanne E. Kelly
Insurer Central Services

W. Thomas Kelly
Insurer Central Services

Thomas P. Kerester
Tax Executives Institute

Donald W. Kiefer
Congressional Research Service

Arthur L. Kimmelfield
Summit, Rovins and Feldesman

Kenneth J. Krupsky
Arnold and Porter

Irwin Litman
NYNEX Corp.

Harris E. Loring III
Apollo Computer Inc.

Donald C. Lubick
*Hodgson, Russ, Andrews, Woods
and Goodyear*

Carl J. Lukach
E.I. du Pont de Nemours and Co.

Frederick L. MacDonald
General Motors Corp.

Rosemary Marcuss
Congressional Budget Office

R. N. Mattson
IBM Corp.

Leif Mutén
International Monetary Fund

Davis W. Nelson
Westinghouse Electric Corp.

William R. Pearse
EAC U.S.A.

Mary Frances Pearson
Ernst and Whinney

David S. Poston
*E. I. du Pont de Nemours
and Co.*

James C. Pugh
PPG Industries Inc.

Stanford G. Ross
Arnold and Porter

Lior Samuelson
Peat Marwick Main and Co.

Raymond A. Schroder
Exxon Corp.

Richard Shapiro
*Oppenheim, Appel, Dixon
and Co.*

Lee Sheppard
Tax Notes

Ethan H. Siegal
Newmyer Associates

Philip G. Simonds
TRINOVA Corp.

Delos R. Smith
The Conference Board

Judith E. Soltz
CIGNA Corp.

Sven Steinmo
University of Colorado

C. Eugene Steuerle
Department of the Treasury

Emil M. Sunley
Deloitte Haskins and Sells

Alan A. Tait
International Monetary Fund

Vito Tanzi
International Monetary Fund

W. A. Warren
Exxon Co., International

Raymond C. Wilson
American Telephone and Telegraph

Participants from Other Countries

Erik Aasbrink
Ministry of Finance, Sweden

Arne Baekkevold
Embassy of Sweden,
Washington, D. C.

Grant A. Bailey
Embassy of Australia,
Washington, D. C.

Stefano Benazzo
Embassy of Italy, Washington, D. C.

Luigi Bernardi
University of Pavia, Italy

John Bossons
University of Toronto, Canada

Ian C. R. Byatt
Her Majesty's Treasury,
United Kingdom

Aldo Cardarelli
Ministry of Finance, Italy

Pierre-Andre Chiappori
Ecole des Hautes Etudes, France

Sijbren Cnossen
Erasmus University Rotterdam,
The Netherlands

Isaias Coelho
Secretaria da Receita Federal, Brazil

Flip de Kam
Social and Cultural Planning Office,
The Netherlands

Paulo de Pitta e Cunha
Ministry of Finance, Portugal

Thomas de Vries
Embassy of the Netherlands,
Washington, D.C.

Michele del Giudice
Ministry of Finance, Italy

David A. Dodge
Department of Finance, Canada

Jens Drejer
Ministry of Taxation, Denmark

Pieter Dyckmeester
Ministry of Economic Affairs,
The Netherlands

Edward A. Evans
The Treasury, Australia

John A. Fraser
Embassy of Australia,
Washington, D. C.

Emilio Gerelli
University of Pavia, Italy

Elio E. Grandi
Italian Industries Association

John Hills
London School of Economics

Keimei Kaizuka
University of Tokyo

Marilyn Knock
Department of Health and Welfare,
Canada

Robert Koch-Nielsen
La Cour and Koch-Nielsen, Denmark

Hendrik Elle Koning
The Treasury, The Netherlands

Gerold Krause-Junk
*Institute für Auslandisches
und Internationales Finance
und Steuerwesen,
Federal Republic of Germany*

John Kristensen
*Embassy of Denmark,
Washington, D. C.*

Karin Kristensen
Ministry of Finance, Denmark

Claes Ljungh
Ministry of Finance, Sweden

Didier Maillard
*Ministry of Economics and Finance,
France*

Thomas Menck
*Ministry of Finance, Federal Republic
of Germany*

Kenneth C. Messere
*Organization for Economic Cooperation
and Development*

Jean-Claude Milleron
*Ministry of Economics and Finance,
France*

Atsushi Nagano
Ministry of France, Japan

Miriam Hederman O'Brien
Trinity College, Ireland

A. O'Donnell
*Embassy of Great Britain,
Washington, D. C.*

Cedric Sandford
University of Bath, England

John H. Sargent
Department of Finance, Canada

Osumu Shimizu
Ministry of Finance, Japan

Donal Thornhill
*Office of the Revenue Commissioners,
Ireland*

Adalbert Uelner
*Bundesministerium fur Finanzen,
Federal Republic of Germany*

Robert Weeden
*Department of Inland Revenue,
England*

Dirk Witteveen
The Treasury, The Netherlands